Crime in Literature

Crime in Literature

Sociology of Deviance and Fiction

VINCENZO RUGGIERO

VERSO

London · New York

First published by Verso 2003

Verso
UK: 6 Meard Street, London WIF OEG
USA: 180 Varick Street, New York, NY 10014–4606

Verso is the imprint of New Left Books

ISBN 1–85984–570–3 Hb
ISBN 1–85984–482–0 Pb

British Library Cataloguing in Publication Data
A catalogue record for this book is available from the British Library

Library of Congress Cataloging-in-Publication Data
A catalog record for this book is available from the Library of Congress

Designed and typeset in Monotype Joanna by Illuminati, Grosmont
Printed in the UK by Bath Press

Contents

Acknowledgements   vii

Introduction   I

1   Atavism and Conflict: Dostoevsky and Camus   9

2   Organizing Crime: Cervantes, Gay and Brecht   28

3   Legal and Illegal Drugs: Baudelaire and London   53

4   Nana, Women and Crime   77

5   Baldwin and Wright: Ethnic Minorities,
Hate and Crime   104

6   Moby Dick and the Crimes of the Economy   135

7   Felix Krull: The Con Man and the Irrationality of
Markets   156

8   Mark Twain and the Corruption of a Town   178

9   Hugo, Mirbeau and Imprisonment   194

10   Manzoni and Legal Suffering   216

References   236

Index   251

Acknowledgements

I have been discouraged by many people from writing this book, mainly colleagues and acquaintances who thought that, once one is safely working in a disciplinary field and is lucky enough to have achieved a career of sorts in it, one had better pretend that the knowledge offered by that field is all a curious human being can aspire to. People who, instead, thought that disciplinary boundaries have to be challenged and expertise in one field tested by broader intellectual curiosity are those who discussed with me the rationale and contents of this book. These are Cynthia Winifred, Ermanno Gallo, Geoffrey Pearson, Giuseppe Mascoli, Letizia Artoni, Lucia Ruggiero, Mary Eaton, Mick Ryan, Ruth Jamieson, Susanne Karstedt and Trevor Bark. I thank them all warmly and I dedicate this book to them – along with, of course, Fyodor Dostoevsky, Albert Camus, Miguel de Cervantes, John Gay, Bertolt Brecht, Charles Baudelaire, Jack London, Émile Zola, James Baldwin, Richard Wright, Herman Melville, Thomas Mann, Mark Twain, Victor Hugo, Octave Mirbeau and Alessandro Manzoni.

Introduction

While some sociologists and criminologists do have time to read fiction, few use it to clarify concepts to themselves, discuss them with colleagues and transmit them to students. Reading fiction appears to be a privilege granted to fortunate academics who succeed in avoiding heavy workloads or persuade their line managers that, after a particularly demanding research project and between hectic semesters, they need an unproductive, soothing, break.

This book uses fiction as a tool for the communication of sociological meaning and the elaboration of criminological analysis. It addresses the issues of crime and crime control through the reading of some classic literary works. It is not a book of literary criticism, but a book written by a sociologist who reads classic fiction sociologically. Although I am aware that this proviso may not thwart the critique of scholars who know every minute detail about the authors and works I consider in the following pages, in pre-emptive self-defence I swear that I would never accuse an author of crime novels or a literary critic of ignoring, say, 'propensity event theory' in criminology. The idea of writing this book slowly took shape after I conducted a series of experiments with groups of students and after testing sociological-literary papers in conferences and academic journals.

A few years back, for example, when invited to deliver a paper on 'Respect in Prison', I found that the best way of affirming that the very title of the conference sounded somewhat like an oxymoron, was to show some etchings produced by Giambattista Piranesi in the eighteenth century and accompany the slide show with some sociological-literary commentary. I argued that to understand the invisible profile of affliction and control in contemporary imprisonment one must look not so much at the rigorous Benthamite technique of space, as at the visionary lines of the 'imaginary prisons' of Piranesi. Those prisons, I suggested, are the absolute opposite of the narrow space, without losing their sense of being a fearful nightmare. Vastness and segregation, emptiness and constriction, coexist and blend; Piranesi's prisons make tangible that which is invisible – the fetters of the mind (Ruggiero, 1991). The space of imprisonment is no longer enclosure, but an unbearable dilatation, an anguishing multiplication of levels, a labyrinthine succession of walls opening onto other walls, a space of temporal infinity, enclosed within itself, mathematically infinite (Yourcenar, 1978).

Later, while researching and writing on business crime, I found some of Daniel Defoe's work extremely inspiring for the identification of another criminological oxymoron, namely 'business ethics'. Looking at eighteenth-century England, I argued that the crimes of the powerful were the object of similar negotiation and redefinition to those of the powerless, and that the ruling groups were concerned not only with drawing the boundaries between acceptable and unacceptable behaviour of those they ruled but also with the identification of the ethics of their own economic behaviour (Ruggiero, 2000b). Defoe's writings, in particular his novels and essays on trade, honest and dishonest economic ventures, and business conduct, revealed to me the difficulties one encounters when trying to grasp what exactly constitutes business crime, how some commercial and productive activities find moral legitimation, and ultimately where the border between acceptable and unacceptable economic practices is to be placed.

The final thrust towards conceiving this book was provided by the realization that Howard Becker, whom many colleagues would not hesitate to describe as a legendary figure in our field, was studying the social and ideological aspects of literature, particularly the work of Antonio Candido, who proved how the boundaries between academic disciplines can be made permeable and fuzzy. Candido resisted disciplinary specialization, and continued to mix imagination and observation, science and art (Becker, 1995). He ended up changing field, and after teaching sociology for almost fifteen years eventually became a professor of comparative literature, an example that was to be followed by authors like Dolin (2000), who quit legal for literary studies, to build explanatory bridges between the mentalities of law and fiction. Dolin argues that canonical fiction serves 'to probe law's nomos, offering adversarial narratives on behalf of those who are marginalized by the criminal or civilian law. Fiction becomes both a legal test site and an unofficial court of appeal' (Sutherland, 2001: 26). Storytelling and literary imagining, in sum, can provide essential ingredients in rational arguments (Lara, 2000).

This author is not joining the traffic from sociology to literary studies, but only reading some classic fiction while revisiting some sociological and criminological discourses and concepts. It has been suggested that the most common kinds of sociological studies in literature seek to relate a period, or a genre, to social conditions, or focus on the relation between the work and the public, or finally investigate the position and social function of the writer (Candido, 1995). This book, instead, discusses sociological and criminological notions while 'telling stories'

(Dow, 1980), some of those classic stories which lie in our minds as if resting, until we decide to put them back in motion by linking them to our daily activities and thoughts.

For fear of offending colleagues I will pretend not to concur with Benjamin (2000a), who claimed that fiction is more important than sociology, because fiction has words, and words conquer ideas. Nevertheless, I must express my appreciation for the freedom fiction offers us in shaping feelings and weighing values. We are used to seeing the world through the lenses of the law, rather than those of values and imagination. The locus where conflicts around good and evil are played are courts, where 'skilled lawyers manage to prove that murderers are not murderers, but something else' (Yehoshua, 2000: xiv). Imagination, in this sense, is elsewhere, where people create words and conquer ideas, sitting at their desk rather than in court: 'I never think, except when I sit down to write' (Poe, 1980a: 41).

Unlike sociologists, artists have a *genius irritabile*, and while possessing a sense of beauty they also have a strong sense of deformity or disproportion. 'Thus a wrong – an injustice – done a poet who is really a poet, excites him to a degree which, to ordinary apprehension, appears disproportionate with the wrong' (Poe, 1980a: 36). Artists see injustice where the unpoetical see no injustice whatsoever. Thus their irritability is not to be confused with 'temper' in the vulgar sense, but associated with clear-sightedness in respect to wrong, 'this clear-sightedness being nothing more than a corollary from the vivid perception of Right – of justice – of proportion'. According to Poe (1980a: 36), finally, 'a man who is not irritable is no poet'.

There is more than irritability in the classic works discussed here, namely a sense of openness from which, as sociologists and criminologists, we have but to learn. It is true that books may be produced for non-practical ends, *gratia sui*, for love, and that we read them for pleasure, for spiritual elevation, to broaden our knowledge, or as a pastime: nobody forces us to read fiction. However, as Eco (2000) argues, reading is not like jogging or doing crosswords. Literary works teach us freedom of interpretation, because the very ambiguity of language spawns multiple readings of texts. In *The Red and the Black*, for example, we are told that Julien Sorel goes to church and shoots Madame de Rénal. After noting that Julien's arm shakes, Stendhal tells us that he shoots once but misses his victim; it is only after he shoots again that the lady falls. We may observe that, because he was shaking, Julien had not gone to the church with the intention of killing, but that he was pushed to murder by a confused passionate impulsion. On the other hand, we may also construe that Julien had indeed the intention of killing, but was shaking only because he was a coward. The text authorizes both interpretations. While closed texts have a hermeneutic truth in them and may teach us a sense of reality and destiny, hypertexts can be changed and rewritten by readers, as they teach us creativity and freedom (Eco, 2002). Examples of such hypertexts are the literary situations presented to readers by Christa Wolf (2001), where we are not given objective situations but are made aware of subjective interactions offering the possibility to participate, through our own subjectivity, or even unconsciously, in the elaboration of the text and in its meanings. Even when writing the histories of Medea and Cassandra, and after painstakingly studying mythology and its different interpretations, Wolf feels free to invent, to intervene and correct texts, a freedom accorded to readers as well (Calasso, 2001). Invention, finally, is also a crucial variable in the philosophical analysis of fiction proposed by Deleuze (1998), according to whom literature is neither expressive nor reflexive, but diagnostic (Buchanan and Marks, 2000). As with philosophy, the task of novels is the creation of concepts, which are always debatable and revisable, because their 'in-between spaces' offer infinite possibilities to readers.

The texts presented in this book offer similar possibilities, selected by this author to highlight some central, specific topics in the study of crime and social control. The book begins by examining the notion of political violence in Dostoevsky's *The Devils* and Camus' *The Just*. In the former, crime is associated with the departure from Christianity, but also with moral insanity and epilepsy. A parallel discussion is conducted of Lombroso's theories, and of his crucial analysis of political offenders as epileptic. Attention is drawn to the fact that the novel, however, also contains Durkheimian hints, when it appears to link crime with the particular contingencies of socio-economic transition in the Europe of the early twentieth century. Reading *The Just*, instead, the prevailing analysis this author detects is that political crime is seen by Albert Camus as the result of cultural and material conflict between social groups. A parallel discussion of conflict theory in sociology and criminology is therefore presented.

Chapter 2 is an analysis of Cervantes' *Rinconete and Cortadillo*, John Gay's *The Beggar's Opera* and Bertolt Brecht's *The Threepenny Opera*. In these works many criminological theories are detected, both of a general and of a specific nature. For example, crime is associated with relative deprivation and Mertonian 'innovation', but also with lack of control. Moreover, different descriptions and theories of organized crime, which are discussed in this chapter, also emerge from the reading of these three classics.

Chapter 3 focuses on Charles Baudelaire's *Les Paradis artificiels* and Jack London's *John Barleycorn*, and attempts a critical evaluation of the concept of 'retreatism' as a deviant adaptation. While this type of deviant adaptation remains a central concept used in traditional analysis of drug use and distribution, the chapter emphasizes the prescience as well as the ambivalence of the two authors vis-à-vis participation rather than retreatism or absenteeism. The chapter also pinpoints the failure of Baudelaire and London to anticipate the outcomes of drug prohibition.

Chapter 4 discusses theories of women and crime and some concepts of feminist criminology while telling the story of *Nana* by Émile Zola. Chapter 5 is devoted to the issue of crime and violent racism in James Baldwin's *Blues for Mister Charlie* and Richard Wright's *Native Son*.

After dealing with various forms of conventional criminality, the book then moves on to analyse some types of white-collar crime, and crime of the powerful. Melville's epic *Moby Dick* is discussed in Chapter 6 as an allegory of industry, describing work conditions, simultaneously praising and condemning profit and management. Here, three different ways of interpreting the crimes of the economy are analysed, all detectable in *Moby Dick*. These suggest notions of intrinsic, extrinsic and organizational crime. Thomas Mann's last novel, *Confessions of Felix Krull, Confidence Man*, is examined, in Chapter 7, against the debate on criminal careers and differential association theory. The presentation of this theory is accompanied by some notions derived from the sociology of organizations, notions that the career of Felix Krull inevitably evokes. In Chapter 8 theories of political and administrative corruption are applied to the analysis of the little classic by Mark Twain, *The Man that Corrupted Hadleyburg*.

Lest readers are led to believe that, after the description of such an array of criminal activities, this author implicitly invokes harsh punishment for perpetrators, the two final chapters deal, respectively, with critical views of imprisonment and of the criminal justice process. Chapter 9 analyses Octave Mirbeau's *The Torture Garden* and sections of Victor Hugo's *Les Misérables*, and offers a parallel discussion of penal philosophies, including retribution, rehabilitation, deterrence, abolitionism and reductionism. Finally, Chapter 10 recounts Alessandro Manzoni's *Storia della colonna infame*. This chapter constitutes a sort of conclusion to the book, as it draws a parallel between the way in which the plague devastating Milan in 1630 was dealt with by the authorities and the way in which contemporary law incessantly needs new 'plague spreaders' in order to seek legitimacy for its operations.

Some literary critics describe techniques, motifs, allegories, latent psychological keys, archetypical characters and fateful ideas (as teachers of sexual education would describe eggs, sperm, membranes and glands) while omitting a marginal detail, namely that what is described may, occasionally, provoke some pleasure (Oz, 2000). This book is the result of my pleasure in reading. As Borges is alleged to have said, while others may boast of what they have written, I take pride in what I have read.

I

Atavism and Conflict:
Dostoevsky and Camus

In a provocative, though realistic, visualization of justice there are no composed and wise judges sacredly pondering on guilt and innocence, but fighters who, respectively, represent the winners of today and struggle to be the winners of tomorrow. The symbol of such justice is not a blindfolded goddess holding a scale, but the assegai of a warrior (Vergès, 1988). When political violence is examined, this symbol is particularly apt, suggestive as it is of a battle between groups, each claiming legitimacy for the use of force.

The analysis of political violence in criminology displays similar paradigmatic shifts to those observed in the analysis of crime in general. Early inquiries of 'political criminality' related this activity to climate, and produced detailed graphs showing that more revolutions occur in the spring and summer than in other seasons. Critics who did not believe that a particular '*fauna or flora criminalis* [was] produced by certain climatic or geological conditions' retorted that revolutions occur when social development clashes with political institutions which do not possess enough elasticity (Bonger, 1936: 56). Such critics contributed to the demise of the positivist school, by moving away from the study of 'delinquents' to focus on the social conditions giving shape to

behaviour officially disapproved of. With anomie theories gaining widespread acceptance, a tradition destined to inspire an ample variety of
analysts was established, both in the field of the sociology of deviance
and in that of the sociology of collective action. Labelling and conflict
theories gave a definitive impulse to this shift, slowly becoming the
prevalent paradigms for the study of political violence.

I will illustrate some aspects of this shift, and its ambiguities, through
the reading of two important literary works, by Dostoevsky and Camus
respectively. I will also suggest that Camus' analysis overshadows with
sophistication that of most criminologists who contributed to that shift.

Let them scream that I am a reactionary

At one point in his intellectual trajectory, Dostoevsky challenges the
progressive movements in Russia and proclaims his faith in regeneration through a return to the tenets of Christianity, as held by the Greek
Orthodox Church. A tragic expression of his conversion is found in *The
Devils*, a novel initially serialized in a Moscow conservative monthly, *The
Russian Messenger*. While playing with the original idea, the author thinks
of having an atheist as the main character, a man who after senseless
involvement in progressive politics finally turns to God, as the ultimate
reason for being. He then abandons the idea and chooses to target the
Westerners, namely the Russian liberals who dream of converting Russia
into a constitutional monarchy on the model of a Western European
country. His invective, however, is also addressed to the more revolutionary movements in Russia, those in which he had previously partici-
pated, and who oppose both the aristocracy and the ascending class of
capitalists. Aware of the reaction that his change of heart might provoke,
he defiantly declares: 'Let the Nihilists and the Westerners scream that
I am a reactionary! To hell with them' (Magarshack, 1971: x).

An event comes to his aid: the murder of a young student in Moscow, and a subsequent investigation leading to the discovery of a revolutionary conspiracy. This had been organized by Sergey Nechayev, at the time a disciple of Bakunin, who had travelled abroad with a false passport and engaged in revolutionary propaganda activity. On returning to Russia he had become the self-styled representative of the World Revolutionary Movement and organized a Society of National Retribution in Moscow. The organization of this society was based on an allegedly wide network of 'groups of five', revolutionary cells unknown to one another, centrally coordinated, for security reasons, by an obscure, omnipotent, committee. Nechayev and friends had murdered a member of a 'group of five' for purportedly refusing to carry out the instructions of the committee.

Dostoevsky's description of Shatov's murder in *The Devils* ([1871] 1971) follows closely the official report of this murder, which along with other episodes led Bakunin himself to break with Nechayev and distance himself from the insane ruthlessness of his group. In his novel Dostoevsky lumps together the aristocracy and the revolutionaries, and his dislike is personified by Verkhovensky, who is presented less as a revolutionary than as a rogue. As for the other revolutionaries, they appear as caricatures, distorted by the author's vague ideas of what a revolutionary movement actually is. 'Indeed, his own violent political views precluded a fair and thorough appreciation of any progressive movement. To him even the mild liberal Stepan is a devil who can just be saved on his death bed by repentance of his former opinions' (Magarshack, 1971: xiii). Only people like Shatov, who like himself abandons his liberal ideas and wholeheartedly returns to the Church, are granted a gleam of salvation. 'Shatov toyed with the idea of denouncing his former associates in the same way as Dostoevsky himself had actually taken steps to denounce Turgenev, the hated aristocrat and atheist, to posterity' (Magarshack, 1971: xiii).

The author feels hatred and repugnance for liberal opponents, but also for the imaginary enemies of Russia, whom he depicts with the dark tones of his own obsession. Europe, in his view, is haunted by a political delirium, and revolutionaries are like actors in a 'vaudeville of hell'. Among these revolutionaries, Stavrogin is an exemplar 'devil': having rejected the ideas he had previously divulged, he becomes indifferent to everything. Nothing enthuses him; he only feels a gelid emptiness. 'If he believes, he does not believe he does. If he does not believe, he does not believe he does not' (Citati, 2000: 331). After being fascinated by 'absolute evil', even evil he now experiences as extraneous. Let us see how this 'vaudeville of hell' unfolds.

Freethinkers and impostors

In St Petersburg a circle of people, who gather around Mrs Stavrogin, start reading progressive papers and magazines, prohibited tracts published abroad, and revolutionary pamphlets. Stepan Verkhovensky is overcome by a burning desire to join the opposition movements, and with Mrs Stavrogin decides to throw himself heart and soul into the new political activity. She announces, at the same time, that she is prepared to found a periodical of her own and devote her whole life to revolutionary publishing. At the evening parties the conversation dwells on the abolition of censorship and on the spelling reform, on the substitution of the Roman alphabet for the Russian one, on the exile of someone the day before, on some public disturbance in the shopping arcade, on the advisability of a federal constitution for the different nationalities in Russia, and on the abolition of the army and the navy. Some also talk 'of the agrarian reform, of the abolition of inheritance, the family, children, and priesthood, the rights of women, of their own splendid houses.... Among that rabble of "new" men there were many impostors' (*The Devils*: 38). It is the activism of such impostors that will facilitate links between this circle and the 'groups of five', generating a mixture of visionary idealism and aimless violence that Dostoevsky binds tightly together. In doing so, as we will see below, he uses some interpretative tools that the positivist school of criminology will later present as a comprehensive corpus of knowledge.

The circle inhabited by these impostors, as it is rumoured, is a hotbed of freethinking, vice and atheism; but it is also a place where participants indulge in the most innocent, amiable and jolly liberal chatter. Whenever overindulging in drink, they grow excited, and on one occasion they even sing 'La Marseillaise'. Dreams of a universal social republic and harmony à la Fourier, however, are shared with murderers and child abusers, the likes of sadistic Mr Stavrogin, who has ascendancy within the group.

The crimes imputed to this circle are those that the positivist school would term 'natural crimes', namely crimes which violate two basic 'altruistic sentiments': pity and probity. The former implies revulsion against the voluntary infliction of suffering upon others, while the latter entails respect for their property rights. According to Garofalo (1914), natural crimes differ from 'police crimes' in that they describe the inner nature of offenders rather than the economic, institutional and normative circumstances leading to the definition of some conducts as criminal. The crimes of the 'groups of five', therefore, have no economic motivation; rather, they are the result of a particular form of morbidity which combines excessive honesty and cruelty. Lombroso (1876: 258) describes political offenders as individuals in need of suffering for something grand, a need produced by 'an excess of passionate concentration in one single idea'. As if hypnotized, these monomaniacs display the typical 'sublime imprudence of nihilists and Christian martyrs', and turn rebellious because oversensitive. Lombroso describes how someone became an anarchist after seeing that a young apprentice had an arm broken by his employer, and how Italian anarchist Caserio was seen crying when discussing the poverty of workers in Lombardy. Political offenders suffer from hysteria, which frequently manifests itself through excessive altruism coupled with excessive egotism, proving that 'this is only a variant of moral insanity' (259).

Leadership and despotism

The most eventful night for the group sees the assassination of the Lebyatkins, the lynching of Lisa by the mob, and an arson attack. These events surprise the members of the organization, who do not see them as consistent with their political programme. They start accusing the hand that guides them of despotism and lack of frankness. They decide to demand a final explanation from him, and if, as has happened before, he once more declines to give it, to dissolve the 'group of five' and to found in its place a new secret society for 'the propagation of ideas'. The new society will be run in accordance with the principles of democracy and equal rights.

The relationship of Peter Verkhovensky, the leader, with the other members of the group is exemplified by his second lieutenant Erkel, who seems to have a mission, or to have instructions from somewhere of an executive character. In fact, 'he had been entrusted with no mission at all … he had merely fallen under the spell of Peter Verkhovensky, having met him only a short time before.' If he had met some depraved sadist and had been persuaded by him, on some socially romantic pretext, to set up a gang and, as a test, 'had been ordered to rob and murder the first peasant he came across, he would most certainly have gone and done it' (The Devils: 539). Erkel is fanatically, childishly, devoted to 'the common cause', but only because he is fanatically devoted to Peter.

To carry out orders was an absolute necessity for his petty, unreasoning nature, which always yearned to submit itself to someone else's will – oh, of course, only for the sake of the 'common' or 'great' cause. Little fanatics like Erkel cannot understand the service to an idea unless they identify in their minds with the person who gives expression to it. (*The Devils*: 540)

When confronted by the other members of the group, Verkhovensky explains that the murder was only committed for personal motives, a robbery turned into killing by clumsy Fedka. He adds that, anyway, there is no reason to be sentimental, because Fedka, quite accidentally, has eliminated a dangerous person for the organization. He then reiterates that individual action should never be allowed to put the common cause in jeopardy: individuals are only links in an endless chain, and everyone owes implicit obedience to the central brain commanding that chain.

Verkhovensky's associates start to show signs of scepticism. Peter keeps drawing a picture of Russia covered with an endless network of small groups. Each of these active groups, while enrolling new members and branching out endlessly, is said to aim to expose the local authorities and to undermine their prestige, to throw the population into confusion, to promote cynicism and public scandals and, finally, by means of fires, to throw the country, if necessary, into a mood of despair.

Aren't those your very words? Isn't that the programme of action you communicated to us as one authorised by the central committee, about which we know nothing at all and which we have every right to regard as entirely mythical? (*The Devils*: 543–4)

Peter insists that members have acted out of reckless self-will, and that they are now exposed to a person who is going to inform the police about them and their organization. Whether the central committee is mythical or nor, now they are all in danger. The prospective informer is Shatov, whose betrayal begs the 'last decision' of the group.

'Oh, let's send him to the devil!', someone says. And would-be repentant Lyamshin adds: 'We should have done it long ago!' Peter proposes that at nightfall, on the following day, Shatov should be lured to a lonely spot to hand over the illegal printing press which he is keeping and which is buried somewhere, and 'deal with him there'. Also, there is a way of averting suspicion completely. He tells members about Kirilov, of his intention, explained later, to shoot himself, of his promise to leave a note behind taking on himself anything the others will dictate to him. It is now interesting to see how Shatov justifies his betrayal:

> Who are the people I gave up? They are the enemies of life, old-fashioned liberals, who are afraid of their own independence, flunkeys of thought, enemies of individuality and freedom, flabby preachers of dead and rotten ideas. What is it they have to offer? Senility, horrible middle-class medi-ocrity, envious equality, equality without self-esteem (The Devils: 575).

Members of the positivist school could not agree more: as Lombroso argues, political violence is caused by extreme egotism hysterically combined with dreams of equality. Such dreams appear as the ultimate justification of a mediocre pursuit of individual aims. Anarchists, Lombroso (1894) claims, are neophiles, and, while embracing all new ideas, only attempt to mask their lack of intellectual independence; they call for collective regeneration because they fear their own individuality.

After Shatov is killed, someone obsessively repeats: 'That's wrong, wrong. That's all wrong!' Lyamshin is caught by violent panic, and suddenly utters an unnatural scream. Peter has to remind the men that their actions must be animated by one aim:

> To bring everything down with a crash: the State as well as its moral standards. We alone will be left, we who have prepared ourselves before-hand to take over the government: the intelligent we shall bring over to our side, and the fools we shall use to carry us on their shoulders. You

must not be shy of that. We must re-educate a generation to make it worthy of freedom. We shall have many thousand Shatovs to deal with. (*The Devils*: 602)

Epilepsy

It is now time for Peter to remind Kirilov to kill himself and take the blame for the murder. He is very anxious and afraid he might suddenly decide not to. Behind this promise there is a theory: by shooting himself, Kirilov will become a god. He explains: 'If there is a God, then it is always His will, and I can do nothing against His will. If there isn't, then it is my will, and I am bound to express my self-will. I am bound to shoot myself, because the most important point of my self-will is to kill myself' (*The Devils*: 586).

In a conversation with another member of the group he also describes the state of mind which has led to his theory. He has 'moments of eternal harmony', he feels a painful sense of gladness, lasting no longer than five or six seconds. It is nothing earthly, but a man in his earthly semblance cannot endure it: he would have to undergo a physical change or die. It is as though one suddenly apprehended all nature. It is much higher than love, and what is so terrifying about it is, if it went on for more than five seconds, the soul could not endure it and would perish. 'In those five seconds I live through a lifetime, and I am ready to give my life for them, for it's worth it. To be able to endure it for ten seconds, you would have to undergo a physical change.' His interlocutor is stunned by the description, and replies: 'You're not an epileptic? I've heard that's just how an epileptic fit begins ... it has been described to me very much like your eternal harmony. Be careful, Kirilov – it's epilepsy!' (*The Devils*: 586–7).

Is this Dostoevsky? Lombroso too stresses that his theory of 'criminal atavism' finds validation when crime is associated with moral insanity and epilepsy. 'With a defective cerebral nutrition, and a failing nervous system induced by epilepsy, morbidity couples with monstrosity' (Lombroso, 1876: 237). Kirilov and his associates, perhaps, suffer from 'cranium sclerosis', brain haemorrhage, pigmentosis of nervous cells, with the inevitable 'fusion of the frontal lobes'.

When the activities of the 'group of five' come to an end, this is not because evidence leads to apportionment of blame, but because one of its members suddenly solves the mystery. Lyamshin locks himself up in his room for hours; he seems to attempt suicide, but does not succeed. He then rushes off to the police, crawling on his knees, sobs and shrieks, kisses the floor, crying that he is not worthy to kiss the boots of the high officials who stand before him. They calm him down and speak nicely to him. He tells them everything, absolutely everything: all the facts, all he knows, anticipating their questions, giving them information about things in which they are not interested and they would never have thought of asking him. It is, again, the act of an epileptic: his face is distorted, his allegiance has suddenly shifted, he displays incongruent, intermittent impulses, the eternal harmony he used to find in the 'group of five' he now experiences in the presence of the police.

Times of transition

The Devils contains, however, much more than some scattered Lombrosian assertions relating political violence to individual pathology or innate maladjustment. Criminologists may distil other categories in the novel, and ardent anomie theorists, for example, may cherish it as a flagship.

The 'group of five', in fact, is situated in a larger social context and is surrounded by political turmoil. All sorts of low-class individuals make an appearance in the novel, and though Dostoevsky makes no effort to hide his aversion for them, he cannot avoid noting how these individuals 'always appear everywhere in troubled times of uncertainty or transition' (*The Devils*: 459). Along with the so-called 'progressives' (his inverted commas), who are always in a greater hurry than everyone else and whose aims, though mostly absurd, are more or less definite, he sees the rabble. 'This rabble, which you will find in any society, usually rises to the surface in every period of transition and is not only without any aim, but also without any inkling of an idea, merely expressing with all its strength unrest and impatience.' This impatient mass of individuals, without realizing it, almost always finds itself under the command of a small crowd of 'progressives', who act with a definite aim, 'and it is they who direct this scum where they like, provided they themselves are not composed of utter idiots, which, however, happens, too' (*The Devils*: 459). The social composition of this 'scum', as presented by the author, may not testify to his sociological acumen, but well describes a transitional anomie which one may regard as the cause of unrest and violence:

> Wretched little Jews with a mournful but haughty smile, guffawing travellers, poets with political tendencies from the capital, poets who made up for their lack of political tendencies or talent by wearing peasant coats and tarred boots, majors and colonels, who laughed at the senselessness of their profession and who for an extra rouble would be ready to take off their swords and leave the army for a job as railway clerks ... innumerable divinity students, women who were the embodiment of the woman question – all these suddenly gained the upper hand among us. (*The Devils*: 460)

The violence of the 'group of five', therefore, might also be interpreted as an extreme manifestation of 'times of transition', when the division of labour, to use Durkheim's (1960) argument, ceases to create social solidarity and becomes anomic.

It would be improper to claim that *The Devils* incorporates, in a literary masterpiece, the crucial shift from early positivism to anomie theory occurring in the analysis of political violence. In his novel Dostoevsky reflects the shift he experiences in his own political and philosophical views, when his return to religion is accompanied by the spiteful rejection of the 'rabble', the 'scum', and the 'liberals' leading them. The Devils, in a sense, mirrors its author's intellectual trajectory: it starts with optimistic joy 'as if the narrator did not know its tragic end' (Borges, 1999: 517).

In the second literary work examined in this chapter an analysis of political violence can be carried out that transcends the shift from positivist to anomie theory, reaching out to touch on conflict theory and surpassing it in refinement.

The Just

Camus' adaptation of Dostoevsky's The Devils bears a more problematical title: The Just, a theatre version of the novel first performed in 1959 (Camus, 1984). The most recent staging of the play was unjustly described as 'embarrassingly dated', as a play 'ready to be consigned to the dustbin of obsolete intellectual theatre' (Wassenaar, 2001: 19). This hasty dismissal is due to the association of political violence with Marxism, therefore with an allegedly obsolete philosophy, an association which ignores the current violent practices in which religious, ethnic or other groups engage themselves. Some contemporary relevance of The Just comes to light if the practices of such groups are borne in mind.

The play tells about the bombing which killed the Grand Duke Sergei, the Tsar's uncle, organized by a socialist revolutionary cell in Moscow. It also focuses on the clash of personalities and ideological justifications surrounding the incident, while the concluding part deals with its judicial aftermath.

'Freedom will remain a prison until everyone on earth is free.' Earnest didacticism characterizes the members of the revolutionary cell, who aim at 'hastening the liberation of the Russian people'. They want the Imperial Court to learn how determined they are to continue their 'reign of terror until the land is returned to the people' (*The Just*: 166). While all members adhere to this broad political programme, their personalities display the contradictions that most political movements and groups invariably experience. Kaliayev, for example, is also called the Poet, a name that some regard as inappropriate for a terrorist, whereas others deem it ideal, for all poetry is revolutionary.

Individualism clashes with the need for collective discipline, as when Stepan begs Kaliayev to let him throw the bomb: 'You know how much it means to me.' The answer is: no, orders are orders. Those not involved in the operation have to wait in their rooms: 'It's hard but those are the rules' (*The Just*: 171). Kaliayev says that during the war the Japanese never surrendered: rather they killed themselves. But he is told that suicide is not an option. To commit suicide, a man must have a great love for himself, whereas a true revolutionary cannot love himself.

Love and hatred, life and death, clash in the mutual antagonizing of Stepan and Kaliayev. The latter says that he loves life and claims that he joined the revolution *because* he loves life! The former retorts that he does not, and that he loves something higher than mere life: he loves justice. 'I have come to kill a man, not to love him' (*The Just*: 175). He is reminded that he will not kill by himself, for no cause. He will kill with the rest of his companions, on behalf of the Russian people! They are all killing to build a world where there will be no killing at all. They must accept their role as criminals, until finally everyone on earth will be innocent.

Sometimes it worries them to think that they are forced to be murderers, but then they realize that their choice will lead them to die too, and this thought reassures them. They feel that they are giving more than they take.

Dora's misgivings make her shake with emotion: just before killing the Grand Duke, Kaliayev, for a moment, will have to look at him. A man is a man: the Grand Duke may have gentle eyes; perhaps he will be smiling and look meekly at his murderer. To which Kaliayev replies: 'It is not him I am destroying... I am destroying tyranny' (The Just: 177).

The first attempt fails, as Kaliayev sees that there are children in the Grand Duke's carriage. He cannot do it, otherwise the revolution will be loathed by the entire human race. He is told that revolutionaries love the human race enough to force revolution on it, to rescue humanity from itself. On the one hand, it is wrong to think that anything is justifiable: 'thousands of us have died to prove that everything is not justifiable' (The Just: 187). On the other hand, the Grand Duke will be killed because his death may help to bring nearer the day when Russian children no longer die of starvation. Kaliayev stresses that, though he is ready to kill to overthrow the tyranny, behind his comrades' words he detects the threat of another kind of tyranny, and if that new tyranny ever comes into power, it will make him a murderer. The revolution has its honour, he concludes. No is the reply: honour is a luxury reserved for those who have carriages.

At the second attempt, the attack is successful, but soon after Kaliayev is identified and arrested. In his cell he speaks to fellow prisoner Foka, to whom he introduces himself as a revolutionary socialist. Foka is stunned, and with unwitting comicality he answers: 'Why did you have to be that? All you had to do was to stay put and you would have had fun. The world was made for you gentlemen.' Didactically, Kaliayev addresses him with: 'If Russia were free you would not be here... we will all be brothers and justice will make our hearts pure and innocent.' But Foka remarks that it 'seems bloody silly getting put in prison for ideas like that'. There is no use talking about brothers; he is a prisoner but he has been given the job of hangman as well. 'I get a year knocked off my sentence for each one I hang… suits me' (The Just: 205–6).

Fighting for life while giving death: this unbearable contradiction unfolds in the last part of the play, when Kaliayev faces execution. Is that the only way he will find peace: in death? So let him die, but quickly, someone proffers. Dora finally explodes: 'Death! The gallows! Oh, it's always death! If death is the only way, then we have chosen the wrong path. The right path leads to life, a life where the sun shines. You can't be cold all the time' (The Just: 221).

Moments before being executed, Kaliayev looks happy: it would be too unfair if he did not find happiness in death when he had rejected it in life. He walks quite calmly to the scaffold, climbs the steps and is 'swallowed up by the darkness'. You can just see the shroud that the hangman puts over his head. And then?

> A horrible thud… Don't you realize that today is the day of our justifi-
> cation! Something has been born today which is our testimony, the
> testimony of us revolutionaries. He is no longer a murderer! A horrible
> thud! That's all it took… one thud and he was plunged back into the joys
> of childhood! (The Just: 226)

It is true that revolutionaries love their fellow human beings, Dora says, but they do so with an unhappy love. They are so cut off from them, shut in their little rooms, lost in their thoughts: and do the people love them? Do they know that they love them? Revolutionaries genuinely love: they give everything, sacrifice everything, without expecting anything in return. They do not remember what summer is like, and in choosing death they also choose eternal winter. There is warmth in the world, but it is not for them: they are 'the just'. Dora wants to find her own justification for that choice, and asks to throw the next bomb, because she is 'no longer a woman, but equal to everybody else'. She shall throw the bomb, and then one cold night she will face the same rope, and everything will be easier.

Group interests and beyond

Conflict theorists express the view that the organized state does not represent the values and interests of society at large, but those of limited groups with sufficient power to control its operations and practices. Conduct norms are not mirrored in the law, which only reflects the norms of the dominant culture (Sellin, 1938). The Just, against this background, could be read as a manifestation, if extreme, of two sets of conduct norms violently clashing. The members of the revolutionary cell are self-appointed representatives of social sectors whose interests diverge from those of the dominant sectors. But let us see in more detail some of the tenets of conflict theory and try to apply them to Camus' play.

The belief that people are fundamentally group-involved beings leads conflict theorists to describe social life as permanent confrontation. Individuals are said to produce associations on the basis of common interests and to pursue them through collective action. These associations or groups are said to engage in a permanent struggle to maintain, or to improve, the place they occupy in the interaction with other groups. Conflict is therefore regarded as one of the principal and essential processes in the continuous and ongoing functioning of society. The conflict between groups seeking their own interests is especially visible in legislative politics, where definitions of acceptable and unacceptable conducts are forged.

> Thus the whole process of lawmaking, lawbreaking, and law enforcement directly reflects deep-seated and fundamental conflicts between group interests and the more general struggles among groups for control of the

police power of the state. To that extent, criminal behaviour is the behaviour of minority power groups, in that these groups do not have sufficient power to promote and defend their interests and purposes in the legislative process. (Vold et al., 1998: 235–7)

Camus' revolutionaries appear to use illegitimate violence confidently because that violence is only defined as illegitimate by powerful groups controlling the legislative process. When they claim that the death of Sergei may put an end to the death of the starving children of Russia, they also optimistically anticipate that soon the social groups they represent will be able to redraw the legislation so that their criminality will be perceived as innocence. The small group in which they operate may be unable to overturn legal definitions in a short period of time, but it is their conviction that the way in which their actions affect the social dynamic at large will catalyse a process of redefinition of criminal behaviour. Similarly, conflict theorists posit that the definition of political activity as criminal results from the challenge to authority through dissent, disobedience or violence, a challenge which is deemed intolerable by the establishment (Turk, 1982).

It is inherently difficult to specify the meaning of political criminal acts, but 'it is generally in the interest of authorities to leave themselves as much discretion as possible in dealing with intolerable political opposition' (Turk, 1982: 62). The 'just' pay with the extreme expression of such discretion, namely execution, and this seems to suggest to them that they have a serious chance of bringing radical transformation to the structure of power. Their activity, however, is not an immanent form of that transformation, the person they kill being a symbol, a replaceable icon of that structure of power, which remains intact. They perform what Turk terms 'the propaganda of the deed', that is to say those acts that may be committed as more or less reasoned tactical moves which justify the occasional destruction of property or lives.

Their 'propaganda' is a revolutionary spark aimed at starting the fire of widespread opposition. 'This type of opposition is calculated, organized, and may lead to either a full-blown revolution or annihilation. In the first instance, the former criminals become the rulers of the new order' (Turk, 1982: 107).

It is exactly on the capacity of the former criminals to become the rulers of the new order that the 'just' harbour contrasting feelings. The new order must also be a moral order if it is not to turn into a new type of tyranny. Of course, 'claims that the more advantaged are such by right, not might' will always be met with counterclaims. It is also true that the struggle for authority is a constant, and 'political resistance, including violence, is therefore a fundamental component of a polity' (Turk, 1982: 167). However, even when revolutionary violence is the only remaining alternative (Roebuck and Weeber, 1978), there is a danger that it will intensify the very inhumanity which it seeks to overcome (Cruickshank, 1984).

Camus, on this topic, adds great subtlety to conflict theory, whose overarching tenets risk excessive simplification. He deplores those revolutionaries who express the 'madness and destructiveness' of their virtue, and whose 'morality' leads to abstraction, blindness, fanaticism and ultimately injustice. The evil of abstraction bears the responsibility for wars, torture, violence (Brombert, 1999: 111). Camus also rejects any form of revolt involving the idea of transcendence, and is critical of doctrines of historical inevitability, which he judges as 'transcendence of men without God'. He is suspicious of ideas that lack human warmth and that eventually imprison and exploit individuals rather than serving or liberating them (Cruickshank, 1984: 18). His lesson to conflict theorists is that there are some political conflicts emphasizing history, and others emphasizing humanity. The emphasis on history destroys all limits to human action, because history itself becomes the supreme judge of morality of that action. Revolutions inspired by a sense of historical inevitability inherit the 'right to punish' that they take away from the defeated, and, after dressing it with a religious mantle, put punishment at the centre of the universe. They adopt a doctrine of culpability for the humans and one of innocence for history (Camus, 1965).

Revolt questions the means through which social justice is achieved; it demands limits, lest the very ideal which it seeks to make active in the world is destroyed. The emphasis on humanity makes revolt creative, and leads it to unity, while the emphasis on history leads to the claim to totality. The 'just' seem to waver between these two types of conflict. While seeking the judgement of history, they also feel that there are limits beyond which their revolt will perpetuate the lack of warmth in which they plan the establishment of a future society. Simultaneously, they replace 'we are' with 'we shall be', thus postponing to the future the precise identification of those limits. They are like most human beings, as Camus (1965: 420) notes, who refuse to be what they are. The question is whether this refusal will lead to the destruction of others and themselves, 'and whether all rebellions will have to be achieved through the justification of universal murder, or whether, without pretending an impossible innocence, they will be able to discover the principle of reasonable culpability'.

2

Organizing Crime:
Cervantes, Gay and Brecht

Miguel de Cervantes, John Gay and Bertolt Brecht do not confuse professional crime with organized crime; nor do they associate the adjective 'organized' with the seriousness of the illicit activity described. The three authors considered in this chapter display a subtle understanding of the structural elements underpinning the identification of 'professional' and 'organized' as two discrete categories of illegality. The works examined below allude to the tensions between structured criminal organizations and independent lawbreakers and the way these tensions influence one another's illegal choice, bringing some light to the definitional chaos surrounding this area of criminal activity.

A brotherhood of thieves

Cervantes' *Novelas ejemplares* may be seen as the author's most mature production, for the highly conscious and refined literary artistry the novellas deploy, and for the admirably terse, vigorous and direct style, a declaration of faith to the apothegm that he uses twice in *Don Quixote*: 'All affectation is bad' (Putnam, 1952: xi). The picaresque *Rinconete and Cortadillo* ([1613] 1952) is indeed an exemplary tale of that refined collection, all the more so if readers see it as a historical account of the underworld of a seventeenth-century town. Set in Seville, then populated by a large variety of nationalities and governed by acutely corrupt administrators, the tale reflects Cervantes' acquaintance with the place and its social make-up, particularly those communities where lawbreaking was a commonly embraced profession and thieves' jargon a shared means of communication.

In Seville, even small boys were ostentatiously armed, in imitation of their elders, perhaps hoping that their noviciate would lead to recruitment by a professional gang and thus into a safe career. A 'brotherhood of thieves' was said to be operating in town, a hierarchical organization led by a prior and a number of consuls who supervised the daily work of bag-snatchers, housebreakers, street tricksters and a range of other predators. The brotherhood had a central warehouse in which stolen goods were kept, and administered a large sum destined for members' wages and bribes for those who helped them when they were in trouble with the law. Recruitment was meticulous and only strong, active, proven Christians were accepted, particularly 'servants of powerful and high-placed individuals and agents of the law'. A solemn oath bound members to mutual loyalty, committing them to endure arrest and incarceration and not to inform on their companions. It is uncertain whether the brotherhood exerted a form of monopoly on theft, though historians do not hesitate to vow that when something was missing from the home of a respectable citizen and *vox populi* said that the devil had taken it, the truth is that the 'devil' was likely to be one of the organization. 'That they have a brotherhood is certain, and it has lasted longer than the principality of Venice; for although the law has caught a few unfortunate ones, it has never been able to run down the leader of the gang' (Putnam, 1952: xii–xiii).

That the members of the brotherhood were thieves and served God at the same time should not sound surprising, considering how this was common in the Andalusian underworld, where a popular proverb went: steal the pig and give the feet to God. Highwaymen had a set of prayers believed to render them invisible to their pursuers, and those who were caught or killed rarely failed to reveal sacred medals on their chests and scapulars on their shoulders.

> Out of such setting Cervantes has drawn vivid types. During his residence there he hardly could have failed to absorb all the colour and the movement of the place, and with the true novelist's instinct he has put the experience to good use. He has also doubtless embodied much that he learned in prison. (Putnam, 1952: xiii)

Cervantes, however, was well aware of the risks of romanticizing bandits and organized criminals, and warned that his prose and ethical goals were so respectable and restrained, so within the bounds of reason and conformable to Christian conduct, that 'no one who reads them, either carefully or carelessly, can possibly be moved to evil thoughts' (*Rinconete and Cortadillo*: 5). Hence the choice of giving the stories the title of 'Exemplary', as all of them, in his view, conveyed some useful example of good conduct. Had Cervantes believed for one moment that the reading of those novellas would arouse evil thoughts or desires, he proclaimed, he would sooner have cut off the hand that wrote them rather than see them published. We are fortunate that that hand remained in its place.

Rinconete and Cortadillo

Our two heroes, after formal mutual introduction, find the ideal grounds for a potential partnership. Asked if he knows any trade, Rinconete mentions: how to run like a hare, leap like a deer, and handle a pair of scissors very neatly. His father is a person of quality, being 'an agent of the Holy Crusade, that is to say, one who sells papal bulls or indulgences, a bulero, or, as people usually say, a buldero' (*Rinconete and Cortadillo*: 10). He used to accompany him at times, and learned the trade so well that when it comes to 'dispensing bulls' he would not take second place to any man no matter how good at it he might be. One day, he says, he came to love the money from the bulls more than the bulls themselves, and, having embraced a bag of it, he made off for Madrid, where he gutted the bag. The men who were in charge of the money went after him, and he was shown little mercy. As he was very young, however, they were satisfied with sending him to the whipping post. Then he started earning his living with cards, 'playing twenty-one in all the inns and taverns between here and Madrid'. He shows the cards, which are worn and filthy, but there is one marvellous thing about them: if one knows how to handle them, no matter how one cuts them, an ace is bound to turn up.

> Let us spread the net and see if any bird falls into it from among the mule drivers in this inn; by which I mean that the two of us will start playing twenty-one as if we were in earnest, and if anyone wants to make a third, he will be the first to leave his money behind him. (*Rinconete and Cortadillo*: 15)

Cortadillo says that his father was a tailor and taught him his trade, and with his ability for cutting with shears he went on to cutting purses. He became tired of his cramped life in a small town and of the lack of affection his stepmother showed him, and so he left and went to Toledo to practise his calling there. In that city he did wonders, 'for there was not a reliquary dangling from a hood or a pocket so well hidden that my fingers did not find it out or my scissors clip it, even though it might have been guarded by the eyes of Argus' (*Rinconete and Cortadillo*: 15). In Toledo he was never caught in the act or chased by constables or turned in by any informer. True enough, there was one

time when a spy who worked both with the officers of the law and
with thieves reported his cleverness to the magistrate, who became so
enamoured of his good qualities that he insisted on seeing him.
However, being very humble, he did not like to deal with important
personages, so he declined the invitation and left the city in haste.

Rinconete and Cortadillo deceive some customers of the inn with
their trick cards and are forced to make a precipitous escape. A group
of men help them run away from those they have duped; their 'gratitude' is expressed by the desire to rob one of the rescuers as well.
Cortadillo cannot refrain from ripping open the valise that one of the
group, a Frenchman, carries up behind him. With his knife he inflicts
so wide and deep a gash that the inside becomes plainly visible and
proves worth taking. The bounty consists of a couple of good shirts and
other clothes, and, before the theft is discovered, they leave obsequi-
ously and grateful. 'And the next day they sold the shirts at the old
clothes market outside the Arenal Gate, receiving for them the sum of
twenty reales' (*Rinconete and Cortadillo*: 18).

After being offered a job as porters, which they find admirably suited
to their trade for the possibility the job offers to enter private houses,
they are then approached by a lad who witnesses one of their thefts.
The lad cryptically asks whether they are 'in the bad books', and, to
the puzzlement of the two, he adds that he finds it odd that, as thieves,
they have not yet gone to Señor Monipodio's custom house. Rinconete
and Cortadillo begin to understand, and enquire if all thieves in town
have to pay a duty. The explanation is given that all have, at least, to
register with Señor Monipodio, who is their father, their teacher and
their protector, 'and I accordingly advise you to come with me and
render him obedience, for if you do not do so and dare to commit a
theft without his approval, it will cost you dearly' (*Rinconete and Cortadillo*:
26).

Monipodio is described as an influential, clever and competent man. So much so that during the four years that he has been the leader and father of thieves, not more than four of them have ended up on the *finibusterrae* (hanged), only some thirty have tasted leather (flogging), and a mere sixty-two have gone over the road (to the galleys). He is 'at the service of God and all good people', and he makes his men serve God too. 'He has commanded that out of what we steal we must give something in the way of alms to buy oil for the lamp that stands before a highly venerated image here in the city' (*Rinconete and Cortadillo*: 30). The religious fervour of his men, however, leads them further: they say their rosary, appositely divided according to the days of the week, and many of them do not steal on Friday or speak to any woman called Mary on a Saturday.

Cervantes' description of the brotherhood's members is detailed, leaving no doubt as to their distinctive subculture. Visually, they can only belong to the colourful and ruthless underworld of Seville: some are swaggering young ruffians with large moustaches, broad-brimmed hats, Walloon ruffs, coloured stockings, and large showy garters. Their swords exceed the length allowed by law, the pistols they carry replace the ordinary daggers, and their bucklers are suspended from their girdles. But these swaggering youths are linked with a variety of 'benefactors', including those who defend them in court, the constables who tip them off, the executioner who shows them mercy, and the person who, when one of them is fleeing through the street and the crowd behind him is crying 'Stop thief! Stop thief!', intervenes to stem the torrent of pursuers by saying: 'Let the poor fellow go, he's had enough bad luck, let him go, and let his sin be his punishment!' (*Rinconete and Cortadillo*: 35).

Law enforcers are an irreplaceable resource for the brotherhood, though they are not rewarded as they would deserve. Monipodio says that his organization is given a whole chicken, while only sparing a drumstick for them. Officers, he admits, do more for them in a day than they do for them in a hundred days. But this is the inevitable outcome of the strict division of labour governing the brotherhood.

The two old, dignified, members standing in a corner of the custom house are 'hornets', and their business is to go through the city during the day and spy out houses that might be burgled at night. They also follow those who withdraw money from the Bank of India or the Treasury, in order to see where they take that money and what they do with it. 'We have another pair, a couple of porters who serve as furniture movers at times; they know the entrances and exits to all the houses in the city and which dwellings are worth our while and which are not' (*Rinconete and Cortadillo*: 52).

After Rinconete and Cortadillo are introduced to Monipodio, they witness a telling episode that adds to their understanding of the function and nature of the brotherhood. A young gentleman storms in and asks why the men have 'made such a botch of the job he has ordered done'. Monipodio replies that he does not know what the circumstances are, but that the member charged with executing the job is present and will give a good account of himself. At that point Chiquiznaque arrives, and his superior asks him if he has carried out the commission in question, 'a matter of a knife wound of fourteen stitches'. 'Which one was that, asks Chiquiznaque, the merchant at the crossroads?' Well, he explains,

> I went up to him, took one look at his face, and saw that it was so small that a wound of fourteen stitches was out of question.... Well, seeing that his face was too small and narrow for the required number of stitches, and not wishing to have my trip for nothing, I gave the cut to a lackey of his, and you can be sure that it was a first-rate one. (*Rinconete and Cortadillo*: 61)

The gentleman who ordered the cut says that the group has not complied with the contract, and that the job has to be completed as required. To which Chiquiznaque replies that this time he will leave so perfect a scar that people will think the fellow was born with it.

Rinconete and Cortadillo learn that the brotherhood is engaged not only in organized theft and fencing but also in the delivery of punishment ordered by customers against enemies or competitors. A member reads a 'Memorandum of slashes to be given this week', and the list includes the merchant of the crossroads, worth fifty crowns, thirty received on account; the alehouse keeper of Alfalfa Square, one dozen heavy blows at a crown each, eight on account, time limit six days; the hunchback tailor, known as the Finch, six heavy blows at the request of the lady who left her necklace with him. They also learn that there is a list of 'Common Outrages' in which the organization specializes: throwing vials, smearing with Juniper oil, nailing up *sambenitos* (indicating heresy) and horns (indicating a cuckold), mocking in public, creating false alarms and disturbances, pretend stabbings, and circulating slanders.

Astounded by the careless manner in which justice is administered in that famous city of Seville, and fearful that the 'members of that infamous academy' would make their work more difficult and dangerous, the two independent thieves leave and seek elsewhere a more apposite environment for their professional development.

A bureaucratic brotherhood?

Monipodio's organization possesses some traits that would comfortably fit traditional definitions of organized crime, particularly those revolving around categories such as continuity and bureaucracy. The brotherhood, as we are informed, has lasted longer than the principality of Venice. Similarly, in the early 1950s, a number of North American agencies suggested that organized crime was formed by one single, albeit segmented, wide group of criminals bound together in a self-perpetuating, continuing conspiracy (Kefauver Committee, 1951). The notion of bureaucracy was also applied to 'crime families', whereby organized crime was described as hierarchically structured, characterized by formal rules and consisting of individuals with specialized and segmented functions within the hierarchy. A few individuals and families were therefore deemed to centralize and coordinate all organized criminal activities (Cressey, 1969).

The brotherhood of thieves led by Monipodio, however, is not only characterized by specific internal relationships between its members, nor simply by a 'principal and agent' model of organization. For, if it is true that the 'principal' of the brotherhood commands a number of agents to take actions on Monipodio's behalf, and that the agents are motivated by monetary reward, the actions taken imply the existence of external actors who, though not part of the organization, establish such meaningful relationships with it that without them the brotherhood would lose its central character. True, its members are 'swaggering ruffians' carrying pistols instead of daggers, but their subculture is perpetuated thanks to the demand from representatives of the official culture for the services they deliver. Monipodio is described as an influential man, and his friends include constables, executioners, and various other people who intervene to hamper those who chase his men after they have committed a theft. The brotherhood, in other words, is defined by both its internal cohesiveness and its ability to interact with external customers and partners (Ruggiero, 2002). Overturning conventional definitions, it has similarly been argued that organized crime consists of 'politicians, law enforcement people, businessmen, union leaders, and (in some ways least important of all) racketeers' (Chambliss, 1978: 9). In some classics of the sociology of deviance there is also awareness that criminal careers in organized crime receive a crucial boost when, after passing from one status to another in the illegitimate opportunity system, members develop a set of relationships with members of the legitimate world. 'Unless [they] can form these relationships, the possibility of a stable, protected criminal style of life is effectively precluded' (Cloward and Ohlin, 1960: 166).

Rinconete and Cortadillo stumble in an organization that rationalizes theft by making revenues more stable and by rendering the related flow of commodities more predictable. In this sense, the organization expresses an implicit preference for frequent small-scale operations rather than infrequent large-scale ones. Hence its stability and perseverance in setting up long-term bonds of mutual interest with official authorities and respectable customers. This, in turn, benefits its members, who can rely on steady income and enjoy a degree of security vis-à-vis the vagaries of demand and law enforcement. As Stigler (1970) remarks, criminals are faced with details regarding their occupational choice which do not substantially differ from those of licit occupations. They have to estimate the possible costs of apprehension, legal defence and conviction, and they may also have to plan or save for periods of ill-ness, unemployment and eventual retirement. The brotherhood is able partly to resolve these problems, hence perhaps its attractiveness to loose ruffians and disorganized little groups of thieves, who join Moni-podio's firm more for want of security than for fear of retaliation. Rinconete and Cortadillo, however, prefer to continue their activity without the protective but stifling interference of the brotherhood, and in doing so they resist, as professional criminals, the pressures for recruitment by organized criminals. Despite the fact that the organiza-tion, as a keen member tells them, has succeeded in drastically reducing the risk of apprehension and the level of occupational risk, they opt for freedom of criminal enterprise, and retain the privilege of simul-taneously planning and executing their own future exploits. We shall see how the tension between organized and professional crime evolves in the literary work examined below.

Here, it is worth noting that the brotherhood described by Cervantes is a structured predatory association that also inflicts punishment on request, thus playing a vicarious law-and-order function. In this sense, the brotherhood is a fictitious or real ancestor of the old Neapolitan Camorra, the organization entrusted with maintaining public order at the time of the unification of Italy, when the regular police had been sent to back up Garibaldi's army (Ruggiero, 1993). It would appear, therefore, that Monipodio's organization is allowed to fill the deficiencies of institutional state power, and to replace this power in the disciplining of conflicts and the tempering of violent excesses. This vicarious function, however, does not seem to survive, as is often suggested (Albanese, 1985), in more modern forms of organized crime. Nor does the brotherhood play the exclusive role of 'protection and trust' provider, in a situation where the state apparatus is unable to provide both (Gambetta, 1992). Cervantes' brotherhood does not regulate the market through the exercise of violence; nor does it create a smooth environment for 'free' transactions to take place. Its violence, meticulously graded in its menu of punishments, is an instrument aimed at the polarization of the market rather than the establishment of free, trustful and fair transactions in it. Let us see how the predatory and violent elements in Monipodio evolve in the activities of Jonathan Wild.

Crime, parasites and the state

John Gay's The Beggar's Opera ([1728] 1986) is more than a parody of the conventions of melodrama, and its historical value is not just found in its offering us, 'instead of the floridly baroque arias of Scarlatti or Handle, English and Irish folk songs; instead of the royal palace or the enchanted island, the alehouse and the prison; instead of heroes and goddesses, thieves and whores' (Loughrey and Treadwell, 1986: 12). It is also a document that, while describing conventional crime, unveils the practice, the rationale and the structure of a criminal enterprise developing common interests with agencies of social order. Moreover, it is a piece of realistic analysis of how organized crime and the official establishment can exchange services and perform a role of mutual enhancement and promotion.

The background to the *Opera* is provided by London's urban space-scape, where new buildings sprang up wherever uncontrolled planning permitted and wherever the provision of adequate light or sanitation could be evaded. The poorer quarters of London, made up of filthy alleys and narrow, dark courtyards 'bordered by ramshackle tenements known as rookeries' (Loughrey and Treadwell, 1986: 13), perpetuated their state while offering a contribution to the wealth of the nation and the maintenance of social order. In one such quarter, the slum of St Giles, more than one house in every four was a gin shop; official commentators praised its inhabitants because the distilling of corn was an important way of supporting agriculture, therefore an activity to be cherished and tenderly preserved. Unfortunately, however, the city space in which such a useful contribution to the national economy was conceived was also a impermeable to surveillance. In the slums, the irregularity of buildings, the alleys and the courts seemed to be intended for the purpose of concealment, so that useful activities could dangerously mingle with parasitic ones. Henry Fielding (1751) describes London as a vast wood or forest, in which a thief may harbour with as great a degree of security as wild beasts do in the deserts of Africa or Arabia.

While policing was chaotic and ineffectual, and if virtually every permanent official involved in the administration of London had to buy their job, prisoners were also required to pay for the cost of their detention, as they were billed for the use of the cell. Trade and its principles penetrated the logic of criminal legislation, shaping crime itself, rather than responding to it. In 1706 an Act was passed which for the first time made the receiving of stolen goods a capital offence (Beattie, 2001). This Act also contained a section encouraging criminals who were prepared to inform on their accomplices: if the evidence given led to conviction, the informer received not only a free pardon but also a reward of forty pounds.

> The intention behind this Act was to break up the gangs of thieves by encouraging them to betray one another, but its real effect was to bring into being a class of professional informers, called thief-catchers or thief-takers, who operated by perjuring themselves and blackmailing their victims. (Loughrey and Treadwell, 1986: 17)

This allowed the criminal law, more than any other social institution, to govern eighteenth-century England without a police force, and explains the resistance of the elite to any drastic legal reform. Hence the rejection of fixed criminal codes establishing determined sentences for precise offences, which still prevails in the country, and hence the inclination of the elite to 'think of justice in personal terms', with the result that mercy and a patronizing attitude are coupled by the spectacle of suffering as righteous institutional vengeance (Hay, 1975).

Organized crime as described in *The Beggar's Opera* is strictly hierarchical in its layout, with the thief-catcher sending his soldiers to steal around the city: if they refuse to go, he reports them to the authorities for some former crime. The new Act, in effect, was fully exploited in its economic potential by the most successful criminal of the period, 'Thief-Taker General of Great Britain and Ireland', Jonathan Wild. His skills, as thief-taker and receiver, led him to become the master of the London underworld, a career that he accomplished by both pushing people into crime and using their crimes as a weapon against them in case they decided to stop serving him. As part of his strategy, he would persuade a member of a gang to inform against one of his accomplices, and then find another member who was prepared to accuse the first, in case he stepped out of line. In this way he would take the money for handing over a criminal and take control of the gangs at the same time.

Jonathan Wild moved adroitly within the realm of the law, and like a benefactor offered help to anyone who had been robbed, inviting them to visit his Lost Property Office. In the office the victims would find that no stolen property was irretrievable and could be returned after settling a fee. As an entrepreneur and employer, he shunned the risks connected with his venture, transferring all potentially negative outcomes onto his employees.

The opera sets off with a song describing all human activity as dishonest, and telling the audience how, through all the employments of life, 'each neighbour abuses his brother, all professions be-rogue one another'. Statesmen are included in the invective, though lawyers compete more directly with thief-catchers, as they act against rogues and for them; for 'tis but fitting that we should protect and encourage cheats, since we live by them' (Beggar's Opera: 43). This is the opening scene, in which Peachum is sitting at the table with a large book of accounts before him. His name reminds us that, like Wild, his trade is to impeach or inform upon his criminal acquaintances for the sake of the reward.

When he shows concerns about the uncertainties of his profession, Peachum is told by his wife not to be too hard-hearted, because he has never had a finer, braver, set of men. Moreover, 'We have not had a murder among them all, these seven months. And truly, my dear, that is a great blessing' (Beggar's Opera: 48). Perhaps for this reason recruitment is lively, with apprentices knocking on his door at all times, and learning the basics of the job in the very first conversation with their supervisor. Peachum tells them to go and read the catechism because, once caught, as first offenders they can have their sentence reduced from death to transportation, a fine, or whipping, if they plead 'benefit of clergy', namely if they show that they are literate by reading a passage from the scriptures.

The protagonists of the *Opera* are convinced supporters of monetary success, as money takes out every spot or stain, and their experience tells them that rich rogues are a fit company for any gentleman: 'the world, my dear, hath not such a contempt for roguery as you imagine' (*Beggar's Opera*: 59). On the other hand, their greed hardly surpasses that of other occupations. As a soldier and a sailor sing: a fox may steal your hens, a whore your health and pence; your daughter rob your chest, your wife may steal your rest... but if a lawyer's hand is freed he steals your whole estate. Perceiving that robbery is generalized, and that they are not more dishonest than the rest of mankind, gang members complain that the laws are only levelled at them. In a tavern near Newgate, where they congregate, discussions revolve around their right to appropriate the wealth that the rich leave inert in their coffers: 'What we win, gentlemen, is our own by the law of arms, and the right of conquest' (*Beggar's Opera*: 68). Echoing liberal philosophical thought, they claim that resources belong to those who convert them into dynamic wealth, and if traditional organized criminal groups boast their ability to make gold out of lice (Ruggiero, 1996), they proclaim their pride for turning lead to gold. Bullets enable them to extract gold from their victims; though, as Macheath admonishes, pistols are their last resort.

As in contemporary groups, 'honour' is a keyword, and is repeated numerous times throughout the opera, providing an improbable rationalization for the activities of the gangs but also a screen for the ruthless competition between them. Dishonourable behaviour, in fact, is the key to success within and without the organization, and such behaviour is deemed innate in all human beings, making criminals ordinary representatives of their species: 'Lions, wolves, and vultures don't live together in herds, droves or flocks. Of all animals of prey, man is the only sociable one. Every one of us preys upon his neighbour, and yet we herd together' (Beggar's Opera: 98–9).

The partnership between Peachum and Lockit, established for the purpose of handing in Macheath to the authorities, reflects the collaboration between Jonathan Wild and the corrupt official agencies that was necessary to the career of thief-takers. In The Beggar's Opera, however, corruption is the permanent feature, the inescapable backdrop for all careers. Hence the explicit allusions to rogues in higher places, to criminal behaviour as universal and, ultimately, to 'justice as unjust' and moral values as a function of wealth and power.

The ending of the Opera is cheerful, but this is only due to the author's efforts to comply with the taste of the times, which required that virtuous characters be rewarded and wicked ones punished, therefore reflecting the fundamentally just nature of God's universe. This notwithstanding, the final word of the beggar cannot avoid reiterating his central thought: 'Through the whole piece you may observe such a similitude of manners in high and low life, that it is difficult to determine whether (in the fashionable vices) the fine gentlemen imitate the gentlemen of the road, or the gentlemen of the road the fine gentlemen' (Beggar's Opera: 121).

Wild versus Sheppard

If Peachum represents Jonathan Wild, the criminal bureaucrat who acts as a conformist 'deviant', Macheath is resonant of Jack Sheppard, the independent, individualistic, rebellious criminal who refuses to conform to the discipline of hierarchical organizations (Moore, 1997).

In the biography written by Daniel Defoe ([1725] 1986), Wild is described as an ambitious man resorting to crime out of sheer laziness. After leaving his wife and infant son, Wild is said to have served as a personal assistant to a lawyer, from whom he learned the secrets of legal affairs, enabling him to start working as a 'setter', namely hunting down and bringing debtors before a court. Wild, in other words, built his criminal career on legally acquired skills and resources, and made crime a supplementary source of advancement for his official, institutional, position. Sheppard, by contrast, was consistent in his search for status exclusively within the underworld and through independently conceived acts of predation. Wild used self-promotion in order to create an image that appealed to respectable people who sought to retrieve their stolen property, and, at the same time, to members of the underworld who ended up becoming his servants (Moore, 1997). While pursuing professional recognition and social acceptance, aspiring to conventional respectability, and insisting that his work was for the benefit of society rather than himself, he also trawled

> the back streets of London in search of the desperate and down-and-out. The more miserable a person was the better; he would be willing to do anything for a chance; and if Wild did help him get set up as a highway man or footpad, he would owe Wild his life and serve him loyally. (Moore, 2000: xvi)

In Henry Fielding's ([1743] 1978) fictional reconstruction of Wild's life, the underworld and the overworld are intimately mingled, and if the author does not accept that Newgate Prison is regarded as the repository of true human nature with its mask off, he suspects that the splendid palaces of powerful people are often no more than Newgate with the mask on. Fielding stresses how honest people prove indignation that 'the same morals be in one place attended with all imaginable misery and infamy, and in the other, with the highest luxury and honour' (1978: xix). In the rules guiding Wild's activity, readers may detect a mixture of maxims suitable for successful criminals and great entrepreneurs alike. These rules include: never do more mischief to another than is necessary, for that mischief is too precious a thing to be wasted; 'know no distinction of men from affection, but to sacrifice all with equal readiness to interest'; never communicate more of an affair than necessary to the person who is to execute it; never trust those who have deceived you, nor those who have been deceived by you; shun poverty and distress, and ally as close as possible with the powerful and rich; never reward anyone for their merit, but always insinuate that the reward is above their merit; virtues, like precious stones, are easily counterfeited, and very few have knowledge or discernment sufficient to distinguish the counterfeit jewel from the real (175). Fielding concludes that, if greatness consists of power, pride, insolence and doing mischief to mankind, then Wild shall stand unrivalled on the pinnacle of greatness.

The greatness of Wild, one should add, can also be seen in an important achievement which eluded Monipodio, namely the elimination of a professional, independent, criminal who did not accept regimentation in a strictly organized structure. Macheath–Sheppard, who refuses to appreciate the advantages of working in such a structured organization, has no escape, and is sentenced to death, while his counterparts, Rinconete and Cortadillo, rove elsewhere to continue their self-planned career.

The organization led by Peachum possesses some of the characteristics that analysts would attribute to contemporary forms of organized crime. While enjoying increasingly larger shares of the criminal market, the organization internalizes those costs which would otherwise be sustained by agents external to it (Schelling, 1967). Violence, for example, is part of such external costs, and members of organized crime may have a collective interest in restricting its use so as to avoid the disapproval of the public (Buchanan, 1980). Peachum's wife, when trying to cheer up her man, who is concerned with performance issues, seems to suggest that the task of a successful organization is to reduce violence to a minimum, and that Peachum should rejoice for having achieved this.

Like Cervantes' brotherhood of thieves, Peachum's firm is well connected with official institutions and respectable citizens, and offers goods and services to both. In this sense, one could argue that alliances and partnerships with the overworld are essential for its prosperity. At the same time, however, its major value-generating source remains dependent on the members of the underworld it manages to recruit. In this respect, one notion of organized crime, particularly applicable to conventional criminal activity, comes to mind. This is that organized crime displays a particular division of labour among its members, based on the growing separation between the task of planning and that of executing. The antagonism between Peachum and Macheath describes the attempt of organized groups to subject independent criminal groups and professional individuals to their control, and to turn them into pure employees with no decision-making role. While in professionally independent groups tasks are collectively planned, profits shared, and further activities collectively attempted, in organized crime there is a low degree of cooperation among its members, or rather an abstract, 'Fordist' kind of cooperation among them. Planning and execution are here strictly separated (Ruggiero, 1996; 2000a). This is what Macheath rejects, and he is punished for it.

While Peachum's organization is heavily reliant on its acolytes for the gathering of revenues, its major characteristic is its parasitic nature, though this is based on the predatory ability of its subordinates. In the rewriting of *The Beggar's Opera* by Bertolt Brecht one can detect a further development of organized crime, where both the predatory and the parasitic element are, though not completely, superseded.

From crime to business

In *The Threepenny Opera* ([1928] 1979), Brecht draws on the plebeian tradition, likening the rules that govern criminal enterprise with those guiding conventional economic enterprise (Meyer, 1973). All layers of society are said to embrace such rules, which Brecht associates with greed and exploitation.

Businessman Peachum claims that his is a combat against the increasing callousness of mankind; therefore he runs a shop where 'the poorest of the poor can acquire an exterior that will touch the hardest of hearts' (*Threepenny Opera*: 5). He is the proprietor of The Beggar's Friend Ltd; he not only allocates the city areas to those begging but also chooses the clothes they have to wear in order to 'touch the hearts' of passers-by. When Filch goes to see him, Peachum understands that he must be 'the bastard' that two of his men have caught, the one who had the impudence to molest people in District 10. He tells him that he got off because 'we had reason to believe you didn't know what's what', but if he is caught again 'it'll be the chop for you, got it?' (7). When Filch is asked what he has to do in order to carry on with his job, he is told that he has to pay a pound. Peachum explains that licences are delivered to professionals only, and pointing in a business-like way to a map of the city, shows how London is divided into fourteen districts. Any man who intends to practise the craft of begging in any one of those districts needs a licence from his firm, Jonathan Jeremiah Peachum & Co. Filch does not have a pound, so they agree on 'ten bob' plus 50 per cent on earnings, to be settled once a week. With the outfit, however, it is 70 per cent. And when Filch asks what the outfit consists of, he is told that it is for the firm to decide. Then he is dismissed: 'You'll start on Baker Street. Numbers 2 to 104.'

Meanwhile, deep in the heart of Soho, Mackie Messer (Macheath) is celebrating his marriage to Polly Peachum, the beggar king's daughter. He is scolding his men, who find it hard to learn that bloodshed must be avoided. He is angry and accuses them of being more like cannibals than businessmen. Their most recent loot from a house is composed of what they describe as junk: a rosewood harpsichord along with a Renaissance sofa. This is unforgivable. Mackie Messer and Polly need a table and a few chairs for the banquet: the bridal couple cannot sit on the floor. The order is therefore given to saw off the legs of the harpsichord, so that a bench can be made. Fortunately, we are not informed about the fate of the Renaissance sofa.

Bandit Messer, however, is also capable of mimicking bourgeois etiquette, and reprimands his men for eating a trout with the knife. After stressing that anybody who does that 'is just a plain swine', he wonders how he will ever manage to 'turn this trash into human beings' (Threepenny Opera: 17). During the banquet he shows that his aspiration to mingle with the elite is not confined to the imitation of its manners, but is based on real contacts with some of its representatives and the establishment of common interests with them. The Chief Sheriff of London, Tiger Brown himself, enters the room, hailed as an old friend. Mackie Messer reminds his acolytes that seldom has he, the humble bandit, made even the smallest haul without giving him, his friend Brown, a share, a substantial share, as a gift and token of his unswerving loyalty, and seldom has Brown staged a raid without sending him a little tip-off.

These contacts in the highest places, however, fail to render the gang invulnerable, and Messer is sold to the authorities by Peachum, who persuades the prostitutes controlled by the former to betray him. When finally in trouble, Mackie Messer feels that his enterprise must continue even without him. He asks Polly to run the business:

> Listen carefully. This is a list of the personnel. First of all, Crook-finger Jake, a year and a half in the business. Let's see what he's brought in. One, two, three, four, five gold watches, not much, but clean work.... Here's Dreary Walter, an unreliable sod. Sells stuff on the side. Give him three weeks' grace, then get rid of him. Just turn him in to Brown... Jimmy II, cheeky bastard; good worker but cheeky. Swipes bed sheets right out from under ladies of the best society. Give him a rise.... Robert the Saw: small potatoes, not a glimmer of genius. Won't end on the gallows, but he won't leave any estate either. (Threepenny Opera: 36)

The entrepreneurial character of Mackie Messer is finally proven by his thought about the investment of his profits. A restrained spender and a cautious investor, he tells Polly to send his illegal revenues to Jack Poole's banking house in Manchester, and confesses that it is only a matter of weeks before he too goes into banking, making this activity the core of his future life. Banking, he says, is safer and more profitable than crime. But for this to happen, the money will have to be taken out of his present business, and Polly has to go to Brown and give him the list of all the thieves who work for him. Within four weeks all that human scum would be safely in the cells at the Old Bailey. Polly is shocked and asks how can he look them in the eye and shake their hands, after taking the decision to inform on them. He replies that he has no pity for those 'gaol-birds', but as soon as they reappear on the scene he calls them gentlemen and talks about honour and loyalty.

Peachum is as ruthless in his career as Messer is cynical and hypocritical in his, and both have very personal views about making it in the market and in court. The former regards all businessmen, and generally those led by the desire to make profits, as morally sound, claiming that laws are made for the exploitation of those who do not understand them, or are prevented by naked misery from obeying them.

The latter, as he approaches the gallows, and before begging everyone for forgiveness, describes himself as a declining representative of a declining group. His criminal career is at an end, like that of artisans threatened by the factory system and its impersonal labour organization.

> We lower middle-class artisans who toil with our humble jemmies on small shopkeepers' cash registers are being swallowed up by big corporations backed by the banks. What's a jemmy compared with a share certificate? What's breaking into a bank compared with founding a bank?
> (*Threepenny Opera*: 76)

Mackie Messer is not aware that this process describes his very career. Minutes before the execution, enter a royal official on his horse, who, as *deus ex machina*, brings a special order from the Queen to have the bandit 'set at liberty forthwith, and raised to the hereditary peerage. The castle of Marmarel, likewise a pension of ten thousand pounds, to be his in usufruct until his death' (77).

Successful and pariah forms of organized crime

Brecht's *The Threepenny Opera* exemplifies criminal activity as both organized and disorganized, both an improvised and a thoroughly planned enterprise. Mackie Messer's men, whom the boss treats as cannibals and trash, may be sloppy and coarse, but they provide the criminal labour Messer needs to gain access to the formal economy and the social elite. Messer capitalizes on predatory crime and his attitude towards his men is highly parasitic in nature, while his interest in 'going clean' through involvement in the financial world leads him, ultimately, to a symbiotic relationship with the conventional economy. His career is rewarded, and enhanced, by the Queen with freedom, a castle and a pension.

It would be inappropriate to suggest that all forms of organized crime are destined to observe a similar development. Messer's men, if not reported to the police, may for example continue their exploits, and while stealing Renaissance sofas whose value they do not comprehend, may remain bogged down in stagnant forms of organized crime. Pariahs of organized crime, they may never make it into the legitimate world, and therefore they may be denied those 'multiple social affiliations' that would improve their life chances (Blau, 1994). These affiliations would simultaneously expand the scope of their criminality, as suggested by Messer as well as Peachum, both intent on demonstrating how the logic of lawbreaking is universal in all entrepreneurial spirits. Macheath–Messer, in entering the elite, may learn the techniques and rationalizations that distinguish elitist criminality, thus being corrupted by, rather than corrupting, it. In criminological jargon, he might use his previously acquired skills in a career as a white-collar offender.

In his notes for directors and actors, Brecht clarifies this point by suggesting that the character of Peachum is not to be cast in the stereotyped formula of the 'miser'. Peachum has no more regard for money than the police chief, and both, in making a commodity of human misery, are merely following the trend of the times (Brecht, 1979). The bandit Macheath, in his turn, should be interpreted as a bourgeois phenomenon.

> The bourgeoisie's fascination with bandits rests on a misconception: that a bandit is not a bourgeois. This misconception is the child of another misconception: that a bourgeois is not a bandit. Does this mean that they are identical? No: occasionally a bandit is not a coward. (Brecht, 1979: 92)

Macheath's dislike, as a good businessman, of the shedding of blood except where strictly necessary alludes to a business principle, like his plan to take the money away from the organization of theft into a Manchester bank. This reduction of bloodshed to a minimum, and this punctilious economizing, aim at ensuring that risk is neutralized or passed on to his employees. He thinks more of exploiting his men than of robbing strangers. His common sense tells him that his own security is closely bound up with that of the official society. 'When he pictures his future he never for one moment sees himself on the gallows, but just quietly fishing the stream on a property of his own' (92).

Some scholars base their definitions of organized crime on the professionalism of its participants, while others follow specifically quantitative lines, thus implying that the number of people engaged in illegal activities determines the degree of their organization. Yet others align the organizational dimension with a variable that is, in the main, temporal: that is to say, the length of time that illicit activities have been going on. Cervantes, Gay and Brecht see, though in different fashions, a continuous competition between professional and organized criminals, with the latter attempting to co-opt the former in their structured activities. While also stressing numbers of participants and continuity, service provision and partnerships with official actors, they attribute the variable 'organized' to specific criminal enterprises and the division of labour within them, rather than to the seriousness of the criminal acts performed. Studying the competitive game in which Rinconete, Cortadillo, Monipodio, Peachum, Wild and Macheath are engaged is a fruitful intellectual exercise for sociologists of deviance attempting to analyse organized crime and law enforcers attempting to tackle it.

3

Legal and Illegal Drugs:
Baudelaire and London

Artistic inspiration and drug use have a controversial relationship. Possession by the Muse may be similar to Bacchic transport, an intense madness that Plato associates with the process of creativity itself: lyric poets are not in their senses when they write. Conversely, drugs may be said not only to impede the creative process but also to hamper Aristotle's 'good life', one that is active, healthy, rational and virtuous. If leading a good life makes humans happy, then addictive behaviour is failure to achieve happiness (Franzwa, 1999). The problem is that many writers achieve a 'good life' without being hampered by drugs, but thanks to them. But does this denote drug users as sinners or sick persons?

Neither the 'sin' nor the 'sickness' models are sufficiently equipped to accommodate a sociological analysis of drug use in literature (Lilienfeld and Oxford, 1999). Without sin many works of fiction would be insipid, as heroes and heroines would lose their 'heroic' aura without a degree of transgression. As for 'sickness', this features frequently as a form of physical and mental rebellion, and many literary characters prove that, as already noted, through pain, one may achieve 'a more than usual clear-sightedness in respect to Wrong' (Poe, 1980a: 36).

Drug use in literature, as well as drug use by writers, is motivated by a variety of factors that change according to individual and collective contingencies (Plant, 1999). The search for pleasure, the mitigation of pain, the desire to gain access to the unknown, or to escape environments devoid of imagination, are all found in fiction, often coupled with the pursuit of a state of 'death within life' leading to something similar to a new childhood (Milner, 2000). The experience of hashish smoking, for example, is for some authors an attempt to achieve a pleasant transitory madness, limited in time and self-controlled, opening up an aesthetic *terra incognita*. The use of drugs, in others, is consistent with the rejection of rational thinking, and therefore of conventional social order, triggering a process in which also the official language, suitable for describing such order, is transcended.

With the exception of isolated fragments, the history of drugs in literature starts with Thomas De Quincey, whose *Confessions of an English Opium Eater* appeared in 1822. Before focusing on the two authors who form the core interest of this chapter, it is worth sketching this history briefly.

Using laudanum, allegedly to alleviate the pains of neuralgia, De Quincey (1985) developed a habit from which he tried, with controversial results, to free himself, leaving us an unprecedented description of the 'opium-trance'. This is like a tumultuous dream full of music and the 'multitudinous movement' of innumerable armies. Whether this battle reflects the author's effort to give up his habit, or describes the pleasant effect of opium eating is hard to ascertain, as he intends both to eulogize the properties of the substance and to demand sympathy for his state of addiction. On the one hand, he hears voices uttering the word 'Death', and awakes crying aloud 'I will sleep no more', as if publicly announcing his resolution to give up. But on the other hand, he praises the joy caused by the drug, which is said suddenly to reveal an abyss of divine pleasures. When comparing alcohol with opium, for example, De Quincey observes that the former brings to the surface the human elements of those using it, and sometimes the animal part of their nature. The latter, instead, confers sovereignty to the divine parts of human nature, providing a cloudless peace to moral sentiments and enlightening intelligence. Is this an explicit theorization of the importance of drugs for artistic creation?

Opium is the milk of Paradise (Coleridge, 1956), and facilitates 'reveries' rather than dreams, leaving users partly conscious, hence in an ideal state of mind to perceive new shapes and colours, and to escape the tyranny of reality. Opium acts on our brain, De Quincey suggests, as if on a palimpsest, where overlapping events and feelings are disentangled: the use of the substance proves that those feelings were not dead, but were only asleep.

The idea that drug use encourages literary productivity is received and perpetuated throughout the nineteenth century. Balzac (1958) emphasizes the capacity of opium to allow time travelling, enabling users to 'get rid of centuries' and see the splendour of ancient cities and peoples. Poe (1980b: 19–20) sees in Ligeia's beauty the radiance of an opium dream, and in Berenicë, who 'roams carelessly through life with no thought of the shadows in her path', a strident contrast with his own addiction. This addiction forces his body and soul to the most intense and painful meditation; it is a 'nervous intensity of interest', a monomania for the 'contemplation of even the most ordinary objects of the universe'. This 'monomania' will also make him an outstanding master in his genre. Alexandre Dumas explains how, when smoking hashish, dreams become reality and reality dreams, so that smokers and writers are compelled to renounce reality forever if they are, respectively, to live well and produce great art (Dumas, 1997).

London gin shops, in the description of Dickens, have no relationship with artistic creation; rather, they symbolize the social privileges enjoyed by those attending them. Handsome glass plates invite customers to taste the liqueurs of the 'Bottle Department', the 'Wine Promenade', the 'Whiskey Entrance' or the 'Brandy Bell', while the shelves leave patrons in a state of pleasing hesitation between ordering a glass of 'The Cream of the Valley', 'The Out and Out', 'The Good for Mixing', 'The No Mistake', or 'The Real Knock-me Down'. These places, however, are 'numerous and splendid in precise proportion to the dirt and poverty of the surrounding neighbourhood' (Dickens, 1850: 124). Gin shops, with their stone balustrades, rosewood fittings and illuminated clocks, often border on the 'Rookery', where cheap, poisonous, drinks are consumed, and where drunkenness 'hurries its victims madly on to degradation and death' (340). As for opium, Dickens's readers are led to associate it less with peaceful reverie than with violent crime (Milner, 2000). In *The Mystery of Edwin Drood* opium smoking is part of the demonic conduct of murderers, and readers end up identifying addiction with profound perversion. Although evil is also hidden behind the routine pettiness of ordinary individuals, and qualifies the meanness of otherwise unremarkable characters, opium incarnates evil to its most spectacular and grandiose degree (Dickens, 1870).

Rimbaud was engaged in a relentless search for the 'deregulation of the senses' and it is likely that hashish lent him frequent support in this pursuit (Delahaye, 1925). Like many of his contemporaries, the poet strives to 'see' beyond himself and the reality surrounding him, and to appreciate the limits of the known in order to trespass them. This search avails itself of all tools capable of working towards the subversion of language: in *Une Saison en enfer* (1873) he gives each vowel a different colour and to consonants different shapes and movement; then, following an instinctive rhythm, he invents poetic verbs which are 'accessible to all senses' (Rimbaud, 1965: 156). His alchemy of verbs is accompanied by the successful attempt to see a mosque where in reality stands a factory, and finally to transmigrate into another being: 'I is another'.

Less fascinated by metempsychosis than Rimbaud, surrealist artists found drugs both attractive and repulsive. Their 'automatic writing', the flow of words and images taking shape unconsciously, did not rely on artificial substances, even if it brought a form of inebriety which recalled that generated by opium. La Révolution Surréaliste contains a number of articles on drugs, but these are not so much focused on the effects of drugs as on the negative effects of drug prohibition. As their argument goes: no law can avert users from craving substances they need more than bread, and which dissolve their ills while giving them life. Artaud (1976: 121) publishes an open letter to legislators, calling them idiots, because they believe in the right to govern human grief, and to medical doctors, whom he addressed as 'imbecilles', says: 'It is not for your love for humans that you talk, but for your imbecile tradition. Your ignorance about human nature equals your imbecility in wanting to limit it.' On the other hand, Breton (1988) appears to distance himself from cocaine through his character Nadja, who after involvement in trafficking and using the substance assures readers that 'it is now over'.

The position taken by surrealist artists is surprising if one considers that, decades before, the likes of Freud ([1884] 1974), whose influence on surrealist art can hardly be denied, described cocaine not only as a panacea for the medical community but also as a potent stimulant suitable for hard workers, a substance producing no artificial effects, but bringing forth a self more natural than nature. Using a dynamometer, he measured the effect of cocaine on the strength of muscles, and finds a marked increase (Driscoll, 1999). Meanwhile Sherlock Holmes, putting such analysis into practice,

Took his bottle from the corner of the mantelpiece, and his hypodermic
syringe from its neat morocco case. With his long, white, nervous fingers
he adjusted the delicate needle and rolled back his left shirtcuff. For some
little time his eyes rested thoughtfully upon the sinewy forearm and
wrist, all dotted and scarred with innumerable puncture-marks. Finally,
he thrust the sharp point home, pressed down the tiny piston, and sank
back into the velvet-lined armchair with a long sigh of satisfaction. (Doyle,
[1890] 1986: 7)

He finds cocaine, which he offers to share with Watson, 'so transcend-
ently stimulating and clarifying to the mind'.

Benjamin ([1928] 1979: 216) attains inspiration and illumination in
smoking hashish: colours grow brighter and objects more beautiful.
Time and space expand to 'regal' dimension: 'Versailles, for one who
has taken hashish, is not too large, or eternity too long.' A concert,
indeed a brass band, seems to be playing, but it is only the blaring of
car horns. Benjamin becomes a physiognomist, or a contemplator of
physiognomies, and fixes his gaze on faces which are remarkably coarse
or ugly. Then he suddenly understands how, to a painter, ugliness can
appear as 'the true reservoir of beauty, better than any treasure cask, a
jagged mountain with all the inner gold of beauty gleaming from the
wrinkles, glances, features' (Benjamin, 1972: 37).

One wanders why the literature sketched so far failed to leave any
substantial trace in the sociology of deviance, and why among the most
pre-eminent representatives of the discipline drug use is invariably
associated with defeatism, quietism, resignation, and ultimately retreatism. These, according to Merton (1968), are manifested in escape
mechanisms which lead drug users to abstain altogether from the re-
quirements of society. Drug users are gathered in the cauldron of
retreatism that includes psychotics, autists, pariahs, outcasts, vagrants,
vagabonds, tramps and chronic drunkards. They all 'have relinquished
culturally prescribed goals and their behaviour does not accord with
institutional norms' (Merton, 1968: 207). In contrast, if we listen to

Benjamin (1979), smoking hashish performs one of the most important exercises in human socialization and the establishment of solidarity. In a 'state of deepest trance', he bumps into two men (ordinary
people or vagrants, who knows?), and in them sees 'Dante and Petrarch';
he concludes that all men resemble each other, they are brothers.

Subcultural theorists, in turn, describe drug users as double failures,
namely as people who have failed to achieve status through either
legitimate or illegitimate means (Cloward and Ohlin, 1960). The works
mentioned above display little notion of retreatism, and drug use,
whether by authors themselves or by the characters of their creation,
is associated with active perception and hectic endeavour. Perhaps, one
exception is Dickens, who seems to be aware that drugs have a social
connotation, whereby some are destined to find destruction in what
others find exhilaration. Some wretched Dickensian characters drown
in alcohol: in a short story the 'drunkard', after an existence of poverty,
misery and starvation, physically drowns in the Thames, while the
wealthy have fun in the gin shop nearby (Dickens, 1850).

Before returning to this and other aspects of drug use in the sociology
of deviance and literature respectively, let us now examine Charles
Baudelaire's Les Paradis artificiels and Jack London's John Barleycorn.

Poison and work

Wine makes the most sordid shack shine; its red vapour resembles
sunset in a cloudy sky. Opium expands things beyond their confines;
it extends limits, deepens time, digs pleasure and fills the soul with
dark joy. These are among the sharp poetic judgements that Baudelaire
addresses to 'poisons', which include wine and opium, but also to a
woman's green eyes, whose poisonous power cannot be matched (Les
Fleurs du mal, in Baudelaire, 1975). All poisons are sweet and terrible old

friends, but it is in particular the bottle of laudanum which quietens
Baudelaire's disgust for the world and the repulsion for the dump in
which he lives. That bottle promises caresses and betrayals, and is capable
of repelling 'the dictatorship of time and the slavery of life'. In *Les
Paradis artificiels* ([1860] 1999), Baudelaire concentrates all his thoughts
on wine, hashish and opium, and the ambivalence one finds in this
work reflects the mixture of motives inspiring his investigation, which
is ethical, poetic and spiritual at the same time. Readers who seek some
social, rational, common-sense materialistic meaning in this writing
will be disappointed, and should bear in mind that Baudelaire regards
materialists, 'who abolish the soul and hell', as interested, lazy persons
'who do not intend to re-live'. This notwithstanding, Baudelaire offers
us a number of surprises, and some of his remarks pop up as unexpected 'wise' statements which he himself would have judged as
embarrassingly materialistic.

Wine gives courage, strengthens the will and brings happiness.
Drinking is a melody, and composers should choose their wine according to the type of music they intend to create. Conscientious comic
opera authors will resort to champagne, whose lightness and sparkling
vivacity will provide the precise inspiration the genre requires. Religious music necessitates Jurançon or wine from the Rhine region,
because their inebriating bitterness is conducive to profound ideas. In
turn, heroic music needs Burgundy, with its severe warmth and its
enthralling patriotic strength.

Wine helps placate remorse, evocate memories, drown grief and
create fantasies: there is some mysterious god hidden in the fibres of
grapes. Who would be so inhuman as to condemn those who, drinking
wine, imbibe genius? Baudelaire tells of how publishers, competing for
the novels of the great Balzac, used to complement sums of money
with crates of French wine.

Wine is like humans: you never know what noble deed or monstrous mischief it is capable of. We have to treat wine as our equal, and to be against it is to be against ourselves. Such intimacy creates poetry: together, humans and wine hover towards infinity, like butterflies, birds and perfumes. But there is more. If one descends lower down to contemplate those mysterious human beings who live courtesy of the refuse of big cities, those who collect the items discarded by the inhabitants of capitals, even there one finds the soothing effect of wine, which helps compose poems and songs. For those who work without joy, fatigue without relief and pain devoid of compensation find in wine a humane leveller, an intellectual golden pleasure. In brief, those who do not drink are either imbeciles or hypocrites, who often boast their sobriety while concealing some unspeakable vice. A man who drinks only water has a secret to hide.

In a blasphemous allegory, wine is attributed the capacity to create a 'third person', and to generate a mystic operation in which the human being, as Father, together with the vegetal god, the Son, produce the Holy Spirit, namely a superior being. And if such a superior being is hard to detect in those whom drinking makes nasty, well, they were nasty even before drinking.

If wine fosters sociability and makes divinities out of humans, hashish is antisocial in nature, though its effects vary according to frequency of use and the personality of users. Baudelaire warns that, due to the intensification of feelings caused by the substance, hashish smokers had better choose favourable circumstances and partners. Happiness and well-being become plethoric, as do sadness and anguish. Hence the suggestion to neophytes to refrain from expressing scepticism: smokers at their first experience with hashish will find themselves in the comical situation where the effects of the substance surface right at the moment when they claim to be impervious to it. First, an irresistible hilarity takes hold of you, and the most common words and ideas assume a new bizarre dimension. This 'gay languidness' and this happy unease do not last long. People who normally are inarticulate become masters in reciting interminable *calambours*, and while ideas become improbable the thread connecting thoughts turns feeble. Only your accomplices manage to follow you. Listening to music becomes a sort of visual exercise, as notes are colourful drawings, causing smokers to wail, or even cry. One feels ill with joy, and does not want a remedy.

Baudelaire describes the second phase as one in which smokers feel cold and hungry, their limbs refuse to move, and their ears develop a selective hypersensitivity which allows the dissection of sound into discrete components. During the course of one hour, smokers live more than one life. It is a calm beatitude, an immobile happiness that resolves all philosophical problems. 'All the hardest theological problems troubling human reason become clear. Every contradiction turns into unity. Man is elevated to god.'

The personality of hashish smokers is subject to a process of destructuring. Baudelaire gives the example of a respectable magistrate, an honourable man whose gravity elicits respect, who, after smoking the substance, starts to dance a wild cancan. That man, who is entitled to judge the acts of others, has learned to dance in secret. In brief, while wine intensifies will, hashish annihilates it. Wine makes us nice and cooperative, hashish only makes people lazy. Wine is for those who work and deserve to drink it; hashish is for those who seek solitary joy, for unproductive layabouts – it is useless and dangerous.

In order to explain the effects of hashish, Baudelaire uses a distinction between two different types of dreams. The first are riddled with aspects of our daily life, of worries and desires that are combined in a more or less bizarre fashion with the objects and activities performed during the day. These are natural dreams: they resemble those who make them. The second type of dreams are absurd, unpredictable, and bear no relation with the character, the passions and the life of the dreamer. These are called hieroglyphic dreams, and represent the super-natural aspect of life; they are symbolic and moral representations generated by the mind of dreamers. The dreams induced by hashish resemble the first type: they never transcend the field of the natural; and while hashish smokers are subjugated by such dreams, in reality they are only subjugated by themselves, their troubles and limitations pre-existing their act of smoking. Hashish smokers will find nothing miraculous in the substance but only their own nature, their tempera-ment and morality. 'Hashish is a magnifying mirror, all right, but still it is only a mirror.' For those who nevertheless do choose to experi-ment with the substance, Baudelaire suggests that the right environ-ment, a house poetically furnished, some good music, and a nice sunny day are highly advisable for the experiment to succeed. All senses are affected: the eyes penetrate infinity, the ears perceive discreet sounds among chaotic noise, while objects take on strange shapes. Misunder-standings follow, sounds turn into colours, while colours become musical. However, there is nothing supernatural in this inebriety: all the analogies present themselves with unusual vivacity; they penetrate and invade the mind in a despotic manner.

> Musical notes become numbers and if you have any aptitude for math-ematics, melody and hramony are turnd into a vast mathematical exercise without losing anything of their voluptuous and sensual character. The numbers breed more numbers and you follow their phases and develop-ment with an inexplicable facility and an agility equal to that of the performer. (Paradis artificiels: 52)

The personality of hashish smokers may temporarily disappear, and objectivity may develop to the point that the contemplation of external objects makes one forget about one's own existence. Smokers become part of the objects they contemplate, and at times they do not feel they are smoking, but rather that they are being smoked. Here they are, then, incapable of working, unable to act, completely drained. This is the punishment they suffer for the prodigality with which they have dissipated their nervous fluid. They disseminate their personality, and it will take them a heroic effort to pull it back together.

Thoughts become rhapsodic, driven around haphazardly like victims to all unpredictable contingencies: hashish is a disorderly demon, whereas opium is a smooth seducer. Hashish is the enemy of a regular life. It is around this judgement that Baudelaire builds his objection to the substance: imagine a nation in which all citizens use hashish. What citizens, what soldiers, what legislators would they be? Smoking hashish is tantamount to abdicating one's will; it is a solitary pleasure making individuals useless to their peers and society useless to individuals. Smokers become self-centred, and precipitate into a bright abyss where all they have to do is narcissistically admire themselves. Hashish is an enemy of art, which does need contemplation, but also requires work. And how is beauty acquired, if not through both work and art?

Baudelaire's analysis of opium is based on his very personal reading, and translation, of De Quincey's memoirs, a book he admires because it breaks 'through that delicate and honourable reserve, which, for the most part, restrains us from the public exposure of our own errors and infirmities.' Baudelaire likes the way in which the English opium eater tears away the 'decent drapery' and shows his moral ulcers and scars. 'There is no crime in opium use, but weakness', he proclaims. Such weakness is shared by professors, philosophers and high-ranking politicians. Manufacturing workers, too, use opium, which is for them an economic bliss: with their wages they can hardly afford beer or other alcoholic drinks. However, even if wages went up, workers would not abandon opium for the 'vulgar joy' of alcohol.

If coarse persons, made stupid by unfulfilling jobs, can find some sort of consolation in opium, what is the effect of the substance on learned and sensitive people? They will be touched with pensiveness. It is true that opium-using careers may start as a therapy, and users be driven to the substance by physical pain. It is also true that, a panacea for all human illnesses, opium is a typical *pharmakon*, namely it cures and poisons at the same time. However, it does not disrupt our mental faculties; on the contrary, it injects order and harmony into our mind. While wine deprives humans of self-control, opium makes self-control easier; 'it is disciplinary in its effect'. Opium does not generate extreme feelings such as unjustified hatred or improbable, sudden love, but it induces a natural, good disposition, and gives the intellect the joy of a cloudless lucidity.

Baudelaire's defence of De Quincey and his habit relies heavily on this alleged intellectual lucidity provoked by opium, which in his view does not hamper but enhances one's capacity to work. Opium, unlike hashish, strengthens one's will; it allows De Quincey to complete his work, and to deliver the manuscripts due to his publishers. De Quincey is described as someone who is burning from the desire to work and the impulse to act, but is stymied by pain. He is likened to a warrior who is forced to immobility, and opium as the substance capable of releasing his energy. However, along with the pleasures, Baudelaire also lists the pains of opium, the intellectual torpor it produces and the manner in which it ties users to a constant dormant state. Dreams are accompanied by anxiety and gloomy melancholy. 'I seemed every night to descend, not metaphorically, but literally to descend, into chasms and sunless abysses, depths below depths, from which it seemed hopeless that I could ever reascend' (*Confessions*: 103). Baudelaire interprets this state of mind as a painting created by an artist dipping the brush in an earthquake or an eclipse. The unbearable proportion assumed by these 'sunless abysses' is matched by the incontrollable dilation of time and space: a century becomes as long as one night, while space is amplified to infinity. Dreams of lakes turning hauntingly into oceans torment opium users. The human face 'brings its tyranny' into these dreams, appearing on the rocking waters of the ocean: 'faces, imploring, wrathful, despairing, surged upwards by thousands, by myriads, by generations, by centuries: my agitation was infinite, my mind tossed, and surged with the ocean' (108). Baudelaire emphasizes the despotic spontaneity of these images, which intertwine with fears of mythological tortures and cancerous kisses given by crocodiles. The 'other' becomes menacing, and is associated by De Quincey with distant, Oriental cultures, in the form of 'the Maley' who visits his nightmares. Fear is also addressed to the 'savage tribes' of Africa, the creatures, trees, usages and appearances of the tropical regions, and the slimy things one finds in the muddy Nile. In sum, opium may help users deal with themselves and others, but eventually, Baudelaire seems to warn, it leads them to a disfiguring hatred for both.

Baudelaire does not believe that De Quincey ever really abandoned his habit: his regained peace and intellect, his final 'triumph' over the substance, is seen by Baudelaire as a concession to 'British insincerity', an artistic sacrifice immolating truth on the altar of public prejudice and decency. Perhaps De Quincey never gave up 'prostrating before the dark idol', and his final triumph is a literary device offering the audience the expected strike of justice that, at the theatre, 'every last act' delivers. Readers would hate to see sinners get away with their sins: the baddies cannot be rewarded.

There is a reiteration of a central theme in Baudelaire's analysis, namely that work, not drugs, makes humans forget the horror of life. Opium eaters receive sympathy as far as their habit puts them in the condition to carry out their artistic or productive activity; as far as, through work, they can look at the moment they were born with less horror than the day they will die. The author returns to this theme in his *Écrits intimes* ([1887] 1975), where one finds the following, resounding, hymn to human activity: 'We have to work, if not for love, then for desperation, because, after all, working is less boring than enjoying oneself.'

Let us see whether Jack London identifies similar themes in his argument about alcohol.

Malt liquor and the people

John Barleycorn is a traditional personification of malt liquor, and also Jack London's favourite drink. In league with the 'Noseless One', he leads to naked truth and death, after giving clear vision and muddy dreams. 'He is the enemy of life, and the teacher of wisdom beyond life's vision. He is a red-handed killer, and he slays youth.' Jack London's *John Barleycorn* ([1913] 1998) is an 'A to Z' of drinking, a treatise on alcoholism, but also an exercise in autobiography and a meditation on the vital lies that make life acceptable (Sutherland, 1998). Whether fictional or truthfully autobiographical, as London himself claims, the book is a classic text in support of prohibitionism, a document that can be used by temperance movements of all times. In 1913 a leaflet calling for the banning of alcohol showed a healthy young man (Jack London himself?) in contrast with a sodden tramp, and invokes the closing down of all saloons. Contemporary prohibitionists, too, might find some inspiration from the book, as the 'tricks and lures' played by John Barleycorn can also be imputed to other drugs, which set the 'maggots of intelligence gnawing', whisper 'fatal intuitions of truth', and fling 'purple passages into the monotony of one's days' (*John Barleycorn*: 2).

Jack London asserts that no organic, chemical predisposition led him towards alcohol, and that it took twenty years of unwilling apprenticeship to make him a problematic drinker. Accessibility of alcohol is singled out as the underlying element of such apprenticeship, along with that important social institution, the saloon, a central place of congregation where men gather as primitives gather around a fire. His confessions revolve around the effects of alcohol on 'normal' individuals, like he presumes himself to be, not on excessivists or dipsomaniacs, in his view a rare breed. The 'normal' fashion in which his habit develops is punctuated by two specific episodes in his childhood. First, he sips the beer he is carrying for his father, because the glass is full to the top and the liquid is spilling on his trousers. Second, he drinks wine offered by Italians, because he fears that all dark-eyed races are sensitive and treacherous, and they would not tolerate his refusal of a glass. 'Bad as the wine was, a knife in the back was worse' (*John Barleycorn*: 16). But it makes no sense to blame the Italians, he corrects himself: everybody in the community drinks. Even the teacher of the little country school he attends, a greying fifty-year-old man, gives pupils a day vacation when he wrestles with John Barleycorn and is defeated.

While forming his first judgements of the world, he finds saloons delightful and desirable places; warm, involuntary stages where men talk with great voices and laugh great laughs. In these places 'life is very live' and sometimes even lurid, for example when blows are struck, blood is shed, and big policemen come shouldering in. These scenes fill the boy's mind, mingling with images of 'the wild and valiant fighting of the gallant adventures on sea and land' (*John Barleycorn*: 24). Besides, reporters, editors, lawyers and judges, who also attend saloons, give these places the seal of institutional approval and social respectability.

As in his novels, London's life is out, at sea, not in stifling environments inhabited by 'work-beasts'. But the way of the sea leads inevitably to John Barleycorn. However, he would rather be an oyster pirate or a convict than a machine slave, and he would rather hold a glass in the company of adventurers than 'sit at my machine ... repeating, endlessly repeating, at top speed, my series of mechanical motions' (*John Barleycorn*: 39). Through John Barleycorn he joins the world of sailors, a glorious company of free souls, who flout restrictions and the law, and carry 'their lives and liberty in their hands' (39). Romance and adventure seem always to go hand in hand with alcohol, but what is the alternative? One cannot seek happiness while reading about some-one else's deeds, rather than one's own, and meanwhile 'slave for ten cents an hour at a machine' (43).

Only with some practice does the young man learn that buying drinks has its rules, and that all take turns 'to treat'. After accepting a glass, he learns to ask his companion if he wants another one, and drinking ends up symbolizing and strengthening comradeship. In this way he wins the friendship of Spider, Pat, Clam, and even Old Scratch, which is remarkable, because Old Scratch is known as a savage who dislikes everybody, and, as his nickname suggests, in fighting likes tearing off his opponent's face. One night he spends $180 on drinks, though that money should have bought him new clothes. But he has no regrets; he is proud to have shown that he can spend like the rest of them. Jack London drinks to be a man among men, but, while being attracted by the likes of Old Scratch, still nurses a childish desire for sweets. At times, he indulges in secret debauches, and, after ensur-ing that the crew is asleep, locks himself in the cabin and lies in bed for long blissful hours, reading and chewing candy.

Slowly, he discovers that there are fortunate men who cannot take more than a couple of drinks without being intoxicated, and unfortu-nate souls who need numerous glasses before 'betraying a sign' or getting the 'kick'. Both types of men, however, show another quality of John Barleycorn, namely that he inhibits morality. 'Wrong conduct that it is impossible for one to do sober, is done quite easily when one is not sober. In fact, it is the only thing one can do, for John Barleycorn's inhibition rises like a wall between one's immediate desires and long-learned morality' (*John Barleycorn*: 54). Before killing, alcohol does even worse: it robs people of power, place and comfort, while crucifying their pride. Alcohol also makes men violent, as London evinces from his saloon-mates who, normally harmless, do 'most violent and lunatic things when they are drunk' (85). Finally, in a 'splendid culmination', John Barleycorn plays his maniacal trick, generating thoughts of suicide in the drinker's mind.

Jack London is able to refrain from drinking, and he does so when, for short periods, he takes conventional jobs and adapts his lifestyle accordingly. Determined to become an electrician, he is convinced by his employer that before acquiring the necessary skills he has to show willingness and stamina in more humble tasks, for example 'passing coal to firemen, who shovel it into the furnaces'. He soon realizes that his job was previously done by two men who were paid more than he is: therefore, he is merely cheapening the price of labour. He feels like a 'work-beast': he works, eats and sleeps, while his mind sleeps all the time. The young man learns that the dignity of manual labour is not what he has been told 'by teachers, preachers and politicians' (123). He heads out on the path of adventure, and to the saloon, again.

After abandoning conventional education, he quickly becomes a successful writer and, initially, feels no desire to drink. He is a socialist, intent on saving the world, and alcohol would assuage the political fervour of his ideals. Fellow writers and political activists do drink, but temperately, and London returns to alcohol for comradeship, politeness and hospitality. Every day, he only drinks after writing a thousand words, but soon he is unable to write if he does not drink first. Finally, he is afflicted with rational pessimism, as alcohol makes him see 'through the shams of life', and face its cosmic meaninglessness.

> The drinker realises that the real reason that he drinks is not to make himself 'good company' but to make other people bearable. Without drink, they would be what Sartre calls them – hell. (Sutherland, 1998: xxxiii)

But after 'tearing the veils from truth' and being shocked by the terrible sight, what really saves him is one remaining illusion – the PEOPLE. Obsessed with the desire to die, he fears he might commit suicide in his sleep, but the PEOPLE save him.

> There was still one fight left in me, and here was the thing for which to fight. I threw all precaution to the winds, threw myself with fiercer zeal into the fight for socialism. (John Barleycorn: 156–7)

However, not many drinkers manage to find something for which to fight; therefore prohibition is the answer advocated by Jack London, who argues that the practice of not leaving arsenic and strychnine lying around should be extended to John Barleycorn. 'Stop him. Don't let him lie around, licensed and legal, pounce upon our youth' (203). For this reason, he votes in favour of the constitutional amendment granting the vote to women in state elections. Despite his intimate opposition to the women's rights movement, which he regards as unwomanly, he trusts that mothers and sisters will vote for prohibition. Women are the 'true conservators of the race'; he votes 'that women might vote' because he knows that they will vote John Barleycorn out of existence and 'back into the historical limbo of our vanished customs of savagery' (203).

The ascent of illicit markets

Jack London uses a typical technique of denial whereby he distances himself from the enclaves of problematic drinkers he describes and to which he, perhaps, belongs. His appeal to 'the people' rescues a narrative which, otherwise, risks altering the message he intends to convey. Lest readers think that John Barleycorn, after all, allows the author to lead an exciting life, to keep humiliating jobs at bay, and ultimately to buy a wonderful villa in which creative work and success are fully enjoyed, 'the people' are invoked to restore the logic originally inspiring the book. His appeal to 'the people' brings plausibility to the author's efforts to erect a barrier between himself and his long-time enemy, the treacherous John Barleycorn, who has spared him but will certainly victimize weaker drinkers. Those who do not possess his inner power are destined to succumb and must be rescued by legislators. Prohibition applies to others, not to oneself; similarly, alcoholism describes fictional characters, not their creators. Like other authors of the same genre, Jack London tells the story of an individual who is unable to control his drug use, while implicitly claiming that he is. In holding this position, however, Jack London is consistent with his particular notion of socialism, a form of social Darwinism which selects strong, healthy, possibly blue-eyed men and entrusts them with the establishment of the system to come. Prohibition, in this sense, will help these men, not him, to achieve the task allocated to them by history. In the future society, saloons will only be known through history books, and will be thought of 'as a quaint old custom similar to bull-baiting and the burning of witches' (John Barleycorn: 204). A completely failed prophecy, London's argument is akin to the stance taken by paternalistic policymakers, who believe in their right, or duty, to suggest what lifestyle drug users should adopt, who fight to liberate users from the slavery of drugs, and through legislation, as it were, force them to be free.

Baudelaire's thoughts are more ambivalent, as shown in his claim that drugs reduce one's capacity to work, but that some drugs, like alcohol, are connatural to humans and help them not only to work but also to live. In *Le Spleen de Paris* ([1864] 1975), he incites everyone to get drunk, 'in order to escape the torture of time'; to get drunk ceaselessly, 'with wine, with poetry, with virtue, with whatever you want'. Despite his condemnation of hashish and opium, however, he does not invoke drug prohibition, perhaps for the revulsion he harbours towards those who invest themselves with the role of delivering moral lessons. Bourgeois morality, to him, resembles the prudish reaction provoked by the view of naked statues in a 'five-franc-prostitute' visiting the Louvre.

As noted above, much classical fiction does not associate drug use with defeatism, resignation or retreatism, but often with reversed notions such as activity and achievement, whether artistic, productive or generally human. Hints of a retreatist argument, however, are found in both London and Baudelaire, for example, in the belief of the former that alcohol thwarts human achievement and in the claim of the latter that creative activity is a drug-free enterprise. On the other hand, London clearly indicates that alcohol allows one to 'retreat' from beastly work, rather than from society and its values. Alcohol is part and parcel of the path of adventure, of life itself, rather than retreat from it. As a prolific novelist he needs drinking in order to keep up with the pace set by publishers. Baudelaire, who praises alcohol and condemns hashish and opium, is at the same time fascinated by De Quincey, whose work would have been impossible without opium.

Jack London can be described as a *moral entrepreneur*, as he participates in a movement of crusading reformers. Like other rule creators, 'he is interested in the content of rules. The existing rules do not satisfy him because there is some evil which profoundly disturbs him' (Becker, 1963: 147). Paternalistically, he wants to help those beneath him to improve their social condition, though those beneath him may not be attracted to the means he suggests for their elevation. Moral crusaders, however, may unwittingly draw support 'from people whose motives are less pure than those of the crusader' (Becker, 1963: 149). Employers, for example, may favour prohibitionism because a teetotal labour force would pose fewer problems in terms of performance and discipline. In this sense, while alcohol allows Jack London to refuse 'beastly work', he seems to imply that prohibitionism would help others to accept it, and by doing so to find salvation.

Neither London nor Baudelaire appear to be aware that drug use is destined to expand well beyond the enclaves of artists and adventurers, becoming the object of frenetic activity, and that the growth of illicit drugs markets will overshadow all retreatist traits of drug use, offering badly paid jobs for some and determining financial success for others. The social world of drug users and distributors, looking at a substantial body of research, is far from being characterized by passivity, and a better understanding of this world may be reached if variables such as status, success, career and activity are taken into consideration (Finestone, 1957; Sutter, 1966; Feldman, 1968; Hughes et al., 1971; Hughes, 1977; Pearson, 1987; Ruggiero and South, 1995). Drug users have been described as 'compulsively hardworking business executives' whose ostensible goal is the acquisition of money, 'but whose real satisfaction is in meeting the inordinate challenge' they create for themselves (Preble and Casey, 1969: 21). The drug scene, in other words, not only provides a euphoric escape from social problems but also offers to some a motivation and rationale for the pursuit of a meaningful life (Bourgois, 1996).

All drugs discussed by London and Baudelaire were, at the time, legally available, and both authors fail to predict the process ahead leading to their being made illegal, let alone the social and economic implications of this process. The former does not anticipate that the brief season of alcohol prohibition, while proving ineffective in reducing consumption, will act as a crucial phase of 'primitive accumulation' for organized criminal groups and shape their eventual involvement in the distribution of other illicit goods and the provision of other illicit services. Baulelaire totally overlooks the economic aspects of drugs production, distribution and use, limiting his observations to the realm of personal, intimate, choice, as if drugs were exempt from the rules of commercial exchange and the law of value. He is not concerned with future developments; therefore he cannot see how the ascent of illicit drugs markets is destined to offer illegal employment to deprived individuals and groups, while offering investment opportunities to those endowed with financial resources.

Jack London associates alcohol consumption with a type of violence that sociologists of deviance would describe as psycho-pharmacological, namely the violence caused by the characteristics of the substance itself. In this sense, his argument echoes contemporary prohibitionists who claim that the legalization of illicit drugs would cause an increase in users and thus in the aggregate violence generated by use. According to Goldstein (1985; 1986), the illegality of drugs causes other two types of violent behaviour, termed economically compulsive and systemic, respectively. The former type emerges when economically oriented crime committed by drug users becomes increasingly difficult because of property protection and target hardening, therefore forcing users to engage in violent offences. The latter type is believed to be intrinsic in drug markets, where interactions between users and suppliers are said to be embedded in violent forms of regulation. Violence, in sum, is said to be a common sanction for failure to honour contracts that by definition cannot be legally enforced, and is threatened or used to deter fraud, betrayal, theft and dishonesty (Arlacchi, 1998). Like contemporary prohibitionists, Jack London neglects the outcome of drug use criminalization, namely the increase in economically compulsive and systemic violence as a result of the illegality of drugs rather than drug use per se.

Jack London and Charles Baudelaire fail to consider that the effects of drug use depend on the quality of the drugs available, but also on the cultural environment, the motivation, and ultimately the range of social options offered to users. In conclusion, both authors appear to explore the properties of drugs and the phenomena engendered by their use, as if such phenomena were similar in all human beings, as if drugs were 'democratic' (Paz, 1990). Drugs are supposed to offer revelations without regard for the 'merits' of the person who uses them. Unfortunately, the dreams induced by drugs in poets and in ordinary people are increasingly different.

4

Nana, Women and Crime

The theatrical event of the year, finally, was about to begin. Everybody had been talking about it for more than six months. It was the premiere of *The Blonde Venus*, an operetta full of astounding music and recitative verve.

Nana, the new star, was going to play Venus, and she was employed, or rather exhibited, by Bordenave, the notorious theatre director who exhibited women while treating them like slaves. During the rehearsal, for example, if Simonne or Clarisse failed to toe the line, he would just kick their backside. After all, he explained, he was there to sell those girls, and he knew 'what the little tarts were worth'. The man was forever hatching plans to lower the artistic sensibility of Parisians, and his behaviour left no doubt as to the level he intended such sensibility to drop. He shouted, spat, slapped his thighs in anger: 'a shameless character with a coarse sense of humour'. To those who congratulated him for his theatre, he replied: 'you mean my brothel!' (Zola, *Nana* [1880] 1972: 21).

Objectively, Nana was neither a good singer nor a skilled dancer. However, she did not need to possess particular performative abilities, because she had something which replaced everything else. Bordenave

could scent it out, and the smell was strong: the audience would find
out, he swore; Nana only had to appear on stage and everybody would
be hanging out their tongues.

The theatre had been turned topsy-turvy by Nana's arrival, and while
a noisy crowd was besieging the box office, with voices competing in
topping one another, her name sprang out here and there 'with all the
lilting vivacity of its two syllables'.

> The men standing in front of the playbills spelt it out aloud; others
> uttered it in a questioning tone as they passed; while the women, at once
> uneasy and smiling, repeated it softly with an air of surprise (Nana: 24).

Nobody knew who Nana was or where she came from. Conjectures,
however, abounded, and talking about her was a pleasure in itself, as
it gave the opportunity to pronounce that name, a caressing sound
which was whispered from ear to ear, easily rolling off every tongue.
The two syllables provided a musical background to a crowd that, by
pronouncing them, compounded its state of gay excitement and good-
natured expectation. A fever of curiosity, as violent as a physical fit,
accompanied the hectic audience into the theatre, with women uncon-
cerned if their dresses were torn and men if they lost their hats.

Gentlemen of unimpeachable appearance repeated: "Nana! Nana!",
while being crushed together; and when a quarrel broke out at the box
office, no one bothered taking any notice, as the growing clamour
caused by the hum of voices made the noise of the quarrelling men a
sort of counterpoint to the bisyllabic chorus heard in the hall. It was
a spectacular explosion of collective facetiousness and crude sensuality.

> The whole of Paris was there, the Paris of letters, of finance and of
> pleasure. There were a great many journalists, a few authors, a number
> of speculators, and more courtesans than respectable women. It was a
> singularly mixed world, composed of all the talents, and tarnished by all
> the vices, a world where the same fatigue and the same fever appeared
> in every face. (Nana: 28)

The operetta showed Diana, thin and dark, with the adorable ugliness of a Parisian street urchin, addressing a ludicrous complaint to Mars, who was deserting her for Venus. Mars was sporting a comical, gigantic plume, and in the background the chorus was formed by a miscellany of funny faces. This was the cuckolds' chorus, invoking Vulcan, the god of cuckolds, whose wife had run away three days before.

On stage, Nana seemed to be admitting with a wink that she had no talent at all, but that that did not matter, because she had something else. When her voice failed her, and she realized that she would never get through the whole song, without getting flustered, she thrust out one hip, which was roundly outlined under a flimsy tunic, bent backwards, so that her breasts were shown, and stretched out her arms. Applause burst from all sides.

> From that moment the operetta was saved, and indeed promised to be a great success. This carnival of the gods, this dragging of Olympus in the mud, this mockery of a whole religion, a whole world of poetry, struck the audience as rich entertainment. (Nana: 38)

The premiere attended by such a distinguished audience turned into a display of voluptuous irreverence, with legend being trampled and ancient images shattered. Jupiter looked like a fool, and Mars was too funny to describe; royalty had been turned into a farce and the army into a joke. Jupiter, suddenly falling in love with a little laundress, expressed his happiness by dancing a mad cancan. Innuendos rained on the audience and were immediately echoed from the stalls with heavier allusions and indecent remarks, until even inoffensive phrases were given obscene twists by loud, vulgar, exclamations.

The audience, in truth, was not only formed by the literary elite of the city but also included Madame Robert, who provided special services to that elite, though personally limited herself to one lover at a time, always a respectable man. Sunk in his seat was then a truant schoolboy, who looked in a state of stupefied admiration. Two men, after the initial aesthetic astonishment, started to recognize the features of that face and the lines of that body, and thought that Nana was the same girl they had seen some evenings standing at the corner of rue de Provence. This recognition was simultaneous with a collective shiver, caused by Nana's parading her nakedness, hidden only by a veil of gauze. One was uncertain whether that nakedness was redolent of an Amazon, with round shoulders and breasts as stiff as spears, or of Venus rising from the waves. Whatever the resemblance, Nana's audacity received no applause; nobody laughed any more. The men's faces were tense and serious, their nostrils narrowed, their mouths prickly and parched. A wind seemed to have passed over the audience, a soft wind laden with hidden menace.

> All of a sudden, in the good-natured child the woman stood revealed, a disturbing woman with all the impulsive madness of her sex, opening the gates of the unknown world of desire. Nana was till smiling, but with the deadly smile of a man-eater. (*Nana*: 45)

Nana's 'deadly smile' filled the entire house with lust.

Naturalism and positivism

The theatre scene I have just described is an example of how Émile Zola interpreted his role as a literary historian of private life under the Second Empire in France, and how he believed the legacy of Balzac, the literary historian of private life under the restoration and the July monarchy, had to be both appropriated and renovated (Lukács, 1989: 85). Zola never spoke of realism, but of naturalism, and implied that novelists had to eliminate all romantic traits from their creative work. In fact, the word 'creative' itself should be avoided here, as Zola's theory on the composition of novels posited the predictability of events following each other in a sort of harmonic, evolutional, order. Depicting reality meant to exclude all extraordinary inventions and implied that stories would unfold with consequential logic, without ever being disfigured by surprise. Novelists, by accepting the basic principle of showing the ordinary course of average lives, were required to kill the hero.

Fiction, in Zola, was tantamount to chemical experimentation, in which imagination had no role to play: literature had to mimic science. Novelists, like chemists combining substances together, had to place characters, with their specific innate characteristics, into a given environment, and observe the resulting individual acts and the consequent collective effects. Although the author, fortunately, never followed his own theories, and bowed to poetic imagination while yielding to pleasant unscientific prose, he perhaps aimed to 'impress a public easily over-awed by pseudo-scientific terminology' (Holden, 1972: 6). Nevertheless, he was genuinely fascinated by the workings of heredity and environment, and how these determined human action and ultimately history. Nana reflects a vivid picture of French society under the Second Empire, a society in which prostitution was not only a service provided to the pleasure-loving, corrupt, men of the elite, but also the obscene symbolic portrayal of a nation. In courtesans and high-class cocottes readers were expected to see Napoleon III's France and its inevitable decline, and in Nana's life its ruinous 'appetite for luxury and facile pleasures'.

Zola was acrimonious with those little actresses hypnotizing a stupid public with 'an obscenity underlined by a wiggle of the hips', and had no respect for those spoiled young men fascinated by trite productions of Offenbach. He singled out the national debauch as the principal cause of the country's humiliation, like Dumas blamed France's defeat on prostitution (Holden, 1972: 7). But why Nana, why 'chercher la femme', as the central locus of imputation for national decline?

Criminological positivism describes women as less evolved beings than men, and thus closer to primitive types, more likely agents of atavistic forms of criminality. At the same time, female crime is seen as more frequent than appearances may suggest, because women are deemed capable of hiding their offences through devious means and by exploiting men's innate chivalry (Heidensohn, 1994: 1000). Taking lack of evidence as the most manifest proof of female criminality, positivism describes normal women as latent criminals, because, following an inverted logic, it is assumed that criminal women show few deviations from normal women (Hutchings, 2001: 110). Like female offenders, Nana is presented as hysterical and irresponsible rather than criminal, as unstable rather than dangerous (Edwards, 1981). Like a minor or idiot, she is feeble-minded, a term whose vagueness contains an elastic capacity of alluding to undefinable social problems caused by some biological imperfection. In any case, she is not a responsible human being embracing deviance as a rational choice. Nana is a positivist character, with her intense criminal activity well hidden, and, as Cesare Lombroso and Guglielmo Ferrero (1893) would argue, her prostitution substitutes for the crimes her male counterparts commit openly. When, with old age, prostitution will no longer offer a professional opportunity, Nana, like other women, will openly display higher levels of crime. However, as we shall see, Nana will not make it to old age, thus leaving this theory unsubstantiated.

Zola and positivist criminologists are equally interested in women as the subjects of high hidden criminality, but also as offenders whose motivations are illegible, as if an inscrutable malaise accompanied their sexuality. As unpredictable human beings, women are perplexing, and positivist minds searching for scientific explanations find these in impurity and disease, associated with the double exceptionality of their being at the same time female and criminal, something that Lombroso has no hesitation in equating with monstrosity. Similar monstrosity, however, has precedents in writings long predating Lomboso's 'scientific' work, as for example in St Mark's account of how Salomé beguiled King Herod and his court with her dancing, and in return for the pleasure demanded that John the Baptist be beheaded (Search, 1957). Herod, when Salomé kissed the head of her victim, finding the taste of his blood the taste of love, was horrified and shouted: 'She is monstrous, she is altogether monstrous' (Wilde, 1974: 347). And is the story of Medea, retold time and again over the past two and a half millennia, not equally monstrous? The woman, abandoned by Jason, and torn by irrational sorrow, wounded pride, rage, jealousy and hatred, concocts a horrible revenge. Pretending to accept Jason's decision, she sends her rival 'a beautiful but poisonous dress, which, when the rays of the sun hit it, burst into flame' (Atwood, 1998: xi).

The monstrosity of female offenders is ascribed to, among other things, hysteria, which according to Lombroso (1876) is twenty times more frequent in women than in men. This condition is caused by moral influences, emotions, fear and maltreatment, but also by diseases associated with 'genital excesses' and hereditary traits transmitted by alcoholic parents. Lombroso's symptomatology lists eroticism among the characteristics of hysteric women:

> This manifests itself through love hallucinations, and with love night-mares preceded by epigastric fits. Eroticism is often so impulsive that hysteric women give themselves without love, for spirit of adventure, for their need to experience unforeseen emotions or for sudden passion. All criminality of hysteric women revolves around their sexual functions. (Lombroso, 1876: 303)

If Nana's eroticism does not make her a manifest hysteric, her personality straddles the borders of a variety of typologies. This is a constant of Lombroso's characterization of female offenders, as if the 'father' of criminology were anxious to predict which individual woman might fall into which category he painstakingly lists (Young, 1996). While contemporary observers may regard positivistic notions with indulgent horror, it may be argued that some such notions never ceased to inform official discourses of women's crime, and that they are perfectly compatible with the interests of crime-control professionals (Smart, 1977). Nana, in this sense, is criminologically correct: she has loose morals and sensuality, and if hers is not the deep voice of a contralto, and though she refrains from dressing up in men's clothes, her bisexuality adds to the excessive eroticism characterizing her deviance and hysteria. She does not manifest monstrosity under the form of brutality or masculinity, but in the guise of shamelessness, which makes her similarly unnatural. 'Shame is as unnatural to woman as it is for mankind to love their enemies, or to bless those that persecute them' (Mayhew and Binney, 1862: iii). Nana, in this sense, is akin to women described by travel writers of past centuries, where the shamelessness of native females manifests itself through polygamy, promiscuity or incest, while perhaps arousing prurient fantasies of sexual hospitality among those observing them (Rawson, 2001).

Hereditary traits

As already suggested, Zola was more romantic than he wanted to admit, and did not really reconcile his theories with his work. Rather than naturalistic, his description of Nana's life is categorically moralistic, and his counter-heroine is deemed responsible for a series of achievements and crimes for which 'the entire "immoral army" of Paris would not be sufficient' (Holden, 1972: 16). Zola thought he could complete the transition from Stendhal and Balzac, the great representatives of old realism, to the new technique of naturalism, requiring that novelists, and for that matter intellectuals in general, did not participate in social conflicts, but were reduced to mere spectators and chroniclers of public life. His political beliefs, however, along with his writing style, belied his apparent commitment to neutrality. He came close to socialism, 'though he never got beyond a paler version of Fourier's utopianism' (Lukács, 1989: 86). His socialistic ideas, perhaps embraced with the 'scientific' certainty of their victorious fate, led him to establish an equally scientific method of enquiry, in which society was conceived as a harmonious entity rejecting the diseases attacking its organic unity. Zola imagined the social cycle to be identical to the life cycle: 'in society as in the human body, there is a solidarity linking the various organs with each other in such a way that if one organ putrefies, the rot spreads to the other organs and results in a very complicated disease' (86). Because he could not always consistently adhere to his own programme, he is said to have become a great writer. Hating and despising far too much the evil, base, forces which permeated the society of his time, he could not remain 'a cold, unsympathetic "experimenter" such as the positivist–naturalist doctrine required him to be' (92). Nevertheless, his hatred for 'evil' was subtly mingled with 'scientific' observations, and the latter provided the needed justifications for the former.

Zola's invective targeted that 'whole society clinging to the skirts of those women', 'those old men debauching themselves' and 'young idiots ruining themselves, some to keep in fashion, some out of infatuation' (Holden, 1972: 9). But his invective included Nana, who was doomed by her social origin and biological make-up and destined to drag in her fall the entire society surrounding her. Zola just did not like Nana. Her house in the Boulevard Haussmann, for example, was vulgar, and the rooms had never been completely furnished.

The vulgar luxury of consoles and gilded chairs formed a sharp contrast with junk-shop furniture such as mahogany tables and zinc candelabra trying to pass as Florentine bronze. All that smacked of the courtesan deserted too soon by her first serious protector and falling back on shifty lovers, and suggested a bad start handicapped by refusals of credit and threats of eviction. (Nana: 49)

Admirers visit her and patiently wait their turn in the hall, and in moments of overcrowding some are invited to take a seat in the kitchen. Visitors include creditors, for despite her popularity Nana's financial situation is far from sound. Having to provide for her son Louis, who lives with her aunt Madame Lerat, she feels the duty to give him the type of life she never had, a feeling she experiences when she goes through her periodical, if brief, fits of maternal love. The morning after the successful premiere, Nana is in urgent need of some money, and when Madame Tricon drops by she pretends to be ignorant of the nature of the woman's relations with ladies in financial difficulties. An unspecified appointment at three o'clock, arranged by Madame Tricon, would bring to Nana the needed sum.

Describing the events of the previous evening to her aunt, Nana grows intoxicated at her own account, while the applause received still echoes in her mind, an applause capable, in her ominous view, of rocking Paris to its foundations. How could anyone have imagined all that when she had been a child playing in the rue de la Goutte d'Or? Madame Lerat shakes her head: no, no one could ever have predicted it. The two women are incredulous, because Nana's background, as a genetic legacy, is temporarily inconsistent with her career, and perhaps because their unspoken belief in that legacy warns them about future, disastrous events. While expecting such ineluctable events to occur, Nana does her best to enjoy what life is momentarily offering her.

The truant boy who was stupefied by her performance is among that morning's visitors. With a bunch of flowers, he introduces himself as George, the son of a renowned aristocratic family. Steiner, the fat banker, is also there, pondering on his chances to beat such determined competitors. Perhaps to grasp the exact terms of such competition, and the potential rewards this might bring. Nana decides to gather her admirers and draw them all together in a late-night dinner party.

At the dinner, with guests only arriving after midnight, sobriety does not last long. The champagne gradually begins to fill everybody 'with a nervous intoxication'. By two o'clock in the morning all end up behaving indecorously.

> The women began leaning on their elbows in the midst of all the plates and glasses while the men, in order to breathe more easily, pushed their chairs back; dress-coats mingled with light-coloured bodices, and bare shoulders, half turned towards the table, took on a silky gleam. (Nana: 130)

Then the guests start telling jokes at the tops of their voices, gesticulating wildly, asking questions which nobody answers, shouting at each other and whirling aimlessly from room to room. A man, who feels that the level of amusement is not sufficiently high, has a brilliant idea and immediately puts it into practice: he takes his bottle of champagne and empties it into the piano. The others are convulsed with laughter, especially after being told that there is nothing better than champagne for pianos: it gives them tone. Meanwhile, 'women were offering themselves with the honesty of good-natured whores'. Nana is upset, though perhaps thinks that what is happening is consonant with her social origin and genetic code. Confirmation of this will follow shortly.

The golden fly

Fat Steiner's efforts to earn Nana's favours are finally successful, but he is only rewarded after buying a country house for his highly contested lover. Nana, in fact, aims higher, to be precise at Comte Muffat, whose

wealth might resolve her problems once and for all. The right opportunity presents itself when the Count accompanies another gentleman
to Nana's dressing room at the theatre. Muffat is overwhelmed by the
powerful perfume lingering in the room, which makes him dizzy. The
way in which Nana is slowly taking possession of him terrifies him,
reminding him of the pious stories of diabolic possession which he has
read as a child. 'He believed in the devil; and in a confused sort of way,
Nana was the devil, with her laughter, her breasts and her crupper'
(Nana: 155). Every part of her body seems to him to be swollen with
vice. But he promises himself that he will be strong: he will know how
to defend himself from that devil. Simultaneously, however, he is as-
sailed by the subtle pleasure haunting 'those Catholics whom the fear
of hell spurs on to commit sin' (156).

In the dressing room, after kissing Nana on the neck, Muffat, feeling as if his head is on fire, decides to walk home. The struggle within
him has completely ceased. The ideas and beliefs of the last forty years
are being drowned in a flood of sensuality.

> While he was walking along the boulevards, the rumble of the last car-
> riages deafened him with the name of Nana: the gas-lamps set naked
> flesh dancing before his eyes – the naked flesh of Nana's lithe arms and
> white shoulders. And he felt that he was completely hers: he would have
> abjured everything, to possess her for a single hour that very night. His
> youth, the lustful puberty of adolescence, was awakening within him at
> last, flaring up suddenly in the frigidity of the Catholic and the dignity
> of the middle-aged man. (Nana: 171)

In her country house Nana reaches a temporary apotheosis, her
economic security being enriched by genuine love. Although continuing her relationship with both Steiner and Muffat, she sinks one evening
'like a virgin' in George's arms, and the young man brings sincere
happiness into her life, which suddenly seems wonderful to her. 'In the
boy's arms she became a girl of fifteen once more, and under the

caressing influence of this new childhood the flower of love blossomed again in a nature jaded and disgusted by experience of men' (Nana: 191). However, the idyll is not to last.

An article published in Le Figaro treats Nana's past with ferocity, while ominously anticipating her future. The article tells the story of a girl descended from four or five generations of drunkards, whose blood is tainted by an accumulated inheritance of destitution and alcohol. Such inheritance has generated in the girl a serious derangement of the sexual instinct. She has grown up in the slums, in the gutters of Paris; and now, tall and beautiful, and as well made as a plant nurtured on a dung heap, she is avenging the paupers and outcasts of whom she is the product. Her rottenness has dangerously fermented and is now spreading around, rotting the aristocracy. She has become a force of nature, a ferment of destruction, corrupting and poisoning Paris with her snow-white thighs. At the end of the article the comparison with a fly is made, a golden fly which has flown up out of the dung, and after sucking filth and death from the gutters is now menacingly buzzing, dancing and glittering like a precious stone, entering luxurious 'palaces through the windows and poisoning the men inside, simply by settling on them' (Nana: 221).

Nana as offender and victim

Lombroso (1876: 278) would apply to Nana his definition of nymphomania, in his words 'characterised by impulses to commit libidinous crimes, rape, and ferocious onanism, performed both in private and in public'. The positivist school of criminology described nymphomania as a maddening force turning girls' pudency into bacchanal urge. Nana's character, however, is multifaceted, and, as readers become accustomed to her 'undeserved' wealth and aristocratic excesses, a twist in the novel shows her back on the street, where she belongs: the high-class cocotte is destined to redescend to the social inferno she thought she had escaped.

After moving in with fellow performer Fontan, Nana begins experiencing the violence of domestic life, and is beaten by her partner, the first time because she has forgotten to shake the crumbs off the sheets after eating in bed with him. Although terrified, she feels that the slap had calmed her down, putting an end to an argument that is going nowhere: 'It was even nice getting a slap, provided it came from him' (Nana: 251). But after the first slap, a new life begins, and for the slightest thing Fontan hits her face, until she grows accustomed to it, and takes the beatings without resistance. Sometimes she screams and threatens him, but then he pins her against the wall and talks of strangling her, which has the effect of making her more amenable. Often, she collapses on a chair and sobs for a few minutes. 'Then she would forget all about it, gaily singing and laughing, and bustling about so that she filled the little flat with the rustle of her skirts' (251).

When Fontan disappears for the whole day, however, Nana learns how to avoid solitude. She meets with her friend Satin and together they visit Madame Robert, who lives in the street where men furtively hurry along, looking up at the windows, and women in dressing gowns seem to be waiting. They also dine at Laure's, a restaurant full of ladies of fifty whose swelling contours are tightly laced by belts and corsets. Other female customers are enormous creatures in their late thirties, with bloated flesh hanging in puffy folds over their flaccid lips, but in the midst of all these bulging bosoms and bellies there are a few slim, pretty girls to be seen. 'These still wore an innocent expression in spite of their immodest gestures, for they were just beginners in their profession, picked up in some dance hall and brought along to Laure's by one of her female customers' (Nana: 257).

After being the victim of yet another beating, Nana is told that she has to provide for herself, which she accepts, offering, in fact, to work for herself and the man beating her as well. She then starts a series of wild forays into the streets of Paris, visiting sordid places and walking muddy alleys, 'in the flickering light of gas-lamps'. She goes back to the tatty dance halls 'where she had kicked up her heels as a girl', and returns to the dark corners on the outer boulevards, where, when she was fifteen, 'men used to fondle her on corner-posts'. With Satin she becomes restless, and the duo soon become known in all the late-night cafés and cheap hotels, whose staircases are always wet with spittle and spilt beer. They would also walk up and down the streets, planting themselves in key locations, crossing the whole city, on rainy evenings when their boots let in water or hot evenings when their bodices cling to their skin. They endure 'long waits and endless walks, jostlings and quarrels, and the brutal caresses of a passer-by taken to some squalid furnished room, to come swearing down the greasy stairs afterwards' (Nana: 271).

Nana has inherited from her parents a deep distrust for the police, but now she has learned to fear them. Her friend Satin keeps telling her that the 'public morals brigade' is formed by thugs and unscrupulous blackmailers who would accept presents, in money or in kind, in exchange for omitting their names from the list of known prostitutes. The police, Satin says, arrest as many women as possible, in the hope of earning bonuses.

> Nana listened to these stories in growing terror. She had always been afraid of the Law, that unknown power, that instrument of male vengeance which would wipe her out without anybody in the world lifting a finger to defend her. She saw Saint-Lazare as a grave, a black hole in which they buried women alive after cutting off their hair. (Nana: 274)

Nineteenth-century descriptions provided by social reformers, whether inspired by their moral or their religious vocation, seem to echo Nana's adventures, especially when our heroine spends her time in dance halls and down-market restaurants. Some specific places frequented by Nana resemble those abundantly dissected in some Victorian writings, which were described as infectious sources of corruption attacking the purity of women and putting their moral weakness to the test (Zedner, 1991). Being more vulnerable, it was suggested, women were particularly prone to fall when entering such places. Nana, on the other hand, is particularly vulnerable, and her family background emerges as an aetiological variable even after she has acquired some degree of wealth and some form of respectability among the elite.

More recent criminological studies of women and crime stand out as, perhaps, among the most interesting developments in the field. Such studies provide a number of critical arguments and viewpoints that readers of Zola may utilize for an appraisal of his analytical shrewdness. These studies remind us of a fundamental distinction which is totally neglected by the creator of Nana. While for Zola, the offences committed by his heroine are associated with biological characteristics, partly determined by social conditions and contexts, criminological studies mainly focus on social roles, expectations and interactions. In other words, if Nana's crimes are seen by Zola as consistent with her 'sex', the same crimes would be seen by contemporary female criminologists as the result of her 'gender' and of her interactions with men.

Criminology and the sociology of deviance are concerned with a number of issues which also emerge from Nana's inconstant, sinusoidal, biographical trajectory. The main issues discussed include why women commit fewer crimes than men, why these crimes are less serious, and why women are less represented in the criminal justice system. As a prostitute, Nana is never arrested; nor does she ever serve a prison sentence. She, therefore, is never given the opportunity of enjoying the advantages of chivalry allegedly accorded to deviant women. At first sight, then, her gender does not seem to be a key variable in her criminal career; nor does it appear to affect the nature and intensity of the institutional responses she elicits. Rather, her low levels of offending, and the nonviolent nature of that offending, might explain her lenient treatment. Only when working on the street does she experience the fear of law enforcers, who totally ignore her, instead, when she works for wealthy, distinguished customers. Does the social setting in which she performs her job affect the treatment she receives more than her gender?

As Heidensohn (1994) argues, modern academic and popular debates address both the issue of chivalry and the issue of women being, under certain circumstances, dealt with more punitively than men. But if the agencies of law enforcement and criminal justice in general ignore Nana's conduct, Zola does not; nor does he appear to consider chivalry as an appropriate value to deal with his fictional character. Perhaps he is convinced that Nana's criminality, like that of other women, increases in transitional periods, when the distance between male and female offenders is reduced, and when women allegedly adopt more masculine types of illegal conduct (Adler, 1975). See, for example, how Nana's illegality assumes the same speculative character that guides the relentless business career of banker Steiner. See also how the decline of Nana reflects that of an entire male society. However, Nana is given additional punishment by her partner, becoming a victim of domestic violence, thus confirming that women who do not conform to conventional roles are more harshly treated, if not formally by institutional agencies, then informally by those they love (Eaton, 1986).

Nana, in sum, confirms that women may suffer more intensely than men the stigma associated with deviance, also because 'there are relatively few positive role models of the good old villain-type for women to emulate' (Heidensohn, 1994: 1018). In this respect, however, it would appear that she is not only the victim of societal misogyny, but that she also develops her own form of misogyny. She feels that her achievements far exceed those of other women, and her refusal of family life and monogamy reveals her clear dissociation from the lifestyle of her subservient female friends, their failure and their subjugation. According to Muraro (1984), female misogyny is not the reflection in women's mind of the misogyny of men. Male misogyny may subside, she argues, especially with the growing assimilation of women in society, and with their consequent 'banalization'. When relationships among women increase in quantity and intensity, as in the case of Nana, conventional distances between them shorten, while real differences become accentuated. If women do not accept patronizing one another, or react with hypocrisy to differences between them, then hate may emerge. A woman may hate another woman when she receives from her a humiliating image of her sex. This is what Nana does, to the point that she desires not to be a woman. In this respect, it is not only the lack of role models of the 'good old villain-type' that Nana experiences; there is a lack of female role models *tout court* for her to emulate. Muraro describes such lack with the following example. Soldiers, immersed in mud, exhausted, filthy, fighting a stupid war, are illuminated by the appearance of their general, who is well dressed, articulate and immaculate in his uniform: they see in him the symbol of what their gender can potentially offer. Nana, like other women, has a poor symbolic image to adopt and internalize, surrounded as she is by individuals of her sex she has no intention of emulating. Hers is the 'misogyny' of an emancipated woman, possessing elements one finds in Patricia Highsmith's (1980) short stories, where for example Pamela, a woman who is against abortion and state childcare, is attacked and killed during a feminist meeting. She also reminds us of a real account by Millet (1971) of a physical clash between a group of feminists, attending a conference on the abolition of prostitution, and prostitutes imprudently invited to that conference.

While some female criminologists find it vital to develop a critique of sexism in order to shape new perspectives on women's crime and to design alternatives to law discourses (Smart, 1977; 1989), others remain sceptical about an 'add and stir' approach, and see the simple mixing of feminism into criminology as unproductive (Heidensohn, 1994). Yet other female scholars focus on marginalization, arguing that women are poorer, and that the typical cycle of offending in which they engage exposes them to differentiated prosecution and punishment (Carlen, 1988), and that, for the same reason, their rehabilitation is more problematic (Eaton, 1993). Dilemmas, however, remain concerning the ability of women, especially those who are socially marginalized, to achieve successful social bonding processes, which would reduce their criminality (Heidensohn, 1985). Finally, while some theorists may suggest that the problem is not women's crime but men's crime, and that the focus should shift to the issue of why women do not commit offences, rather than why they do (Stanko, 1993), others would endorse the view that criminological conceptualizations of gender and crime, and explanations of the specific institutional treatment inflicted on women offenders, are inconclusive.

Zola, in contrast, resolves such dilemmas by rooting Nana's criminality in her genetic patrimony, and his desire to punish her transcends the vagaries of her career. High-class cocotte or street prostitute, Nana is doomed by the author's 'scientific' study of her innate make-up. Nana sells sex in exchange for money; she also enters the social subculture and organization in which such practice makes sense, but she does not suffer the social process labelling her 'a prostitute and the consequences of involvement in prostitution, such as increased police surveillance, reduced economic opportunities and increased poverty'

(Phoenix, 1999: 6). She is not persecuted by official agencies, poverty or social stigma, except when she works on the streets; however, she suffers the vindictiveness of her creator.

Final retribution

Nana is not destined to end her career and her life in the streets; Zola gives her further opportunities to ascend again, in order to make her final fall more painful. Former lover Comte Muffat comes back into her life, and she convinces him to finance theatre impresario Bordenave's latest work, in which she demands to play a part, this time as a respectable woman, not as a courtesan. 'She had had enough of high-class tarts' (Nana: 298). Her performance is disastrous: how could Zola make her succeed in such a part? Thereupon, Nana makes her final choice. She plunges into a hectic private lifestyle, re-establishing a reputation as fashionable host and becoming the 'beneficiary of male stupidity and lust'. Her new, sumptuous, house becomes the scene of evening galas, though the Louis Seize diligently scattered in the rooms hardly temper the vulgarity of those gatherings. While lavishing the most fervent promises of fidelity on Muffat, she continues her affairs, both with young George, who has also returned, and with Satin, with whom she spends tender afternoons, exchanging endearments and mingling kisses with laughter.

The two women often plunge into an 'orgy of reminiscences':

> They used to have frequent fits of chattering of this kind when a sudden urge to stir up the mud of their childhood would take hold of them; and these fits always occurred when men were present, as if they were giving way to a burning desire to smear them with the dung on which they had grown to womanhood. (Nana: 333)

In a resentful, if composed, outburst, Zola finds it despicable that, amid fine gentlemen with their great names and their ancient traditions of respectability, the two women can sit face to face, exchanging tender glances, 'triumphant and supreme in the tranquil abuse of their sex, and their open contempt for the male'. Worse still that those gentlemen are amused and applaud them.

The clash between Zola and Nana continues when the woman starts to read a novel that is causing a sensation at the time. It is the story of a prostitute, and Nana inveighs against it, declaring that it is all untrue, and 'expressing indignant revulsion against the sort of filthy literature which claimed to show life as it was – as if a writer could possibly describe everything' (Nana: 336). This trenchant critique of naturalism is accompanied by more gentle blows dealt by Nana's guests against Zola's 'criminological' theories: to claim 'irresponsibility in certain pathological cases meant that there were no criminals left, but only sick people' (340).

Nana is punished with an unwanted pregnancy, which strikes her as 'a ridiculous accident', a bad joke, a piece of bad luck. She feels an unpleasant sense of surprise, because her sexual parts, as Lombroso would have it, have been deranged, so they are not expected to make babies. 'Nature infuriated her, with this intervention of solemn motherhood in her career of pleasure – this gift of life in the midst of all the deaths she was spreading around her' (Nana: 385). However, she has a miscarriage, which one might read as rehabilitation or double punishment, or as a natural fact of life.

Nana soon returns to dazzle aristocratic Parisian life with her splendour, rising higher than ever on the scale of vice, dominating the city with her insolent display of luxury. Her contempt for money makes her openly squander fortunes. One of her lovers, Philippe, is arrested, charged with having stolen twelve thousand francs from the funds of his regiment. For the last three months, due to Nana's financial insatiability, he has been taking small sums in the hope of being able to

pay them back, concealing deficits with forged documents. George
attempts suicide, stabbing himself with the scissors he finds in her
bedroom, leaving an unpleasant stain of blood on the carpet. 'The
growing needs of her life of luxury sharpened her appetite, and she
would clean a man out with one snap of her teeth' (Nana: 434). Her
bedroom has become a public place, while the Comte falls victim to a
sensual tempestuous wind and his brain plunges into unfettered, 'delirious fantasies of the flesh'. The sleepless nights with Nana trigger a
thirst for bestiality, a mania for 'walking on all fours, growling and
biting'. At times he is a dog:

> She would throw her scented handkerchief to the far end of the room,
> and he had to run and pick it up with his teeth, dragging himself along
> on his hands and knees. 'Fetch it, Caesar! Well done; good dog…'. And
> he loved his degradation, enjoying the pleasure of being an animal. He
> longed to sink even further. (Nana: 442)

One evening Nana insists on the Comte visiting her dressed in his
formal uniform of court chamberlain. When he appears in all his su-
perb glory, she roars with laughter and teases him mercilessly. Faced
with his sword, cocked hat and white breeches, the dress-coat of red
cloth trimmed with gold, the symbolic key hanging on its left-hand
skirt, Nana launches herself into a ruthless attack of irreverence against
pomp and grandeur, and, for the joy of humiliating him in the official
dignity of his uniform, she shakes him and pinches him, shouting: 'Get
a move on, chamberlain!' Finally, at the peak of her excitement, she
kicks him in the rear. 'Every kick was a heartfelt insult to the Tuileries
and the majesty of the imperial court, dominating an abject and frightened people' (Nana: 442).

Nana's 'labour of ruin and death' has now reached completion. The
'golden fly' that came from the dungheap of the slums, carrying the
ferment of social decay, has poisoned all those men simply by alighting

on them. Her mission has been accomplished: she has avenged the beggars and outcasts, the dangerous classes, of her world. And while, as it were, her sex rises in a halo of glory and blazes down on her prostrate victims like a rising sun shining down on a field of carnage, 'she remained as unconscious of her actions as a splendid animal, ignorant of the havoc she had wreaked, and as good-natured as ever' (Nana: 453). The gentlemen's scepticism towards the new criminological theories, and Zola's theories, has been proven wrong.

Leaving the carnage behind, Nana then spends some time in Cairo and Russia, and once back in town she is inflicted with the final, lethal, punishment: she contracts smallpox. The treasures she brought back from her journey remain locked in fifty-two boxes, at the station, as a form of appropriate restitution of undeserved wealth. In the hotel room where she spent her last hours she is visited by a variety of acquaintances, who having delayed their arrival find her dead. They stay a while, and only before leaving decide to glance briefly at the corpse. When the brass candelabrum is lit and placed on the bedside table next to the corpse, the dead woman's face is finally revealed. They all run away, horrified at the sight of what deserves a full quotation.

> What lay on the pillow was a charnel-house, a heap of pus and blood, a shovelful of putrid flesh. The pustules had invaded the whole face, so that one pock touched the next. Withered and sunken, they had taken on the greyish colour of mud, and on the shapeless pulp, in which the features had ceased to be discernible, they already looked like mould from the grave. One eye, the left eye, had completely foundered in the bubbling purulence, and the other, which remained half opened, looked like a dark, decaying hole. The nose was still suppurating. A large reddish crust starting on one of the cheeks was invading the mouth, twisting it into a terrible grin. And around this grotesque and horrible mask of death, the hair, the beautiful hair, still blazed like sunlight and flowed in a stream of gold. Venus was decomposing. It was as if the poison she had picked up in the gutters, from the carcases left there by the roadside, that ferment with which she had poisoned a whole people, had now risen to her face and rotted it. (Nana: 470)

Women, crime and fiction

The collapse of a social system is symbolized by the rotting of a female body, belying Zola's oblique admission of discomfort, and defeat, vis-à-vis women's sexuality. Zola perhaps was concerned with the limits of male power over females and how these limits made men vulnerable to manipulation. 'The courtesans turned the tables on their clients, but always within the larger political context in which their clients retained their superior economic power – the power to buy a woman's sex' (Naffine, 1997: 120–21). Some female criminologists advocate the need to use fiction as a source of meaning for both womanhood and women's criminality. Opposing literary naturalism, and for that matter realist criminology, they claim that reality and meaning are not there, in the world, waiting patiently to be recorded by objective observers. Novelists and criminologists – as external observers – contribute to the making of reality and meaning according to the ideological and cultural framework shaped by their role and occupation. 'We, as meaning-makers, are obliged to deal with meanings already constituted (by others) for us, but we also play an active part in reconstituting those meanings as we pass them on' (Naffine, 1997: 122). Realism, while polemically advocating the concrete against the abstract, materialism versus idealism, implies on the one hand the impatience of one sense of practical, and on the other a tone of limited calculation typical of politicians and businessmen (Williams, 1976). The sense of practical and limited calculation, in turn, may reduce the analysis to surface observation, thus making realism prosaic, a device to evade the real (Ruggiero, 1992). It is curious how some criminologists, echoing Zola, while studying the conducts of others, find redundant the study of the way in which their perceptions affect the phenomena they observe, and how they neglect the fact that by interacting with the subjects observed

they actively constitute frames of meaning (Giddens, 1976). Both Zola
and these types of criminologists feel uncomfortable when facing the
social mechanisms that produce what they regard as knowledge.

In a logical extension of these arguments, Naffine (1997: 122) stresses
that, 'if the making of meaning is already a creative process, then there
is no hard division between the creative nature of writing about crime
fact and the creativity involved in crime fiction'. On the other hand, if
scientific discovery requires creativity, how can it be distinguished from
the accomplishments of works of imagination?

> To understand crime is to engage in a positive act of creation – some-
> thing requiring invention and imagination. The feminist criminologist is
> not simply reporting on the phenomenon of crime, but positively con-
> structing that body of knowledge ... our understanding of this crime
> [rape] depends on certain critical assumptions about the nature of rela-
> tions between the sexes, and so our understanding is a product of a
> certain way of looking at heterosexuality that can be constructed quite
> differently from a feminist perspective. (Naffine, 1997: 122)

Nana displays the characteristics of other fictional femmes fatales:
she is apparently normal and respectable, but her appearance disguises
her true criminal nature. An obscure and inscrutable object of desire,
she resembles other female anti-heroines whose enigmatic nature embodies 'lower-order female criminals, and ... the sense of the unreliability of women, their incipient criminality as a species, which
featured in a whole range of discourses concerning women and crime'
(Hutchings, 2001: 93).

Sensation novels were preoccupied with the nature and the criminogenic character of the family, where the private – namely women –
entertain problematic relations with the public, namely men. This
literature had an important effect, in the sense that it described how,
behind a façade of harmony and dull happiness, desires and unsatisfied
urges ended in explosions of uncontrollable violence (Flint, 1993).

Creative work about crime by female writers, however, provides a subjective shift which implicitly rejects prevailing images of women. While appealing for a better world for women, which is itself instrumental in the creation of better images of women (Cornell, 1993), feminist crime writing distances itself from orthodox crime fiction, where sexually active women are often, by definition, wicked and untrustworthy (Bird and Walker, 1993). Detectives invented by women, for example, are kinder and languid, at times androgynous; whereas virility is depicted as stupidity (Heilbrun, 1994). This is the result of women writers 'intruding' in a male field, returning their gaze, while contesting their position as privileged observers (Butler, 1990).

In Nana, sexuality and gender are depicted as pathology, a figurative analogy which is also prevalent in many nineteenth-century tales of seduction, where sentimental narratives are underpinned by a mixture of sex and murder (Davis, 1957). Without women, their sexuality, and their ultimate death, such narratives would be hollow, and, if they failed to display their corpses, would convey a message of unacceptable relativism, with males and females sharing the blame. Whether women are murdered by their inexperienced, exasperated lovers or, like Nana, by the revengeful events plotted by their authors, it is always because they have corrupted the men surrounding them; they have undermined male reason, putting themselves outside the moral frame, therefore becoming deserving victims (Knox, 1998). There is a frequent conjunction between femininity and death in tales of seduction, and Nana follows the rule, and, with the destabilizing nature of her sex, she shows similarities with women in sensational novels who take whatever they can from men − their money, their house, their family, or their reason. 'Largely, then, Woman became the representation of nightmare, not of reason. In the discourse of murder, sex is Woman and sex is Death: therefore, Woman too is Death' (Knox, 1998: 22). Think of some of the most disturbing stories written by Edgar Allan Poe (1980b), where prostitution, abortion and infanticide coalesce and where seduction, abandonment, sexual violence and murder provide thrilling counterpoints. In 'The Mystery of Marie Rogêt', Poe depicts woman as a criminal whore 'infecting men with disease and driving them to crime; woman as betrayed victim of male lust and so driven to criminal extremities; and woman as the precipitator of the violence visited upon them' (Hutchings, 2001: 97).

It is true that, to some extent, male writers' models of female detectives are not rare in the mass-publishing 'pulp markets of the nineteenth century'. But these female detectives are presented as funny and clumsy, especially when taking pleasure in manly sports and excelling in boxing: 'a female engaged in a masculine occupation, especially when the Amazon uses fist-cuffs and excels at sports, must have been regarded as a titillation to the predominantly male readers' (Munt, 1994: 4). Through a process of 'intrepid infiltration', female writers introduced sufficient irreverence to temper the genre's conventional masculinity. Utopian models of female agency emerged, while humour, parody and transgression challenged male authority myths.

When Zola was making claims to objective scientific truth, the literary world was becoming increasingly accessible to women; it was also turning into a site of gender contestation (Hutchings, 2001). *Nana* remains a classic novel, 'criminologically correct' for its times, and fruitfully open to contestation by female criminologists and novelists: a gift that may help us clarify our understanding and misunderstanding of women and crime.

5

Baldwin and Wright:
Ethnic Minorities, Hate and Crime

When African-American writer W.E.B. Du Bois undertook the exploration of how his people were perceived within American society, he chose a central metaphor to describe their 'invisibility'. This was conveyed by the image of a 'veil' separating them from white society, a veil whose existence he personally experienced during his student years. It was a small thing which, nevertheless, all of a sudden burst like a revelation upon him. In the school he attended, on the hills of New England, boys and girls used to buy gorgeous visiting cards, ten cents a package, and exchange them. 'The exchange was merry, till one girl, a tall newcomer, refused my card, refused it peremptorily, with a glance' (Du Bois, 1996: 4). He realized that he was different from the others, shut out from their world by a vast veil that he had no desire to tear down. Rather, he held all beyond it in common contempt, 'and lived above it in a region of blue sky and great wandering shadows'. Later, he was to encounter numerous whites who saw him not as a person, but as a 'problem', people who said foolish and awkward things, attempting to show kindness and open-mindedness, but revealing the distance separating them from him (Gibson, 1996). They would say that they knew an excellent black man in their town, or that the Southern outrages disturbed them, though in fact they meant to pose a simple question: how does it feel to be a problem?

Ethnic minorities as a 'problem' appear in criminological analysis as offenders and, to a lesser degree, as victims, generating debate around marginalization, violence, institutional racism and other related issues. The works of James Baldwin and Richard Wright examined in this chapter offer an excellent array of literary material to revisit such issues.

The Bible and the gun

James Baldwin's *Blues for Mister Charlie* (Baldwin, 1964) is a play based, very distantly indeed, on the case of a black youth who was murdered in Mississippi in 1955. The murderer was eventually acquitted, while his brother, who helped him in the killing, became later a deputy sheriff. Baldwin tells us of the difficulties he encountered in drawing valid portraits of murderers, by whom he is baffled and terrified. With one part of his mind he hates them and would be willing to kill them. Yet, with another part of his mind, he is aware that no man is a villain in his own eyes. Something in the man knows – must know – that what he is doing is evil; but in order to accept the knowledge the man would have to change. 'What is ghastly and really almost hopeless in our racial situation now is that the crimes we have committed are so great and so unspeakable that the acceptance of this knowledge would lead, literally, to madness' (Baldwin, 1965: 10). Murderers, then, in order to protect themselves from madness, strive to put their acts at a distance, and, while compulsively repeating them, enter a 'spiritual darkness' which no one can describe.

Baldwin stresses that American people in general are responsible for those murders, because they lock one another in the prison of their respective colour (Campbell, 1991). They persuade murderers that black people are worthless human beings, and that it is the sacred duty of whites to protect the honour and purity of their tribe.

The play takes place in Plaguetown, the plague being racism, on a stage divided by an aisle between Whitetown and Blacktown, and the action among blacks takes place on one side of the stage, with the action among whites on the opposite side. There is an initial gunshot, and Lyle appears on stage carrying and then dropping Richard's body as though it were a sack. His first line is: 'And may every nigger like this nigger end like this nigger – face down in the weeds!' (*Blues*: 14).

A funeral follows, and we learn that Richard was the son of Meridian (the priest) and grandson of Mother Henry. A friend of the victim, Lorenzo, finds no comfort in the religious ceremony: a young man has been butchered, and there they are, sitting in the house of 'this damn almighty God' who only cares what happens to white people; 'that white man's God is *white*'. It is that white God, he says, that has been lynching them, burning them, castrating them, raping their women, and robbing them of everything that makes humans human. Now, why are they sitting there, in His house? 'If I could get my hands on Him, I'd pull Him out of heaven and drag Him through this town at the end of a rope' (*Blues*: 15–16). Juanita warns that such violence would make their community no better than those who murder them. To which Lorenzo retorts that he does not want to be better than them: better at what, he asks, better at being a doormat, better at being a corpse?

After years of nonviolent protest and demonstrations, black people have been allowed access to that 'crummy library downtown' which was already obsolete in 1897, and where nobody goes anyway; who in town reads books? They can also go to that big movie palace, but many of them can leave without Yul Brynner and Doris Day, especially if at the same time they cannot get licensed to be electricians or plumbers, they still cannot walk through the park, and their children cannot use the public swimming pool. Lorenzo concludes: 'We still can't vote, we can't even get registered.... And these people trying to kill us too. And we ain't even got no guns. The cops ain't going to protect us' (*Blues*: 16).

Meridian says that he will not rest until the man who killed his son is brought to trial. He mentions Parnell, a white journalist, who has proven to be a pretty good friend to all of them: 'He is the only white man in this town, who's ever really stuck his neck out in order to do – to do right.' Parnell has fought to bring the culprit to court, but Lorenzo is distrustful, and remarks that when a white man is a *good* white man, 'he is good because he wants *you* to be good. Well, sometimes I just might want to be *bad*. I got as much right to be bad as anybody else' (*Blues*: 17). Parnell joins the group to disclose that a warrant is being issued for Lyle's arrest. As for convicting him, Juanita is realistic: 'You're asking for heaven on earth. Why should they convict him? Why him? He's no worse than all the others. He's an honourable tribesman and he's defended, with blood, the honour and purity of his tribe!' (18).

When the action moves to Whitetown, we learn that Lyle is a shopkeeper and sells his goods to black people, who make his living. Parnell is also his friend, and goes to tell him that he is going to be arrested. He explains that several circumstances force the chief of police to act, and that he would not if he could think of some way not to. This is because the chief of police 'wouldn't arrest anybody except blind beggars and old coloured women if he could think of any way not to – he's bird-brained and chicken-hearted and big-assed' (*Blues*: 23).

Lyle does not understand all the fuss. The victim was a 'nigger' who went up north and got ruined, then came back south to cause trouble. He also knows that he was a dope fiend. 'He probably got killed by some other nigger – they do it all the time – but ain't nobody even thought about arresting one of them? Has niggers suddenly got to be holy in this town?' (*Blues*: 24). He has got nothing against coloured folks, he says, but he will not mix with them. He does not believe in mixing; he just wants to defend his woman from them.

Before being murdered, Richard had returned to his town, after being in the North, where he saw no signs saying that blacks 'cannot do this and cannot go there'. He had started to think again about the death of his mother, who he believed did not fall but was pushed down the steps in the hotel where she worked. He had felt his father to be a coward for having accepted the official version of the death and for not having taken a pistol 'and gone through that damn white man's hotel and shot every son of a bitch in the place'. Mother Henry had warned him that he could not see white people as the cause of all the suffering in the world. But Richard had become angry: 'Oh yes. They're responsible for all the misery I've seen, and that's good enough for me. It's because my Daddy's got no power that my Mama's dead. And he ain't got no power because he is black.' Mother Henry did not need to worry; hatred was not going to make him sick, but make him feel well. He was going to learn how to drink it – a little every day in the morning, and then a booster shot late at night. He was going to re-member everything: his mother's and his father's face that day, Aunt Edna and all her little deals, all those boys and girls in Harlem, all the pimps, whores and gangsters and all the cops.

> And I'm going to remember all the dope that's flowed through my veins. I'm going to remember everything – the jails I been in and the cops that beat me and how long a time I spent screaming and stinking in my own dirt, trying to break my habit. I'm going to remember all that, and I'll get well. I'll get well. (*Blues*: 32)

After the flashback showing Richard's anger, the play is suggestive of episodes of violence and the town seems enveloped in a threatening atmosphere. Some white people are seen one night attempting to tamper with the gas pipes of a house in the black community, and as the dogs howl they are seen running away. Lorenzo explodes again: they are defenceless, and no defence will be found by falling on one's knees and using Bibles as breast shields! Meridian's peaceful confidence is also shaken, as he is no longer sure whether he should dissuade his people from arming themselves. Parnell, however, suggests that if the blacks were armed they would be slaughtered. The Christian faith returns to be questioned: would black people have embraced this faith if they had not been black? Perhaps they had to become Christian in order to have any dignity at all: since they were not human in human eyes, then they could be human in God's eyes. But, on the other hand, what is the point of this big struggle? Where is the hope? If Mister Charlie – namely all white people – cannot change, then neither the struggle nor God can bring change.

In Whitetown, meanwhile, discussions are taking place around recent developments. In the past, some say, they had some minor trouble from time to time, but it did not amount 'to a hill of beans'. Black people were nice then, and they could always help to catch another black. Reverend Phelps adds:

> Their minds have been turned. They have turned away from God. They are a simple people – warm-hearted and good-natured. But they are very easily led, and now they are harkening to the counsel of these degenerate Communist race-mixers. And they don't know what terrible harm they can bring on themselves – and on us all. (Blues: 56)

Whitetown, in brief, feels in danger; in particular, husbands fear that their women could be raped, because 'niggers have got one interest, and it is just below their belly bottom'. In this part of town everybody knows that Lyle, before being accused of murdering Richard, had an affair with Old Bill's wife, a black woman; and he has never been arrested for the killing.

As the play unfolds in its rhapsodic style, we see Richard and Lorenzo having an argument with Lyle, in his shop, and Richard knocking the white man down and so deriding him: 'Look at the mighty peckerwood! On his ass, baby – and his woman watching! Now who you think is the better man? Ha-ha! The nastier race!' (Blues: 80).

In court Richard is described as a drug addict, who not only knocked down a defenceless shopkeeper but also tried to rape his wife. The judge asks Meridian whether he has brought up his son according to the precepts of the Christian Church. If he had not, the father could be, therefore, deemed an unwitting 'accomplice' of the victim. The man admits that both he and his son had serious reservations concerning the behaviour of Christians, for the way they treated black people. He is told that perhaps the difficulties Richard had in accepting the Christian faith were due to his father's use of the pulpit as a forum for irresponsible notions concerning social equality. 'Perhaps the failure of the son is due to the failure of the father.' But on social equality Meridian has precise views:

> I am afraid that the gentleman flatters himself. I do not wish to see Negroes become the equal of their murderers. I wish us to become equal to ourselves. To become a people so free in themselves that they will have no need to fear others, and have no need to murder others. (Blues: 106)

The judge admonishes him, reminding him that he is in court, not in the pulpit, and clearly states that the man is responsible, directly responsible, for his son's tragic faith. But how can a white judge consider his son's death tragic faith? 'For you, it would have been tragic if he had lived' (106).

> I tried to help my son become a man. But manhood is a dangerous pursuit, here. And that pursuit undid him because of your guns, your hoses, your dogs, your judges, your law-makers, your folly, your pride, your cruelty, your cowardice, your money, your chain gangs, and your churches! (Blues: 107)

After Lyle is found not guilty, he explains how he has killed the black young man. He had found him and asked him to apologize, and as a consequence of his stubborn refusal to do so he had shot him dead, because as a white man he could not be disrespected by a black man. In the final scene Lorenzo and Meridian seem to have reached an agreement that they too will not accept being disrespected in the future. It all began with the Bible and the gun, and perhaps it will also end with the Bible and the gun. The black priest, like an old pilgrim, hides a gun in the pulpit, under the Bible, and accompanied by Parnell, the white journalist, joins yet another anti-racist march.

Hate crime

A crucial element in the definition of racist violence is the recognition that victims are perceived as representatives of specific communities, and that they are not victimized in their capacity as individuals, but as individuals belonging to a real or imagined alien group (Witte, 1996). Belonging to such a group designates victims as Them, as opposed to Us, while the violence inflicted becomes evidence of the inferiority of those targeted. In a logical ellipsis, therefore, the fact that victims suffer violence signals their status as individuals deserving it. According to a similar logic, a social or ethnic group may be compelled to follow menial occupations and its inferiority be inferred by the fact that its activity is confined to such occupations.

Work focused on violent racism highlights the social processes underlying this conduct. It is argued that racial characteristics often justify discrimination and harassment, and become associated with exclusion. Physical violence is the end result of an ongoing, dynamic process, fuelled by perceptions of racial characteristics, and 'cannot, therefore, meaningfully be reduced to an isolated "incident", but must be kept in context if it is to be understood and responded to effectively' (Bowling, 1998: 285). Discursive practices of racial exclusion, in this perspective, underpin endemic, pre-existing violence, which precise incidents and attacks only make visible. *Blues for Mister Charlie* provides a powerful literary example of this dynamic, with racist exclusion permeating the scene throughout the play, to the point that when violence explodes, even in the form of murder, it is perceived as just another element of exclusion.

An expansion of the concept of racist violence is offered by the notion of hate crime, on which criminological debate is increasingly oriented to focus. The term 'hate crime' is employed to describe conflicts that entail criminal acts motivated primarily by racism, homophobia and anti-Semitic (or anti-Christian and anti-Muslim) attitudes and beliefs. It is argued that hatreds based on identities, lifestyles, cultural values and tastes 'appear to have a historic continuity and keep simmering across generations'. Such hatred is said to constitute a reservoir of biases and bitter memories that can trigger violent antagonism, particularly 'in times of hardship' and when prodded by unscrupulous political leaders (Kelly and Maghan, 1998: 2). Violence used by terrorist and fundamentalist groups is included in the definition of hate crime, and it is felt that this type of crime is the result of communities failing to assimilate to each other and developing aggressive nationalist, religious or ethnic fervour. Contemporary societies are said to experience an intensification of such aggressive fervour, as increased movement of people across borders fuels anxiety and strife among social and national groups.

Variants of hate crime include what are described as state-sponsored violent offences, in which perpetrators act, directly or otherwise, on behalf of official state agencies. In doing so they appear to provide an illegal extension to institutionally ingrained feelings and a parallel power of social control addressed to despised communities. This type of hate crime aims to perpetuate exclusion and insecurity among the groups victimized, and is exemplified by neo-Nazi violence against migrants and refugees in European countries. Groups committing such violent offences may feel that the state and its criminal justice agencies, given their passivity, indirectly condone such offences, and may also be encouraged by their anxious nationals who express discomfort towards newcomers and the inability of their system to receive them (Harnishmacher and Kelly, 1998). Hate crime, in these cases, is less the signal of social disorganization and disconnection than the expression of collective resentment towards change expressed by a righteous, protected, violent minority.

However, the motives of the perpetrators may not be associated with specific political affiliation, or, to be precise, with sophisticated frameworks of thought: James Baldwin identifies as *Mister Charlie* all white people who, like Lyle, express extremely prosaic views on others and who are finally led to murder exactly by their prosaic, commonplace, intellect. Violent racism, in this case, is accompanied by hate speech involving not only the murderer but also the white community surrounding him. Ritual forms of communication within this community provide informal support for extreme behaviour, as utterances proclaiming the inferiority of a group both convey shared ideas and offer justification for consequential forms of conduct.

It is recognized that the term 'hate crime' refers to a whole range of conducts and related motives stimulating offenders. Traditional, historic, racial violence, for instance, stems from different motives than hate crime addressed to newcomers (Levin and McDevitt, 1993). Likewise, crime resulting from religious hate differs from violence caused by economic resentment or by a 'morality of vengeance' addressed to lifestyles perceived as pernicious (Hamm, 1994). Hate crime may be associated with the lack of legibility of the other, a situation which may be equated with chaos (Ruggiero, 2001). Racism provides a comfortable escape from chaos; it is the result of fear, both an effect and a cause of the invisibility of the other, who is therefore turned into the enemy, constructed as dangerous, undignified, albeit perhaps because political and cultural barriers make them invisible. In reality, They are not dangerous because they are so different from Us, but because they are too similar to Us. They are killed because We want to convince ourselves that they are Other to Us. 'The conflict between us and them is less the effect of our differences than the attempt to establish such differences' (Escobar, 1997: 42). In a typical established–outsider relationship, hate crime gives expression to a stigma addressed against the latter as a person of lesser human worth. In this way, while the perpetrator finds refuge in his race or nationality and protects himself from uncertainty, the victims may be induced to think of themselves as inadequate in human terms (Elias and Scotson, 1994). Responses of victims to hate crime include a variety of emotional reactions such as anger, fear, sadness, powerlessness and suspicion (Barnes and Ephross, 1994). Lowering one's expectations in economic, social and political terms is another possible response. This, in turn, may perpetuate the exclusion and 'difference' which are the apparent causes of the crime in the first place.

The expansion of the notion of hate crime, with the inclusion of violent offences committed by individuals who are relatively less powerful than their victims, denotes a significant shift in the appreciation of the social contexts in which such crime occurs (Perry, 2001). While the concept of racist violence entails a background characterized by a large power asymmetry between offenders and victims, the concept of hate crime, with such expansion, tends to leave aside altogether issues to do with power (Blee, 2001). James Baldwin's play describes violent crime committed by an individual who is well able to control the outcome of his conduct due to the social, political and institutional resources at his disposal. Hoping for his conviction, as Juanita says, would be like expecting heaven on earth. Racist violence, in other words, is carried out by individuals or groups who are granted a variety of choices and a range of potential actions to carry out. These individuals or groups have the ability to choose the objectives and modalities of their action, and the means to make their choices realistic. They are able to predict the outcomes of their acts because their asymmetric position in society gives them more opportunities to control their relationships with those on whom their action will impact. In the second part of this chapter we shall see how violence performed by a vulnerable actor is not accompanied by such ability.

What should be noted here is that, however, both the studies specifically focused on violent racism, and those dealing with hate crime in general need to be complemented by attempts to explain the dynamics whereby these conducts become recognized as crimes. The nonviolent rallies and antiracist marches alluded to in *Blues for Mister Charlie* echo analytical efforts to explain how certain categories of social actors become categorized as 'legitimate victims' of violence. Social-problems theorists, for example, have demonstrated that what becomes recognizable as a social problem is the product of practical and political activity. 'The construction of social problems often includes a rhetoric of victimization that shapes public and legal definitions of who is and is not harmed unjustly' (Jenness and Broad, 1997: 173). Meridian tragically asks what sins have his forefathers committed that must be expiated 'by chains, by the lash, by hunger and thirst, by slaughter, by fire, by the rope, by the knife, and for so many generations, on these wild shores, in this strange land? Our offence must have been mighty, our crime immeasurable' (*Blues*: 82). He comes to the conclusion, while joining the final political march, that one possible reply is expressed through collective claims bringing attention to their condition as 'legitimate victims' unjustly harmed.

Fear

When Simone de Beauvoir visited Harlem in 1947, the conditions of black people did not greatly differ from those in Mississippi that inspired James Baldwin. She felt a force pulling her back – fear.

> Not mine but that of others – the fear of all those whites who never take the risk of going to Harlem, who feel the presence of a vast, mysterious, and forbidden zone in the northern part of their city, where they are transformed into the enemy. I turn the corner of one avenue and I feel my heart stop; in the blink of an eye, the landscape is transformed. (de Beauvoir, [1954] 1999: 34)

She had been told that there was nothing to see in Harlem: it was only a corner of New York where people had black skin. She saw nothing frightening, but felt that fear was there: 'Crossing the street is, for me, like crossing through layers and layers of fear' (35). For the wealthy bourgeois it was natural, she thought, to be afraid venturing into a neighbourhood where people were hungry: they were strolling in a universe that rejected theirs. Situated in the heart of New York, Harlem weighed on the conscience of whites like original sin on Christians, and the average American, so concerned with being in harmony with the world, knew that beyond those borders he or she would take on the hated face of the oppressor, the enemy. Americans, de Beauvoir wrote, were frightened by that face: they felt hated, and knew they were. 'It's themselves they're afraid to meet on the street corners' (36).

It was because of this moral discomfort, not fear, that she was happy to be escorted to the Savoy by Richard Wright. He met her at the hotel, attracting unseemly attention among customers in the lobby. Had he asked for a room there, he would have been rejected. They chose to eat in a Chinese restaurant, because it was very unlikely that they would refuse to serve them there.

After de Beauvoir had admired black men dancing, with those movements unrestrained by an armour of Puritan virtue, she thought she understood 'how much sexual jealousy can enter into the white Americans' hatred of these quick bodies' (de Beauvoir, 1999: 38). In a sense expressing a form of long-established Parisian 'negrophilia' (Archer-Straw, 2000), she went as far as saying that whites were bitter because they saw blacks as 'freer and happier'. She soon learned that her friend and colleague Richard Wright deplored the kind of attraction towards blacks felt by many whites in the North, especially in New York.

> These whites defined blacks as the antithesis of American civilization. Magnificently gifted in music and dance, full of animal instincts (including an extraordinary sensuality), carefree, thoughtless, dreamers, poets, given to religious feelings, undisciplined, childish – that's the conventional image of blacks that these whites readily contract. And they are 'drawn to' blacks because they have projected onto them what they would like to be but are not. Those who feel the greatest fascination are people who feel most deeply deficient themselves. These 'nigger lovers', as southerners would call them, are for the most part embittered, ill, neurotic individuals, weaklings eaten up with a sense of inferiority.... Wright finds this attitude pernicious because it tends to maintain the gulf between blacks and whites. (de Beauvoir, 1999: 353)

This gulf between blacks and whites is described by Richard Wright in the Introduction to his *Native Son* (1981), whose meanings, as he says, were not clear to him until they literally spilled out upon the paper. There are two worlds, the white and the black: white and black schools, businesses, graveyards and gods.

> The separation was accomplished after the civil war by the terror of the Ku Klux Klan, which swept the newly freed Negro through arson, pillage,

and death out of the United States Senate, the House of Representatives, the many state legislatures, and out of the public, social, and economic life of the South. The motive for this assault was simple and urgent. The imperialistic tug of history had torn the Negro from his African home and had placed him ironically upon the most fertile plantation areas of the South; and when the Negro was freed, he outnumbered the whites in many of these fertile areas. (*Native Son*; Wright, 1981: 13)

The denial of political rights, however, was not enough, and disenfranchisement was supplemented by a whole panoply of rules, taboos and penalties designed not only to ensure peace, a euphemism for complete submission, but to guarantee that no real threat would ever arise. 'To condition him to hope for little and to receive that little without rebelling' (14).

Rebellion against rules and taboos could lead to lynching, and the reason for the lynching, Wright explains, was usually called 'rape', 'that catchword which has garnered such vile connotations that it can raise a mob anywhere in the South pretty quickly, even today' (*Native Son*: 15).

But why draw a picture of a black boy like Bigger Thomas, the protagonist of *Native Son*? What would white people think? They had drawn similar pictures for a long time, and the novel would only provide reasons for the strengthening of their prejudices. And yet, though this consideration made the task difficult, Wright knew that he could not write of Bigger convincingly if he did not depict him as he *was*: that is, 'resentful toward whites, sullen, angry, ignorant, emotionally unstable, depressed and unaccountably elated at times, and unstable even, because of his own lack of inner organization which American oppression has fostered in him, to unite with the members of his own race' (*Native Son*: 24). Bigger's conduct would re-enforce the beliefs of the whites who occupied the lower ranks of the social hierarchy, who would be happy to situate black people beneath them, to whom they felt automatically superior. The other classes, in their turn, would be happy to see 'poor whites' using their energies against the blacks instead of against them, those 'poor whites' who were so busy 'keeping blacks in their place' that they did not 'try in any positive way to win a better place for themselves'.

Before introducing Bigger, the author notes that white men encouraged black youth to engage in petty larceny, because in that way they proved they could not ascend to the moral level reserved for whites. Generally, Southern racists encouraged immorality in blacks by showing extreme indulgence for all profligate behaviour within the black community. A black man who killed another black man was only lightly punished by the courts, while any transgression against whites was punished severely. And yet, in reading *Native Son*, perhaps the black professional classes would feel ashamed of Bigger, because they had escaped his fate, and were unprepared to be reminded of the lowly, shameful depths of life above which they enjoyed their bourgeois lives. 'Never did they want people, especially white people, to think that their lives were so much touched by anything so dark and brutal as Bigger' (*Native Son*: 26).

Richard Wright also feels compelled to show how oppression has shaped Bigger's relationships with his own community, with which the boy has no link of solidarity or sentiment of common pursuit. Moreover, he is forced to locate his character in a city,

> an indescribable city, huge, roaring, dirty, noisy, raw, stark, brutal; a city of extremes: torrid summers and sub-zero winters, white people and black people, the English language and strange tongues, foreign born and native born, scabby poverty and gaudy luxury, high idealism and hard cynicism.... A city where people have grown so used to gangs and murders and graft that they have honestly forgotten that government can have a pretence of decency! (*Native Son*: 29–30)

Wright has some work experience in the South Side Boy's club, 'an institution which tried to reclaim the thousands of Negro Bigger

Thomases from the dives and the alleys of the Black Belt'. There he has
the opportunity to observe a range of Biggers in all of their moods,
actions and haunts. There he feels that wealthy people and the institutions representing them are not really concerned about black youth,
and that their kindness is prompted by a selfish motive: they are paying
him to distract all Biggers with ping-pong, checkers, swimming, marbles
and baseball in order that they 'might not roam the streets and harm
the valuable white property which adjoined the Black Belt' (Native
Son: 30).

The author is also spurred to write Native Son because his previous
work made 'even bankers' daughters' weep and feel good. Nobody had
to weep over his new novel: it would be hard and deep and readers
had 'to face it without the consolation of tears'. Commenting on sociological findings that inspired his work, Wright (1945: xix) remarks that
in order to understand such findings 'you may have to wrench your
mind rather violently out of your accustomed ways of thinking'. In
Black Metropolis (Drake and Cayton, 1945), as in Native Son, there is no
attempt 'to understate, to gloss over, to doll up, or make harsh facts
pleasant for the tender-minded'.

Bigger is an American because he is a native son; but he is also an
unwitting black nationalist, though in a vague sense, because he is not
allowed to live as an American. He is unable to offer any articulate
verbal explanation for what he does. In a dark part of his life there is
an 'objectless, timeless, spaceless element of primal fear' which exercises an impelling influence upon his acts. Accompanying this first fear
is an urge towards ecstasy, complete submission, and trust. 'The springs
of religion are here, and also the origins of rebellion.' And in a boy like
Bigger, young, unschooled, whose subjective life is 'clothed in the
tattered rags of American "culture", this primitive fear' is 'naked,
exposed, unprotected by religion or a framework of government or a

scheme of society whose final faiths would gain his love and trust; unprotected by trade or profession, faith or belief; opened to every trivial blast of daily or hourly circumstance' (*Native Son*: 28–9).

Let us see how the fear felt by Simone de Beauvoir in Harlem translates into that forging Wright's character and his deadly acts.

Toppling skyscrapers

It is an ordinary morning in the life of Bigger and his family; they get up in the one room that is their home. The two boys have to keep their faces averted while their mother and younger sister put on enough clothes to keep them from feeling ashamed; the mother and sister have to do the same while the boys dress. A huge black rat squeals and leaps at Bigger's trouser leg and snags it in his teeth, hanging on. The mother performs the daily nagging at Bigger, her eldest: they wouldn't have to live in that dump if he had any manhood in him.

> All you care about is your own pleasure! Even when the relief offers you a job you won't take it till they threaten to cut off your food and starve you... If you don't stop running with that gang of yours and do right you'll end up where you never thought you would... And the gallows is at the end of the road you travelling, boy. (*Native Son*: 47)

Bigger shuts his mother's voice out of his mind. He hates his family because he knows they are suffering and he cannot help them. He refuses to face the shame and misery of his own and their lives, and though living with them in that misery he has built a wall protecting him from fear and despair. Without that wall, the squalid spectacle surrounding him would force him to kill himself or someone else. To erase that spectacle from his view he 'acts tough'.

During the customary gathering with his group of friends the possibility of robbing Blum's Delicatessen is discussed. It looks like an easy job: from three o'clock to four o'clock in the afternoon there is no policeman on duty in the area, and it should be safe. In the past they have only 'raised' newsagents, fruit vendors and, at times, apartments. Also, they have never held up a white man before. Robbing black people is easier and safer, because the police become suddenly inadequate when black people victimize one another. For months they have talked about robbing Blum's shop, but something seems to dissuade them. Perhaps the robbery would symbolize the violation of the ultimate taboo, in the sense that they would trespass into an alien territory, 'where the full wrath of an alien white world would be turned loose upon them' (Native Son: 52). In short, the robbery would be more than a sheer matter of money; it would be a challenge to established rules, which they are both eager and afraid to break.

Bigger moans that white people have things which are denied to him, and that they do things he cannot do. To him it is like living in a prison, cut off from the world, that he peeps at 'through a knot-hole in the fence'. He would bet that white people's mattresses are stuffed with dollar bills, and that they don't even have to turn over in their sleep: 'a butler stands by their beds at night, and when he hears them sigh, he gently rolls them over' (Native Son: 58). His anger makes him feel that he is going to do something he cannot help.

The gang arrange to meet prior to the robbery, to refine the last details, but Gus is late. Bigger is furious, and when his friend finally arrives a fight breaks out. Perhaps Gus's delay is deliberate, because he is scared and wants the whole plan to collapse. Or perhaps Bigger is even more scared, and attacks him just to divert his friends' attention from his own fear.

> His confused emotions had made him feel instinctively that it would be better to fight Gus and spoil the plan of the robbery than to confront a white man with a gun. But he kept this knowledge of his fear thrust

firmly down in him; his courage to live depended upon how successfully
his fear was hidden from his consciousness. ... The moment a situation
became so that it exacted something of him, he rebelled. That was the
way he lived; he passed his days trying to defeat or gratify powerful
impulses in a world he feared. (*Native Son*: 80–81)

Bigger is then employed by Mr Dalton, a supporter of the National
Association for the Advancement of Colored People. This regular occupation will not temper his fear. Mary, the daughter of his benefactor,
'runs around with a wild and crazy bunch of reds'. What are Communists like, anyway? What makes people Communists? Bigger remembers
seeing many cartoons of Communists in newspapers, and always 'they
had flaming torches in their hands and wore beards and were trying
to commit murder or set things on fire' (*Native Son*: 105). People who
act like that, he ponders, are crazy, and all he can recall having heard
about Communists is associated in his mind with trade unions, strikes,
old houses, people speaking in whispers, and darkness.

As a chauffeur, Bigger drives Mary and her friend Jan to town, and
in his perception the two are awkwardly nice to him. They treat him
not only as a human being, but even as a friend, and they ask to be
taken to 'one of those places where coloured people eat'. Bigger takes
them to Ernie's Kitchen Shack. They also want to see how black people
live, and perhaps visit their homes. Is this affectation or the genuine
interest of revolutionary dreamers? All Bigger knows is the paralysing
depth of his embarrassment, which turns the generosity he is offered
into a studied, inimical display. Mary and Jan praise the blacks, for
their possession of 'so much emotion'. What a people!

If we could ever get them going. We can't have a revolution without
them. They've got to be organised. They've got spirit. They'll give the
Party something it needs. And their songs – the spirituals! Aren't they
marvellous? Say, Bigger, can you sing? (*Native Son*: 117)

As the evening comes to an end, the effects of alcohol start showing in Mary's speech and motions. Later, she is totally unable to walk up to her room, and Bigger finds it natural to take her upstairs, where, while he is laying her on her bed, he sees Mrs Dalton, the blind mother of the girl, enter the room. She cannot see him, yet he is frightened: should he knock her out of the way and run? Mrs Dalton calls her daughter, who is by now asleep, but the smell of alcohol she emits is reassuring: late though it may be, at least the girl is at home. Bigger is petrified, and, while the blind lady addresses her daughter one last time, he covers Mary's face with a pillow. The girl dies. With lucid horror he thinks he has to dispose of her body. The best solution he can find is burn it in the large furnace in the basement of the house; its insufficient size requires that the body be beheaded.

> Though he had killed by accident, not once did he feel the need to tell himself that it had been an accident. He was black and he had been alone in a room where a white girl had been killed; therefore he had killed her... There was in him a kind of terrified pride in feeling and thinking that some day he would be able to say publicly that he had done it. It was as though he had an obscure but deep debt to fulfil to himself in accepting the deed. (*Native Son*: 144)

Fear made him fight Gus: he mistrusted him as much as he mistrusted himself. Fear of failing at the decisive moment made him opt for a motiveless clash with his friend, and he felt that the white race ruling him determined that fear, and ultimately shaped the relations he had with his own people. Fear, again, makes him an involuntary murderer, a new status for him, a status accepted with indifference as well as regret, because the murder was unplanned; it just happened as though his participation in it were unnecessary.

> But of the whole business there was one angle that bothered him; he should have gotten more money out of it; he should have planned it. He acted too hastily and accidentally. Next time things would be much

different; he would plan and arrange so that he would have money enough to keep him a long time. (*Native Son*: 168)

But it is not too late: given that Mary has disappeared, he decides to turn the killing into a kidnapping, and writes a letter to Mr Dalton asking for ten thousand dollars as the ransom for her release. He signs the letter 'the reds', so that it appears that the subversive girl's friends are looking to raise money for their conspiratorial activity. However, he needs an accomplice, at least for the final stage of his plan, when the money will be handed over. His choice falls on Bessie, his girlfriend, who works in the homes of white folks, and feels that she lives their lives, not her own. She works long hours, hard and hot hours seven days a week, with only Sunday afternoons off; and when she does get off she needs something to make her feel that she is 'making up for the starved life' she leads, she wants to get drunk. Her craving for sensation is what Bigger likes in her, and most evenings he gives her the liquor and she gives him herself (177). She wants 'fun, hard and fast fun', but even for her starved life the kidnapping is too much.

Bessie tells Bigger his plot has no chance of succeeding, and as soon as he is found out will be accused of rape. But rape, Bigger feels, is not what one does to women.

> Rape was what one felt when one's back was against a wall and one had to strike out, whether one wanted or not.... He committed rape every time he looked into a white face. He was a long, taut piece of rubber which a thousand white hands had stretched to the snapping point, and when he snapped it was rape. But it was rape when he cried out in hate deep in his heart as he felt the strain of living day by day. That, too, was rape. (*Native Son*: 267)

Bessie's uncertainty turns her from a potential accomplice into a dangerous witness. He kills her, and again feels 'a queer sense of power', because *he* has done this, *he* has brought all this about. In all of his life the two murders are 'the most meaningful things that had ever happened to him'. He is now living, truly and deeply, no matter what others might think. For the first time he has the chance to recognize the consequences of his actions as his own, and feels free 'in this night and day of fear and murder and flight' (Native Son: 279). In running away he feels the need to face his acts in all their fullness, and to shout his satisfaction in front of those whose hate for him is 'so unfathomably deep' that, after they have 'shunted him off into a corner of the city to rot and die', they could turn to him, as Mary had that night in the car, and say: 'I'd like to know how your people live.'

When Mary's bones are found in the furnace the hunt begins. The Black Belt is invaded by five thousand police, supplemented by three thousand volunteers. After the news spreads that a black man has murdered a white girl, several hundred black employees throughout the city are dismissed from their jobs. They work for Jews, Italians and Greeks, who own almost all the businesses in the Black Belt. 'Most Negro businesses were funeral parlours; white undertakers refused to bother with dead black bodies' (Native Son: 289). When he is caught, Bigger is dragged away by his feet; he awakens in prison, where the first visitor cannot but be a preacher. He knows what his words are without listening; 'it was the old voice of his mother telling of suffering, of hope, of love beyond this world. And he loathed it because it made him feel as condemned and guilty as the voice of those who hated him' (320).

Bigger then meets Jan, who also pays him a visit, and feels that that white man believes in him, and the moment he feels this he also feels guilty again, but in a different way now. Suddenly, this white man has come up to him,

> spoken a declaration of friendship that would make other white men hate him: a particle of white rock had detached itself from that looming mountain of white hate and had rolled down the slope, stopping at his

feet.... For the first time in his life a white man became a human being to him; and the reality of Jan's humanity came in a stab of remorse. (*Native Son*: 326)

He knows, however, that he will be killed, and this is why, when in court, he wants to put an end to that unequal fight. But his lawyer tries in all ways to achieve that which he regards as the best outcome under the circumstances, namely life imprisonment instead of the death penalty. Prison would give him the freedom he never had. The very building in which he would spend the rest of his natural life would be the best he has ever known. Steel bars between him and the society he offended would provide a refuge from hate and fear.

In a memorable defence speech, the lawyer claims that, in a sense, it is fortunate that the defendant has committed one of the darkest possible crimes, for if one looks at his life one can understand how subtly and yet strongly that life is linked to everybody else's. There is an original wrong committed against him, a wrong which has engendered the 'hot blasts of hate' and the 'monstrous and horrible crimes' now brought to justice. This is not to say that the defendant is 'an unfortunate victim of injustice', because the very concept of injustice rests upon a premiss of equal claims. Inequality is therefore the mastermind of those crimes.

> We planned the murder of Mary Dalton, and today we come to court and say: 'We had nothing to do with it!' But every school teacher knows that this is not so, for every school teacher knows the restrictions which have been placed upon Negro education. The authorities know that this is not so, for they have made it plain in their every act they mean to keep Bigger Thomas and his kind within rigid limits. All real estate operators know that it is not so, for they have agreed among themselves to keep Negroes within the ghetto-areas of cities. (*Native Son*: 430)

The hate and fear that inequality have inspired in Bigger, woven into the very structure of his consciousness, into his blood and bones, into the hourly functioning of his personality, have become the justification of his existence. 'Every thought he thinks is potential murder', 'every sunrise and sunset make him guilty of subversive actions'.

> Every movement of his body is an unconscious protest. Every desire, every dream, no matter how intimate or personal, is a plot or a conspiracy. Every hope is a plan for insurrection. Every glance of the eye is a threat. *His very existence is a crime against the state!* (Native Son: 434)

The consciousness of Bigger Thomas, he continues, and of millions of others more or less like him, white and black, 'forms the quicksand upon which the foundations of our civilisation rests'. And in a final invective, which sounds eerily contemporary, he launches the following warning: 'Who knows when some slight shock, disturbing the delicate balance between social order and thirsty aspiration, shall send the skyscrapers in our cities toppling?' (Native Son: 436).

The violence of the violated

Criminological analysis attempts to explain the large disproportion between whites and non-whites upon whom are inflicted institutional punishments, including custodial sentences (Tonry, 1995). While suggestions are made that the different ethnic groups are differentially treated by criminal justice agencies, discussions also take place around the hypothesis that 'rates of crime are much higher among certain ethnic minority groups than among the white majority' (Smith, 1994: 1045). Authors who focus on differential treatment note that all stages leading a problematic situation to be defined as crime, and all stages of the criminal process dealing with it, are affected by biased perceptions and actions resulting in harsher treatment of minorities. For example, the higher propensity of victims to report offences committed by minorities as opposed to those committed by whites is deemed one of the causes of the overrepresentation of minorities in the criminal justice system, as is the readiness of the media to turn sporadic illegal acts into constructions of patterned, widespread, racialized forms of criminal conduct (Hall et al., 1978). Furthermore, problematic interaction between minorities and the police is regarded as a crucial cause of these minorities being targeted and criminal charges being brought (Scarman, 1981; McCrudden, Smith and Brown, 1991). Finally, unequal treatment in court is indicated as the main factor accounting for the disproportionate presence of minorities in penal institutions (Hood, 1992; Gelsthorpe and McWilliam, 1993; Hudson, 1993; Jefferson, 1993; Reiner, 1993).

Other contributions to the debate on minorities and crime hinge on the social circumstances leading to the criminalization of certain behaviours and to specific racially oriented legislation. Drug prohibition, for example, is attributed a shadow agenda, in that it gives politicians the opportunity to manipulate racist and xenophobic fears (Gordon, 1994), as 'foreigners' are depicted as ruthless producers and distributors of drugs destined for use by defenceless 'natives'. Punishing crack-cocaine users more harshly than users of pure cocaine is said to reflect institutional discrimination in allegedly neutral penal processes, as crack users are more likely to be black than cocaine snorters. The war on drugs is said to be, in reality, a war declared against the ethnic minorities inhabiting the inner-city areas of Western countries, and is imputed to be an endemic form of racial discrimination. 'The fact that drug dealing in the city, unlike that in the suburbs, often goes on in public areas guarantees that law-enforcement efforts [are] directed at young black and Hispanic men' (Miller, 1996: 81). In the same vein, changes in criminal justice procedure are also seen as possessing an in-built element of differential treatment which is destined to generate increasing overrepresentation of minorities in the justice system. The proposal, in

Britain, to abolish the right of defendants to be tried by a jury is one such case. Because the procedural change applies to offences such as minor theft, assault and criminal damage, such change is said to affect black people more adversely because they are overrepresented in these offence areas – not least because they are more likely than white people to be stopped, searched, arrested and charged. 'To remove their right to request trial by jury, therefore, and put them up for summary trial before magistrates, who are perceived to be on the side of the police, is to deny them one of the few remaining legal safeguards against unfair treatment' (Sivanandan, 2001: 3).

Students addressing the issue of the higher prevalence of crime among minorities, irrespective of criminalization processes, focus on the relationship between poverty and delinquency. Indebted to the 1920s ecological tradition of the study of deviance, some authors propose a theory of *deviant places*, aiming to achieve 'an explanation of why crime and deviance are so highly concentrated in certain areas' (Stark, 1987: 904). Among the factors characterizing high-crime areas and urban neighbourhoods, population density, poverty, transience and dilapidation of buildings are pinpointed as salient.

> Depending on a neighbourhood's combination of factors and its responses to these, the problem of crime will vary. In brief, as neighbourhoods provide differential opportunity structures and differential motivations for crime and deviance, they simultaneously attract deviant and crime-prone people while they repel the least deviant as mechanisms of social control are diminished in presence and impact. (Barak, 1998: 198)

High crime rates among minorities, in conclusion, are due in large measure to the area in which minorities reside, rather than to their race or the differential institutional responses to their offending.

As noted above, this hypothesis· constitutes an extension of the analysis provided by Chicago sociologists, who, in the 1920s and 1930s, identified 'transitional zones' in the urban environment where crime and deviance were more likely to be found. As new migrants sought to join family and acquaintances, it was argued, they were attracted to such zones, where prevailing social conditions and subcultures would perpetuate illegality (Thrasher, 1927; Shaw, 1930; Whyte, 1943). With the expansion of migratory movements and simultaneously of criminal economies, however, physical location may become less significant a variable, as illegal goods and services provided by minorities are not confined to their own communities. In this respect, authors adopting a neo-colonial model of analysis focus on structural oppression and alienation rather than location, and in the explanation of crime by minorities they take into account race as well as class differences, along with institutional responses to it (Tatum 1996). In brief, neo-colonial analysis posits that structural exclusion and perceived oppression 'result in higher levels of alienation and in higher inter- and intrapersonal levels of crime and violence' (Barak, 1998: 209). It is worth discussing in what types of crime and violence minorities are most likely to engage.

Some authors submit that, in illicit markets, tasks requiring a limited set of skills are usually left to ethnic minorities, who therefore operate in risky conditions, are underpaid, and have poor prospects of career advancement. This is due to, among other things, the particular attention to which they are subjected by law-enforcement agencies. Competing indigenous criminal groups provide additional hurdles to their career in illegality. In sum, prejudices and disadvantages prevailing in the official economy are said to be also present in the criminal economy, where benefits for minorities are met with exorbitant human and social costs (Ruggiero and South, 1995; Bourgois, 1996). Ethnic minorities are said to face costs of illegal choice which exceed those faced by indigenous populations. This leads to the definition of most criminal activity by minorities as 'self-inflicted criminality', because in their criminality it is difficult to distinguish clearly between offenders and victims (Ruggiero, 2000a).

In reading *Native Son* such considerations may be extended to violent crime, provided violence is regarded as one of the options among the criminal opportunities accorded to individuals and groups. In this perspective, violence perpetrated by powerless offenders is not separated from that performed by powerful actors, and the institutional makeup in which violence erupts is seen as an apparatus which, while distributing roles, also apportions 'violent opportunities' to all. Bigger Thomas is violent, but the costs he pays in using violence as a means of social interaction are the highest one could pay, namely his own life. The violence available to him is destructive but also self-destructive. Borrowing a concept from economics, one could say that if violence is available to all members of a given society, the *diseconomies* of violence are higher for the underprivileged members of that society – like Bigger – than for others. The costs of Bigger's violent acts are therefore internalized. In a celebrated analysis, Benjamin (1979) argues that some forms of violence are 'foundational and conservative', in the sense that, whereas on the one hand they may introduce new collective rules and shape new components of legitimacy, on the other hand they may just reproduce existing rules and components. Other forms of violence lack such attributes; those performing it are therefore doomed. Groups and individuals, in sum, negotiate their right to use violence, and their success is determined by the acquisition of such right in the form of achievement of a symbolic 'contract' whereby their violent behaviour generates benefits. Bigger is unable to achieve such a contract, and his violence is 'imitative' because it multiplies the violence of which he perceives himself a victim; in this 'mimetic rivalry' he is the predestined loser (Girard, 2001).

Finally, Bigger epitomizes an anti-essentialist conception of racial identity: his being black, in other words, is neither 'racial' nor 'biological', but something *purely social* (Gilroy, 1993). Hence his incapacity to acquire any benefit from his 'mimetic rivalry' is similar to similarly marginalized and powerless individuals belonging to other ethnic groups. The problem facing America, says Wright (1945: xxvi), transcends the problem of black people, which is but a small though highly symbolically important part of it. Similarly, in the sociological literature he cherishes, he sees much more than the anatomy of black frustration; he finds proof of 'how any human beings can become mangled, how any personalities can become distorted when men are caught in the psychological trap of being emotionally committed to the living of a life of freedom which is denied them' (xxvi). With *Native Son* the author sets off for a literary journey which

> situates the philosophical and political problems of black America in the provocative progression from a mode of literary realism defined by race to a metaphysics of modernity in which notions of racial particularity appear trivial and inconsequential. (Gilroy, 1993: 164)

In conclusion, Baldwin's character is the victim of hate crime, and is victimized for his belonging to a real or imagined group. He learns very early that he is different from white people and that there are pregiven precise limits within which he is able to act. But even before learning this, he starts to react to, and at the same time to be dominated by, his condition. Fear is what he feels in the voices of his people, like a premonition of his fate (Baldwin, 1993). Wright's character is not its mirror opposite: he does not enact hate crime against an individual because that individual belongs to a group perceived as inimical. Unlike those who engage in such crime, he is unable to control the effects of his actions. His fear leads him to crime, but prevents him from mastering his future through choices which may bring change to his present condition. His is self-destructive, reactive violence, the violence of a man without choice, the 'violence of the violated' (Kundnani, 2001).

6

Moby Dick and
the Crimes of the Economy

> The harpoon was darted; the stricken whale flew forward; with igniting
> velocity the line ran through the groove; – ran foul. Ahab stooped to
> clear it; he did clear it; but the flying turn caught him round the neck
> … and he was shot out of the boat, ere the crew knew he was gone.
> (Moby Dick, Melville, [1851] 1998: 581)

Only death brings Captain Ahab's obsession with the great white whale
to an end, an epilogue as frenzied as his desire to destroy it. His maniacal
command of a commercial undertaking turns his voyage into a mission
of vengeance and self-destruction, and the whale who has already
maimed him brings the final disaster: Ahab goes down with his ship,
which 'like Satan would not sink to hell till she had dragged a living
part of heaven along with her, and helmeted herself with it'. All
collapses, 'and the great shroud of the sea rolled on as it rolled five
thousand years ago' (Moby Dick: 582).

Melville's allegory of evil and madness inspires generation after
generation of critics, each interpreting the dark epic of Moby Dick
according to their cultural purposes and the underlying ideological concerns of their time. Hailed by some as the first true American novel,
it is dismissed by others as the ravings of a madman (Selby, 1998).
When the book, originally The Whale, was half way through the press,

Melville wrote: 'the tail is not yet cooked – though the hell-fire in which the whole book is broiled might not unreasonably have cooked it all ere this' (Letter to Nathaniel Hawthorne, 29 June 1851; Melville, 1998: 601). The 'hell-fire' which gives birth to *Moby Dick* can be viewed as a combination of many contrasting things: the author's deep moralism, or his blasphemous nature; his coherent search for truth, or his insane reverie; his determination to censure the American dream, or to endorse it; and finally his fervent desire to condemn economic power, or to advocate its legitimacy.

This chapter sets off by reviewing some such contrasting interpretations. It then focuses on one specific, controversial, aspect of *Moby Dick*, namely the images the novel conveys of acceptable and unacceptable economic practices. Melville's novel, in other words, will be examined as a complex moral diagram in which the author outlines his concerns about the achievements and destructiveness of economic undertakings, the development of productive forces and power, and ultimately the distinction between legitimate enterprise and the crimes of the economy.

Genius or madman?

Some early reviewers of *Moby Dick* highlight the originality of its concepts and the splendour of its descriptions, matched by the author's genius for moral analysis. The duplicity of the book, however, encourages an ambivalent reception. One anonymous reviewer describes *Moby Dick* as a mixture of ravings and useful knowledge flung together 'salad-wise'. Unflatteringly, Melville is regarded as a member of the 'incorrigibles' who tantalize readers with indications of genius 'while they constantly summon us to endure monstrosities, carelessness, and other such harassing manifestations of bad taste' (Anonymous, 1851: 1113). Accusations that the author is not so much unable to learn as disdainful of learning the craft of artists are coupled with reviews identifying such craft in the intrinsic doubleness of his book. Moby Dick, it is argued, includes romantic fiction and factual statements in the same work, making it impossible to categorize:

> It may be pronounced a most remarkable sea-dish – an intellectual chowder of romance, philosophy, natural history, fine writing, good feeling, bad sayings – but over which, in spite of all uncertainties, and in spite of the author himself, predominates his keen perceptive faculties, exhibited in vivid narration. (Duyckinck, 1851: 403)

In Moby Dick one could see two if not three books rolled into one. First, readers find detailed information on whales and whaling, and, in particular on the great sperm whale. Second, the novel analyses the relationships between the different characters sharing the fate of their ship. Third, the book is a mixture of moralizing essay and rhapsody in which 'quaint conceit and extravagant daring speculation' are interwoven (Duyckinck, 1851: 404). Among enthusiasts, Salt (1892: 252) stresses Melville's ability to cast to the winds all conventional restrictions and engage in the 'prodigality of his imaginative vigour'. In this view, Moby Dick is much more than the wild story of a voyage of vengeance: beyond the quenchless feud between a fierce old sea captain and a particular white sperm whale of renowned strength and audacity, the book 'has a mystic esoteric significance which lifts it into a wholly different category' (Salt, 1892: 254).

If Moby Dick contains all those malicious elements which are both inside and outside 'portentous' individuals, it is also a 'hunt, the last great hunt', as D.H. Lawrence proclaims in his Studies in Classic American Literature (1923), noting that the hoary, unspeakably terrible whale, of course, is a symbol. But of what? 'I doubt if even Melville knew exactly. That's the best of it' (Lawrence, 1923: 158). The hunt, Lawrence suggests, may be an allegory of American industry, its fanaticism and maniacal exploitation of nature, a hunt which is doomed: 'Something seems to whisper it in the very dark trees of America. Doom!'

> The Pequod went down. And the Pequod was the ship of the white American soul. She sank, taking with her Negro and Indian and Polynesian, Asiatic and Quaker and good, businesslike Yankees and Ishmael: she sank all the lot of them. (Lawrence, 1923: 174)

Lawrence's impatience with Melville is prompted by his conviction that the artist is much greater than the man, the latter being a tiresome New Englander, as solemn and serious as Captain Ahab, who 'stumps about in an ivory stump, made from sea-ivory'.

> Moby Dick, the great white whale, tore off Ahab's leg at the knee, when Ahab was attacking him. Quite right, too. Should have torn off both his legs, and a bit more besides. (Lawrence, 1923: 161)

According to other views Moby Dick, as a great work of art, occupies a privileged space, reaching beyond the realm of meaning. For E.M. Forster, Melville's book is a 'prophetic song', and delivers mystery, rather than meaning (Forster, 1927). One of the first great mythologies created in the modern world, Moby Dick mixes science, exploration, entrepreneurial daring and an obsession with dominion over nature (Mumford, 1929). It embodies an exaltation of individualism and conquest directed against what is described as evil. Melville wrote in the mid nineteenth century, when confidence in economic development was at its highest, and when the prevailing American icons were strong-willed men who seize the land and gut the forests. These men, like Ahab, seem to be impervious to enjoyment and blind to everything but their pursuit, undaunted by fear or sympathy, and confident that their will coincides with human destiny. They are 'liable to regard other men as merely arms and legs for the fulfilment of their purposes, and [are] arid and exhausted in their burnt-out souls' (Matthiessen, 1941: 442). Moby Dick, in brief, is the reflection of American myths of the frontier, of rugged individualism, and of the disaster brought by self-enclosed economic pursuit carried to the extreme (Selby, 1998).

Freedom, which is among such myths, can produce tragic outcomes, as in the case of Ahab, who expresses not the will to be free, but the will to overwhelm nature. Moreover, whaling itself is an industry, and the Pacific Ocean is a sweatshop, with the crew occupying the lowest sector of paid labour (Olson, 1947). And democracy, yet another myth, appears to be disfigured by the authoritarian hierarchy controlling the crew. The captain is a mixture of oppressor and justified criminal (Reynolds, 1992).

Moby Dick is indeed a story of the whaling industry, of the skills and heroism of those who make such industry powerful. It contains precise characterizations of free enterprise, workers and managers: wages, profits, occupational hazards and absentee owners are all there (Chase, 1949). However, the novel is also a tormented search for the limit beyond which freedom, democracy, enterprise and industry amount to criminal conduct.

Suggestions that the analysis of myth and symbol is the key to understanding Moby Dick are coupled with arguments around the value of the novel as a modern mythology, in which Americans are depicted as Adams in a new Garden of Eden (Murray, 1951; Lewis, 1955; Selby 1998). Formalist and humanist approaches are also attempted, and Ahab becomes the personification of an aesthetics of doubt, a man immersed in a constant haze of speculation which compounds, rather than reduces, the uncertainty of his motives (Buell, 1986). By linking Moby Dick with the cultural condition of nineteenth-century America from which the book arises, impetus is given to cultural materialistic and deconstructive analysis. It is stressed that the act of reading Moby Dick is never ideologically innocent: the way in which one reads it 'betrays a reading

of America and its culture' (Selby, 1998: 115). For example, when
Ishmael, a crew member who is both 'welded' to and disturbed by his
captain, asks 'Are the green fields gone?', he alludes to the moment of
transition from an agricultural to a commercial and industrial society.
The whaling industry symbolizes, and sets the pattern for, a new
economic order in which nature is systematically exploited for profit
(Gilmore, 1985). Moreover, *Moby Dick* exposes the chaos of needs and
fears which breed in the marketplace, 'the same marketplace that drove
[Melville's] father to bankruptcy, insanity, and perhaps unconscious
suicide. *Moby Dick* is obviously a man's book, about a man obsessed
with avenging his shattered manhood'. Obsessed Ahab resembles those
insensitive executives 'whose heartlessness ends in a heart attack'
(Leverenz, 1989: 281).

The line

Melville's characterization of 'good hunting evil', of men coming to
terms with the new economic order, and the catastrophic outcome of
their efforts, hides an important dilemma: as a man 'avenging his shattered manhood', Ahab sees in his missing limb the effect, and at the
same time the cause, of his search for a limit beyond which individualism, self-interest and ultimately economic activity lead to destruction.
In analysing how Melville offers a variety of views on this issue, I
would like to focus on 'the whale-line', which symbolizes both the
boundaries between acceptable and unacceptable economic practices
and the weapon with which these boundaries are defended.

'The Line' is the title of a short, central chapter of *Moby Dick*; it
consists of a detailed description of the fatal spear destined for whales.
The whale-line is 'magical, sometimes horrible', made of Manila rope,
handsome and becoming to the boat; it is a 'golden-haired Circassian

to behold' (*Moby Dick*: 287). The rope, which at first sight does not seem so strong, in fact bears the weight of three tons, and must be kept perfectly coiled. Because the 'least tangle or kink in the coiling would, in running out, infallibly take somebody's arm, leg or entire body off, the utmost precaution is used in stowing the line in its tub' (*Moby Dick*: 288). This weapon causes 'repeated whaling disasters – some few of which are casually chronicled – of this or that man being taken out of the boat by the line, and lost'.

> For, when the line is darting out, to be seated then in the boat, is like being seated in the midst of the manifold whizzings of a steam-engine in full play, when every flying beam, and shaft, and wheel, is grazing you. It is worse; for you cannot sit motionless in the heart of those perils, because the boat is rocking like a cradle, and you are pitched one way and the other, without the slightest warning. (*Moby Dick*: 290)

The whale-line, which folds the whole boat in its complicated coils, is very dangerous to use and its magical, horrible character can backfire on those using it. The 'line' attempts to draw a distinction between civilized virtue and destructive barbarism, but in using it the harpooners realize the uncertainty not only of the effects they are likely to produce but also of the very reasons for using it. In brief, the hunt for the whale, which alludes to the dichotomy between proper and perverted economic enterprise, is as tangled as the 'line', and the crew and captain end up compounding the ideological uncertainty which they try to dispel. The captain crosses the 'boundary', because he usurps the system for his own private mission of vengeance. In turn, the crew decline to choose between acceptable and unacceptable economic practices, and choose to adopt both. With this in mind, let us try to untangle the different notions of crime and enterprise which are hidden in *Moby Dick*. I would like to suggest that the novel presents us with three different concepts of the crimes of the economy, and I would respectively term them: an *intrinsic*, an *extrinsic*, and an *organizational* concept.

Crimes intrinsic to the economy

Ahab summons his crew and, holding up a golden coin, announces
that 'this Spanish ounce of gold' will be given to 'whosoever of ye
raises me that same white whale' (*Moby Dick*: 164). This 'round thing
made of gold' triggers intense competition among the whalers, who
realize that the coin is worth sixteen dollars, 'and at two cents the cigar,
that's nine hundred and sixty cigars' (444). The logic of this competition emerges in a significant episode in which Pip, a member of
the crew, is thrown into the sea while pursuing a whale, but manages
to hold on to the boat, wrapped in several turns of the 'line' around
his chest and neck. His fellows attribute the incident to Pip's negligence,
and consider whether to free (and thus save) him, or not. First they
curse him, because they have been stopped in their hunt, and then,
'business-like', they argue that they cannot afford to lose whales: 'a
whale would sell for thirty times what you would, Pip, in Alabama'.
Although Pip is eventually saved and the whale is lost, his colleagues
indirectly remark that, 'Though man loves his fellow, yet man is a
money-making animal, which propensity too often interferes with his
benevolence' (424).

That these men are pursuing the 'unknown evil' which is also part
of their own enterprise is clearly indicated in the analogy between the
'frantic morbidness' of Ahab and the 'intelligent malignity' of the whale.
The legendary white whale is ubiquitous, and is encountered in opposite latitudes at the same time. He is also immortal, 'for immortality is
but ubiquity in time' (*Moby Dick*: 185). His magnitude, eerie colour, and
deformed lower jaw elicit terror, and accounts of his viciousness describe
how he swims in front of his pursuers and suddenly turns around to
launch his treacherous attacks. Ahab is equally vicious, and cherishes a
wild vindictiveness against the whale, ending up identifying with his
enemy, with that 'monomaniac incarnation of all those malicious

agencies which some deep men feel eating in them' (187). All protagonists share a degree of responsibility for the ruthlessness of the whaling
industry: the captain for being intent on an audacious, supernatural
revenge; his crew, made up of mongrel renegades, morally feeble casta-
ways and cannibals, for helping him in his pursuit; and finally the
whale himself, whose whiteness conveys terrible nightmares.

The whalers' killing device is an 'indifferent' weapon, the bearer of
their destiny, in which free will has no role. In this sense, their undertakings are the result of an uncontrollable mechanism, of a necessity
which is inscribed in the economy, an economy which incorporates
crime. Killing is a duty, and duty and profit go hand in hand (Moby
Dick: 224). Before dying, a whale that is part of a herd, tormented to
madness, offers a sinister spectacle of such necessity: entangled in the
harpoon line, he violently shakes his tail, 'wounding and murdering his
own comrades' (400). The same necessity leads the whalers to eat the
meat of their prey: 'a steak, a steak, ere I sleep!', shouts Stubb, one of
the crew. While the banquet takes place, thousands of sharks swarm
around the dead whale to 'feast on its fatness'. The notion that crime
is intrinsic in the economy could not be more clear than in this collective act of biting, chewing and swallowing: while the butchers are
cutting parts of the whale, the sharks are gazing up like hungry dogs.
In brief, it is 'a shocking sharkish business enough for all parties' (301).
The cook of the ship argues that, though sharks are nature, all men
have a shark in them, and by governing it they become angels. All,
sharks and men, 'fill their damned bellies till they burst' (304). Could
we have a clearer allusion to the market?

Melville's metaphor of the economy and its crimes continues with
the macabre description of the dead whale dragged in the sea by the
ship, with sharks fighting each other around the carcass, snapping at
one another's bloody wound:

> They viciously snapped, not only at each other's disembowelments, but like flexible bows, bent round and bit their own; till those entrails seemed swallowed over and over again by the same mouth, to be oppositely voided by the gaping wound. (*Moby Dick*: 311)

The feast, therefore, includes autophagy, within an economy which celebrates itself in the horrid and mocking funeral of the whale. Finally, the sea-vultures too join in 'all in pious mourning, the air-sharks all punctiliously in black or speckled' (317).

The notion that crime is intrinsic in the economy finally returns in the captain's lament that he would like 'to feel something in this slippery world that can hold' (*Moby Dick*: 480). This slippery world, the sea – or, for that matter, the market – is governed by a nameless, inscrutable, unearthly thing, a hidden lord and master, a remorseless emperor. The invisible hand of liberalism commands Ahab against his will, 'recklessly making me ready to do what in my own proper, natural heart, I durst not so much as dare': market forces, with their invisible power, lift Ahab's arm (550). Even after dying nobody would want to be left to such forces, tossed 'like something vile to the death-devouring sharks' (488).

This reading of *Moby Dick* resonates with analyses suggesting that the crimes of the economy are not forms of deviance from, but are rooted in, the economy itself and that the market is the prime repository of illegal conduct. Think of authors stressing the necessity of violations in the economic world (Clinard, 1979), or remarking that in analysing crimes of corporations we are ultimately led to condemn the very nature of the free enterprise system (Pearce, 1976). Similarly, orthodox Marxist commentators argue that the cause of crime is ultimately to be found in the class structure, in competition, accumulation and surplus value – in brief, in capitalism. In this view, the economy must commit crime to survive. Surely, whether and how crime rates in general follow a precise pattern related to the economy is still a matter for criminological debate. Some authors, for example, see offending as a permanent feature of the economy, while others try to identify cycles of offending, which are somehow related to cycles of accumulation (Box, 1983; Passas, 1990). Both, however, concur in regarding the crimes of the economy as part of business routine. In a sense, a list of supporters of this view could even include Sutherland, whose seminal study of large businesses (1983) led him to conclude that the ideal businessperson and the large corporation are very much like the professional thief. Their violations of law are frequent and persistent, and they do not lose status among their associates when violating laws.

> In this respect, also, they are akin to the professional thieves, who feel and express contempt for police, prosecutors, and judges. Both professional thieves and corporations feel contempt for government because government interferes with their behavior. (Sutherland, 1983: 95)

The reading of Moby Dick attempted so far echoes this view, which is reiterated in a recent contribution in the following terms: 'There are various ways in which it is possible to argue that market forces are criminogenic' (Slapper and Tombs, 1999: 136). However, a different reading of Moby Dick may bring to mind other analytical suggestions.

Crimes extrinsic to the economy

Human labour, its energy and intelligence in modifying matter and creating value, is the positive hero of Moby Dick, an economic epic which also features a negative hero, namely the uncontrollable outcomes of that labour. As in other modern epics, a strategy is adopted which allows for the 'projection of violence outside oneself' (Moretti, 1996: 25). Moby Dick possesses a 'rhetoric of innocence' in which the necessity of violence in the economy is recognized, as is 'the necessity of its disavowal for the West's civilized consciousness'.

> Masking mechanisms are not lacking: violence is exercised not upon human
> beings but upon animals, indeed upon the metaphysical creature that is
> Moby Dick; and the hero, as and more than in Faust, is split between the
> innocuous Ishmael and the satanic Ahab. (Moretti, 1996: 26; my stress)

The presence in the novel of a major hero and a secondary one
appears to allude to the difficulties Melville encounters in attempting to
devise such masking mechanisms. Ahab is aloof, enclosed in his own
delusions and obsessions, while Ishmael expresses values and attitudes
that he confidently assumes many readers will share (Tanner, 1988).
Both interpret modern factory conditions, but while one embodies the
ruthlessness of power, the other genuinely, and perhaps naively, believes in the importance of reciprocal dependence fostered by the
economy. The two heroes, in brief, have yet to find masking mechanisms which would simultaneously absolve their respective, contrasting
conduct. Let us consider some examples of the contradictory process in
which they are involved.

Ahab threatens to kill a member of the crew for making a silly
remark on his ivory leg: 'Down, dog, and kennel!… Then be called ten
times a donkey, and a mule, and an ass, and begone, or I'll clear the
world of thee!' (Moby Dick: 128). The victim of such abuse is torn
between accepting and challenging it: he dreams that he is being kicked
by his captain and that it is an honour to be struck by such a great
man, by his beautiful ivory leg. But then he is tempted to murder him
while Ahab is resting. Similarly, Ishmael remarks that the captain
addresses everyone in 'condescension or in terrorem', and that he illegiti-
mately uses his role for private ends. Ahab incarnates an 'irresistible
dictatorship'.

> For be a man's intellectual superiority what it will, it can never assume
> the practical, available supremacy over other men, without the aid of
> some sort of external arts and entrenchments, always, in themselves,
> more or less paltry and base. (Moby Dick: 149)

The secondary hero, Ishmael, who is also the narrator, ponders that superstition may often give potency to 'idiot imbecility', and describes how the officers, while having dinner with Ahab, look like terrified children, in awful silence, 'afraid of the sound of the hinges of their own jaws' (*Moby Dick*: 153). Against dictatorship and oppressive hierarchy, Ishmael advocates cooperation and the principles of honest collective work. He is there to chase whales, he says, and if one with a crooked jaw comes in the way, fine. However, he is not there to help his commander in his personal revenge. Moreover, there is no point in taking revenge on a 'dumb brute', who belongs to the forces of nature: it is madness, it is blasphemous. To which Ahab retorts: 'Blasphemy? I'd strike the sun if it insulted me.' Mad? He is indeed: 'I am demoniac, I am madness maddened!' (171).

In taking distance from his captain's conduct and motives, however, Ishmael is often contradictory. He is aware that Ahab deviates from some vaguely perceived rules whereby individualism and self-interest cannot be stretched beyond the routine exercise of business, because business, in itself, already offers abundant opportunities for individualism and self-interest to prosper. He sees Ahab's will as far overtaking necessity. For example, he is disturbed by the lurid oath and toast called by his commander, when Ahab invites everybody to drink and repeat with him: 'God hunt us all, if we do not hunt Moby Dick to his death!' (*Moby Dick*: 170). But then he admits that 'a wild, mystical, sympathetical feeling was in me; Ahab's quenchless feud seemed mine' (181). Later he retracts by distinguishing between the motives of the crew, who 'were bent on profitable cruises, the profit to be counted down in dollars' and the intent of the captain, who is engaged in 'an audacious, immitigable, and supernatural revenge' (190). Ahab is excessive, consumed as he is 'with one unachieved revengeful desire'. 'He sleeps with clenched hands; and wakes with his own bloody nails in his palms' (205). Finally, Ishmael seems to condemn the whaling industry as a whole, when he remarks that 'there is no folly of the earth which is not infinitely outdone by the madness of men' (394). But in a conclusive celebration of labour, solidarity and collective achievement, he almost sings:

> Squeeze! Squeeze! Squeeze! All the morning long; I squeezed that sperm till I myself melted into it; I squeezed that sperm till a sort of insanity came over me; and I found myself unwittingly squeezing my co-labourers' hands in it, mistaking their hands for the gentle globules. Such an abounding, affectionate, friendly, loving feeling did this avocation beget; that at last I was continually squeezing their hands, and looking up into their eyes sentimentally. (*Moby Dick*: 427)

Ishmael's criticism of Ahab's excesses diverts him, though not completely, from criticizing the whaling industry itself (Moretti, 1996: 32). His condemnation wavers because he is unable to establish whether it is the logic of that industry which creates the Ahabs or whether the captain's excesses are the result of a subjective, pathological, drive. Ishmael's dilemmas remind one of Weberian concerns about the complexity and ambiguity of organizations. Max Weber (1947) stresses that organizations are inspired by a body of abstract rules which guide the pursuit of a corporate group or industry. These rules are said to be located within the limits laid down by legal precepts, though individual initiative may at times modify both rules and precepts. There is a 'spirit of formalistic impersonality' guiding the behaviour of organizations and their officials, a spirit which presents itself *sine ira et studio* – without hatred or passion, devoid of affection or enthusiasm. Norms, therefore, indicate duties without regard to personal considerations, their amorality being a guarantee for the rational and effective running of bureaucracies and industries. But on a number of occasions, Weber seems to detect a 'substantive irrationality' in the outcome of what seem to be entirely rational norms, which he pessimistically ascribes to personal ambition. Surely, Ahab is full of *ira et studio*; he is incapable of running his business with a spirit of formalistic impersonality. His constant violation of the official rules, however, can only partially be attributed to the industry in which he is involved, and his crimes are mainly extrinsic to that industry.

Criminological analysis would locate this interpretation somewhere between 'differential association' and 'propensity event theory'. Criminal behaviour, as suggested by Sutherland (1983), is learned in a communicative process in which specific techniques of committing crime are transmitted along the attitudes, rationalizations and motives underlying that behaviour. On the one hand, therefore, Ahab's conduct is caused by the structure of the industry and embedded in the very culture of the firm he leads. On the other hand, his offending, though culturally induced, is also caused by lack of self-control. Propensity event theory, in this respect, posits that individuals endowed with the lowest self-control are likely to commit the majority of crimes, irrespective of the type of offence (Gottfredson and Hirschi, 1990). Applying this theory to the analysis of embezzlement, Green concludes that offenders do not display their criminal conduct in one episode only, but manifest their low self-control in a career punctuated by a variety of offences. More specifically, they manifest the following symptoms:

> 'Risk-taking', or a quest for exiting and dangerous behaviour;... low frustration tolerance; physicality ... immediate gratification, or impulsivity; and self-centredness – looking out for oneself first or tending to blame oneself last. (Green, 1993: 104)

Does Ahab not manifest similar symptoms? His behaviour straddles the specific boundaries which, in his business, separate 'approved from not totally disapproved rules', to use Weber's expression. In the final reading of *Moby Dick* we shall see how the ambiguities of Ahab's behaviour and its ambivalent reception among his crew can be interpreted in purely organizational terms.

Organizational crime

It seems impossible to strip the hunt for the whale of 'that strange imaginative impiousness' characterizing it. The motives of the hunt, the place it occupies in the national economy, and the very make-up of the whaling industry appear to entice those involved to be 'eager, impetuous and savage'. Ahab himself is fully aware that the 'permanent constitutional condition' in which he operates is sordidness, and that the savageness of his crew may slowly breed 'a certain generous knighterrantism in them' (*Moby Dick*: 217). In brief, the captain understands that some organizational aspects of his enterprise lead to a number of contradictory aims while satisfying diverse needs. The crew cannot be strictly held 'to their one final and romantic object', because they would turn away from that object. In a telling example, Ahab describes his crew as akin to Crusaders of old times, who 'were not content to traverse two thousand miles of land to fight for their holy sepulchre, without committing burglaries, picking pockets, and gaining other pious perquisites by the way' (217–18). The crew, like himself, are participants in an organization which maintains its nominal purpose – the hunting of whales – while encouraging the pursuit of other ends. In this sense, the official ends of the organization are intertwined with its operational ones. Let us see some specific examples.

According to written and unwritten regulations, if a whale is struck by one vessel, and then escapes to be killed by another vessel, it must be shared equitably between the two. However, violent disputes arise due to the innumerable different circumstances in which regulations do not clearly apply. After the chase and capture of a whale, for instance, its body may become loosed from the ship because of a violent storm. The whale may drift and 'be retaken by a second whaler, who, in a calm, snugly tows it alongside, without risk of life or line' (*Moby Dick*: 405). The distinction between 'fast-fish' (which 'belongs to the party fast to it') and 'loose-fish' (which 'is fair game for anybody who can soonest catch it') is never straightforward. Controversies between whalers are generated by a vague code of conduct which seems deliberately designed to prompt abuse. But abuse finds immediate rationalization in Ahab's thoughts. What was America in 1492 but a loose-fish? What was Poland to the Tsar? Greece to the Turks? India to England? All loose-fish. And 'what is the great globe itself but a loose-fish?' (409). Illegitimate conduct, in sum, leads to evolution and development.

The whaling industry possesses an organizational form which offers a repertoire of possibilities and actions, and a number of related techniques and rationalizations, irrespective of their legitimacy. Arbitrary, unorthodox practices can be adopted and, simultaneously, the official aim of the existence of that industry can be maintained. In a most exemplary episode of this engrained doubleness, Ahab's ship meets the *Rose-Bud*, a whaler led by a Frenchman on his first voyage. Through an interpreter who farcically mistranslates the conversation, a member of Ahab's crew mocks the French captain, to the point of leading him to believe that the whale which is fast to his ship may cause illness and death. The sting is worded by the interpreter as follows:

> Only yesterday his ship spoke a vessel, whose captain and chief-mate, with six sailors, had all died of a fever caught from a blasted whale they had brought alongside.... He vows and declares, Monsieur, that the other whale, the dried one, is far more deadly than the blasted one; in fine, Monsieur, he conjures us, as we value our lives, to cut loose from these fish. (*Moby Dick*: 417)

The naive captain is quickly persuaded to leave his prey to the con, who 'proceeded to reap the fruit of his unrighteous cunning', while 'his boat's crew were all in high excitement, eagerly helping their chief, and looking as anxious as gold-hunters' (418).

This reading of *Moby Dick* echoes analyses positing that systems and organizations rely on a normative order and a factual order simultaneously. The former refers to a given set of ends, rules or other norms. Breaking down such normative order may result in an order in the factual sense – that is, a situation where organizations and the system in which they operate reproduce themselves despite the apparent 'chaos from a normative point of view' (Parsons, 1982: 98). The normative and the factual order coexist in the economic conduct of Ahab and his crew, and illegality is one of the options available to them. Some analytical tools devised by the sociology of organizations may be helpful for the understanding of this conduct. *Moby Dick* shows that the whaling industry possesses 'operative goals' as well as 'official goals'. The latter constitute the general purpose of the industry as presented in official statements, while the former 'designate the ends sought through the actual operating policies of the organisation; they tell us what the organisation is actually trying to do' (Perrow, 1961: 856). The contrast between these two types of goal mirrors the multiplicity and conflicting nature of organizational goals in a general sense. The crimes of the economy, in this perspective, are part of the operational goals of industries and organizations. These do not threaten the existence of industries and organizations adopting them; on the contrary, the tension between goals is a sign of health, and helps ensure ready channels for strategic change and flexibility (Ruggiero, 1996; 2000a). Operational goals, in brief, are innovative, and may lead to the discovery of new practices of accumulation which supplement official ones. Put differently, the term 'innovation' belongs to the vocabulary of economics as well as to that of the sociology of deviance (Merton, 1968). Finally, Ahab's ship adopts a 'technology of reason' along with a 'technology of foolishness' (March, 1990). The notion of foolishness should convey that of playfulness, which in turn entails a temporary relaxation or suspension of rules. The sting against the French captain is one such act of playfulness, as the temporary absence of rules allows Ahab's crew to explore new possibilities, indeed to innovate. The sociology of deviance defines as innovative the conducts which adopt illegitimate means for the pursuit of legitimate goals (Merton, 1968). While innovating, Ahab suspends his consistency and espouses a transitional hypocrisy: the whaling industry is required to ignore the gulf between the values it officially embraces and those it actually adopts.

Conclusion

Ahab can be seen as a captain of industry who tries to master nature even in the depths of the ocean (Marx, 1964). Re-reading *Moby Dick* one finds a wealth of illuminating points and controversial issues which would be of enormous interest to scholars drawing a research and discussion agenda in the field of environmental criminolgy. Think of the notion of a 'green field' of study for criminology and the concerns about the 'destructive effects of human activities on local and global ecosystems' (South and Beirne, 1998: 147). Moreover, think of judicial investigation into, and consequent criminological analyses of, corporate crimes such as the illicit dumping of industrial waste, and the partner-ships taking place in such crimes between white collar and conven-tional offenders.[1]

Surely, each age and each reader will find their own symbols in *Moby Dick*, as one would expect when faced with a 'world text', a universal book which generates a clash of different meanings. In such books allegory runs amok, 'through the limitless polysemy that opens these texts to innumerable future interpretations, making them the first open works of the modern West' (Moretti, 1996: 88). When everything collapses, Moby Dick remains alive, bringing its enigmas and prompting new interpretations around the world.

In this chapter I have addressed issues related to acceptable and unacceptable economic practices in Moby Dick, trying to identify some interpretations of the crimes of the economy underlying Melville's novel. I have followed three sets of the author's concerns, all present in the text. These three sets of concerns, or layers of meaning, allude to the crimes of the economy as being respectively intrinsic, extrinsic and organizational. I have mentioned criminological interpretations and analyses which echo these layers of meaning: was Melville an unwitting criminologist? I believe that Melville was rather an excellent novelist striving to draw, like many of his contemporaries, the limit beyond which economic initiative, individualism, hierarchy and industry bring social and human disaster. Melville was perhaps unaware that his concerns were also those tormenting political philosophers and economists throughout the nineteenth and into the twentieth century. Marginalists, for example, resolved Melville's dilemma by positing the workings of a self-quenching mechanism by which a person's desires switch off when satisfied. The economic man is not rapacious, they argued, but is a rational being subject to self-regulating principles: as appetite declines with eating, diminishing marginal utility restrains greed and 'tells him when he has had enough' (Douglas and Ney, 1998: 35). Ishmael, after all, is saved by a ship which abandons the hectic hunting of whales to try and rescue a missing child: it is the 'devious-cruising Rachel' which brings, along with the great white whale, Melville's criminological dilemmas into our time.

Note

1. In the collection edited by South and Beirne (1998: 147) examples of what a green criminology might embrace include matters as diverse as 'animal abuse; the ill-health wreaked on communities by the dumping of toxic waste; and the potential or actual devastation inflicted on the environment and on animal and plant life by the machinery of war, either in actual use or in its testing'. For an analysis of so-called eco-mafias in Europe, and the partnerships between traditional organized crime and representatives of the official economy in the illicit disposal of industrial waste, I would like to mention the report published by Legambiente (2000), an Italian environmental organization. Finally, on the specific connection between environmental, safety and health issues, with a focus on the chemical industry, see Pearce and Tombs (1998).

7

Felix Krull: The Con Man
and the Irrationality of Markets

Thomas Mann draws for his confidence man on the autobiography of a Romanian adventurer, Georges Manolescu, a 'prince of thieves' whose very surname, to readers of neo-Latin mother tongue, suggests 'swiftness of hand'. In his memoirs, Georges combines detailed accounts of the exploits performed by his hands with a spiritual commentary of his predations. A globetrotter of deception, he justifies his acts with the claim that the world wants to be deceived. Once incarcerated, he escapes, robs an elderly lady in the South of France, and marries a German countess in Italy, where he poses as a Hungarian gentleman.

Thomas Mann's character, however, brings in Felix's name less the ability of his hands than the prophetic happiness of his fate: he possesses a felicitous swiftness of the soul which permits him to indulge in moral vagaries and predatory acts as if these fell beyond the 'banal' distinction between legitimate and illegitimate conduct. His self-proclaimed fineness and attractiveness make him believe he is favoured by heaven. Misfortunes and sufferings seem an exception to the natural order, 'a cloud, as it were, through which the sun of my native luck continued to shine' (*Confessions of Felix Krull, Confidence Man*, Mann, [1954] 1997: 13).

During his first visit to a theatre, Felix Krull develops a particular understanding of himself and the world. Struck by a crucial illumination, he visually experiences what is to become the guiding principle of his future career. The main actor on the stage is a 'grease-smeared and pimply individual'; his witticisms are vulgar, and yet in the twilight he appears to be a charmer. At close inspection his face is covered with frightful pustules, yet he is able – with the help of grease-paint, lighting, music and distance – to move before his audience 'with such assurance as to make them see in him their heart's ideal and thereby to enliven and edify them infinitely' (Felix Krull: 35).

Is Krull the epitome of the entrepreneur, or an elegant confidence man? Does he represent the moral decadence of the bourgeoisie, or its very unhindered ascent? His career is punctuated by the identification of transitory ethical values, destined to be superseded or ignored. Norms of conduct are established only to be flouted once the surrounding circumstances change. In this sense Krull is beyond moral judgement; his behaviour nullifies ethical assessment because it leads to high achievement. Krull may be a playful invention on the part of Thomas Mann, who perhaps never really intended to charge his hero with particular metaphorical meaning (Hamburger, 1996). Nevertheless he left us a text which plays with our feelings about market economies and entrepreneurial classes, success and deceit, fraud and enjoyment of self. While some may read in that text the indictment of, and scepticism towards, 'declining' bourgeois society (Lukács, 1964), in contrast others may see Felix Krull – and for that matter the entire oeuvre of Thomas Mann – as the expression of a self-proclaimed apolitical author, the triumph of a literary man against the corrosive enthusiasm for progress (Mulhern, 2000). But what type of homo oeconomicus does Krull represent? And why should playfulness be excluded from the characteristics of successful entrepreneurs and con men?

Early signs

Felix's father owns German champagne-producing company Engelbert Krull, though the bottles produced display the French label 'Loreley extra cuvée'. He also sprinkles his conversation with French phrases such as 'c'est ça', 'épatant', 'parfaitement'. While Felix extols the virtues of that bubbling golden sap which is destined to rise to the upper world and bring sweet inebriety, his godfather Schimmelpreester intimates that champagne should be forbidden by law. He tries to understand what sort of vinegar goes into that brew, or is it petroleum? The producer had better look out for the police, he advises. In the reply of the father one can detect an element of the philosophy of his son: as an entrepreneur, he is obliged to give customers that which they want, namely an illusory good charged with symbolic value, if devoid of genuine quality. Schimmelpreester himself is not immune from deceit, as he is commonly addressed as 'Herr Professor', though it is doubtful whether he is officially entitled to this distinction. His name, after all, reminds everyone that nature is only mould (*Schimmel*) and corruption, and he is a high priest (*preester*) of nature.

Felix aspires to become a high priest of free will, and, seeing the world as something great and infinitely enticing, worthy of all his efforts and solicitude, he experiences a secret joy which derives from the possibilities offered by his 'simple acts of will'. His confidence as a high achiever goes as far as attempting to control the contraction and expansion of his eye pupils, and when succeeding in this task he feels a terrifying joy 'accompanied by a shudder at the mystery of man' (*Felix Krull*: 16).

Achievement, however, remains related to the perceptions of others, who view it through the lens of their expectations: a repulsive worm may be mistaken for a glorious butterfly, and Felix takes example from the theatre actor, who limits himself to responding to the unanimous desire of the audience to be deceived. As a child he indulges in the playful activity of imitating his father's handwriting until he is able to wield a steel pen with the swiftness and sureness necessary to reproduce his signature. This is not the only device allowing him to stay away from school; he is also capable of making himself ill, in order to escape that 'small square house' where his boyish soul is subjected to 'slavery and fear'. The family doctor is both credulous and willing to act complicitly, with his smiles and winks aimed at leading the patient to admit to playing sick, school sick. But Felix rejects this shameful partnership out of pride and contempt. The doctor is an unworthy disciple of Aesculapius, ambitious and stupid, and has achieved his title 'through personal influence, exploitation of wine-house acquaintances, and the receipt of patronage' (Felix Krull: 43). His obsequiousness is exemplified by his practice of receiving patients in order of the wealth possessed, rather than in order of arrival.

For this reason, in response to his complicitous offers, Felix prefers to act all the more ailing and helpless, his cheek hollow, his breathing short and irregular. 'I was quite prepared to go through another attack of vomiting if needs must; and so persistently did I fail to understand his worldly wisdom that in the end he had to abandon this approach in favour of a more scientific one' (Felix Krull: 44). Relying on the fact that the medical profession is not different from any other, and 'its members are, in the most part, ordinary empty-headed dolts, ready to see what is not there and to deny the obvious', Felix resorts to his 'will'. He enters a state of mind of intense excitement which overwhelms him to the extent of producing, in combination with the abhorrence of the drudgery of a day in school, a genuine state of illness.

It would be vulgar to describe this as pure deception, Felix explains, because lies hiding higher truths are not lies but the product of a lively imagination waiting to enter the realm of the actual and palpable world. This lively imagination is at the basis of everything Felix accomplishes; all is the result of endurance and self-conquest, and is therefore to be regarded as achievement of a high moral order.

When Felix does go to school he passes a shop where he likes stocking up on sweets, fruit drops and barley sugar. This place of delights is replete with row upon row of hams and sausages of all shapes and colours, cocoa and tea, glass bottles of honey and jam; it is crowded from floor to ceiling with other eatables such as smoked mackerel, flounders and eels, displayed on platters to tempt his appetite. Among the sardines, the jars of caviar and foie gras, the plump chickens, the smoked salmon, the bundles of asparagus and truffles, this Promised Land also offers 'fine biscuits, spice cakes piled in criss-cross layers, and glass urns full of dessert chocolates and candied fruits' (Felix Krull: 48). Is this a dream or a fairytale? When Felix enters the shop, despite the bell announcing his presence, no answer is given to his 'Good day'. While his mouth waters, his hand grabs a fistful of pralines; he runs out, and in seconds is safely around the corner. Is this theft? Only habit and mental indolence would designate this highly personal deed, shining with 'newness and originality', with such a cheap, paltry word. Once Felix identifies the time when the shop is usually unattended, he repeats his 'original deed' frequently, and his forays bring an anticipation of the sweetness reserved by life for him.

Thomas Mann and Max Weber

This childish, if invaluable, apprenticeship is destined to lead Felix through a brilliant career of fraud, and to share the lifestyle and wealth of the European elite of his time. While Krull's trajectory is ascendent, that of the most celebrated creation of Thomas Mann, the Buddenbrooks, is descendent. The Buddenbrook family show their decline in the un-equivocal neuroses of their members and even in the decay of their teeth. Their spiritual collapse, however, which is accompanied by the failure of Thomas Buddenbrook to revive his firm and mend his intel-lectual and emotional life, provides a sudden opening, when he reads Schopenhauer's *The World as Will and Representation*. The great satisfaction with which he is filled echoes Felix's discovery of the art of acting and the power of will. Both characters, according to Lukács (1964: 17), express the bitter opposition to Schopenhauer harboured by Thomas Mann, who 'could not paint a better picture of the philosopher as the apostle of decadence'. We shall see later how parodistic this picture is. But where do similarities between *Buddenbrooks* and *Felix Krull* stop and differences emerge?

If the Buddenbrooks experience a painful economic and moral decline, Felix is the very offspring of a family in decline, his father having succumbed to competitors and his mother and sister having finally reconciled themselves to the idea of seeking a job. Felix starts his career as a waiter, and only the certainty that his inner force will lead him to be waited on in the future tempers the resentment he feels for his customers. Both the Krulls and the Buddenbrooks epitomize the triumph of bourgeois appetite and, simultaneously, of the manipulation of image, concerned as they are with the *déhors*. Thomas Buddenbrook's existence is no different from that of an actor, as he stubbornly clings to the determination to preserve appearances, making his life a constant irritating pretence (Heilbut, 1995).

In the Buddenbrooks one finds a mixture of piety, thrift and cunning, as their obsession with image and pretence is channelled into a form of religious asceticism. While some members of the family are irreverent towards 'sacred things', others inherit from previous generations the motto 'Work, pray, and save'. All, however, combine introspection with

economic achievement and connect commerce with faith. Even when
decline is under way, when religion becomes a mere consolation for
embittered losers, and 'pious slogans become the last mutterings of con
men', taste for business survives and faith endures, at least as introspection (Heilbut, 1995: 106).

Thomas Mann claims that his discovery of the modern capitalistic
businessman as an ascetic individual devoted to his career and duty
does not derive from the reading of Max Weber's *The Protestant Ethic and
the Spirit of Capitalism* but is the result of his own intuition. However, in
the Buddenbrooks' concern for the *déhors* one finds the echo of Weber's
annoyance at the ceremonial opening by prayer of political conventions
and business gatherings. Religious affiliation is an issue always posed
in Mann's description of the bourgeoisie, as well as in Weber's analyses
of businessmen (Goldman, 1988; 1992). 'To what church do you belong?' is the question encountered by entrepreneurs establishing themselves and making new social contacts, as if faith could guarantee respect
of credit relations. In a personal communication Weber tells of a sales-
man who concedes that, although 'everybody may believe or not believe as they please', he would be extremely cautious in dealing with
a businessman not belonging to any church: 'I wouldn't trust him with
fifty cents. Why pay me, if he doesn't believe in anything?' (Weber,
1948: 303). Admission to a congregation is recognized as a guarantee
of the moral qualities required in business matters, and ultimately
determines the creditworthiness of acolytes.

Both the Buddenbrooks and Felix Krull, though in a different fashion,
are bearers of an 'inner-worldly form of asceticism' which values self-
esteem, individual motives and self-interest, and their conduct is inspired
by a methodical, rational way of life which, in Weber, 'given certain
conditions', paves the way for the spirit of modern capitalism. Both
epitomize the values that Max Weber incorporates among the historical

foundations of modern individualism, those values which are 'placed in the service of maintaining and propagating the bourgeois Puritan ethic, with all its ramifications' (Weber, 1948: 321). The Buddenbrooks, however, in their conventionalism, endorse the validity of a form of hypocrisy that is instrumental in the diffusion of values and principles without which 'capitalism today, even in America, would not be what it is' (Weber, 1948: 309). Felix Krull instead adopts a form of hypocrisy which is purely opportunistic, though consistent with the forging of means for the acquisition of wealth which, as Weber puts it, are 'beyond good and evil'. Both types of hypocrisy are examined by Weber, and both are included among the historical foundations of individualism and business. Means that are 'beyond good and evil' are not only used by entrepreneurs guided by Weberian substantive rationality; they are also those put in place by adventurers who are substantively irrational and untouched by the spirit of 'formalistic impersonality'.

Krull is the other face of the Buddenbrooks, and his exploits are a supplement to the conduct of entrepreneurs and rulers. Charlatans and businessmen possess similar picaresque characteristics, and Thomas Mann seems to suggest that along with 'working, praying and saving' success also arrives through pleasure, invention and foolishness.

The lightness of enterprise

Felix's father commits suicide after the collapse of his firm, but such an event seals rather than annuls his pleasurable existence. His mother, after the economic decline, endorses the belief that the bright opportunities of life only reveal themselves 'after that truly cleansing catastrophe which is correctly called social ruin' (Felix Krull: 75). Adversity arouses the spirit of initiative: because her personal account at the Bank of Commerce is not entirely exhausted, she follows the advice to rent rooms to boarders and lodgers. She has long experience in feeding and entertaining guests, and knows how 'to make a pudding out of crumbs and a tangy hash out of day-before-yesterday's leftovers'. She will continue living as she always has, only her guests will be asked to pay. 'It will simply be a matter of your patience and good humour producing an atmosphere of cheerfulness and comfort among your clients, and I should be much surprised if your institution does not prosper and expand' (75). Felix's sister Olympia, having learned to sing during the years of prosperity, will be sent to a friend in Cologne who will have no problem finding her an occupation in a 'light-opera troupe'.

One could not conceive of more un-Weberian characters: as Olympia and her mother embrace the career of 'entertainers', the lightness of their occupation appears to exclude introspection and thrift. Felix himself confesses to being haunted by emotions and fancies, which he groups under the heading 'The Great Joy'. Even at his nurse's breast he remembers experiencing sensual pleasure, indicative of the eagerness of his nature. That his gifts for the delights of love 'border on the miraculous' and 'exceed the ordinary' find confirmation in the secret relationship he establishes with the housemaid Genovefa, who is in her early thirties when he is sixteen. Felix's desires encounter no serious resistance, perhaps because the maid, in satisfying him, is 'not only performing a domestic duty but advancing her social position' (Felix Krull: 53). Felix's sexual exploits are a parody in action of some of Schopenhauer's principles. Schopenhauer's concept of the 'will', contrary to rationalistic analyses, is not associated with the pursuit of worthy values and goals, but is rooted in experience. 'The elementary experience of our will, according to Schopenhauer, lies in our corporality, or more precisely in our ability to move our bodies' (Joas, 1996: 118). In his philosophy of nature, Schopenhauer conceives of 'will' as a force moving all living creatures and ruling the entire cosmos. Felix applies this principle *ad litteram*, mingling his social ascent with his bodily activities performed with a succession of partners.

As for the Weberian traits of his personality, one has to bear in mind Weber's awareness of autocracies emerging from rational authorities, and irrational entrepreneurs from severe Puritans. Felix, too, irrational and autocratic though he may be, can initiate economic ventures *sine ira et studio*. His 'great joy' is destined to intersperse his biography as a frequent occurrence, until the very last page, and constitutes no obstacle to his entrepreneurial career. This career remains, however, consistent with his thoughts about life: a Protestant 'heavy and exacting task that has been assigned to us, one which we have in some sense chosen and which we are absolutely obliged to carry through with loyal perseverance' (*Felix Krull*: 67). True, little Weberian austerity can be detected in the evening gatherings that Felix witnesses as a child, where wine is served until the small hours, dancing and games are only 'a pretext for kissing and fondling', and *décolleté* ladies bend low 'over the backs of chairs to give the gentlemen exciting glimpses of their bosoms' (20). On the other hand, one may well claim that playfulness, 'great joys' and other exhilarating emotions are part of the entrepreneurial spirit, and that economic actors are never completely rational. Similarly, the entrepreneurial career of Felix mirrors the notion that commodities are produced and survive 'to no purpose', and that economic production as a whole applies the doctrine of the collector 'who liberates things from the curse of utility' (Adorno and Benjamin, 1999: 107).

The entrepreneurial style of the Krulls, however, appears to epitomize more than mere eruptions of irrationality within careers otherwise conformed on substantial rationality. Their social position is from the outset that of 'deviant insiders', as proven by the lies of Krull the entrepreneur about the quality of his champagne. Felix follows in his father's footsteps, adding original elements to his deviant position. His situation in the small town where he lives becomes suspect, disgraceful. He is the object of 'dark and contemptuous glances', because of his disreputable family, as the son of a bankrupt and suicide, and an unsuccessful student. He is hurt and withdraws from the streets. Although expelled from the relatively privileged environment in which he lives, and looked down upon by his former peers, he can make a comeback by means of innovative activities, because he harbours memories of his past high status. Being both outside and inside the official order makes him experiment with new undertakings and economic explorations (Kerr et al., 1964; Hagen, 1980; Ruggiero, 1996). He is tantalized by power, to which he has only partial access, although he has a degree of access to resources – because his gifts, looks and 'will' enable him to establish relationships with individuals who control resources. The ambiguity of his behaviour, which is necessary for innovative economic enterprise to take place, maintains a distinctive lightness, allowing his exploits, in a Weberian fashion, to hover above and 'beyond good and evil'.

Felix is both respectful and irreverent towards bourgeois conventions; while never failing to utilize his personal skills fully, he nevertheless seems to violate the norms of what is deemed rational economic behaviour. But on closer inspection, his deviation from rationality is perfectly consistent with that behaviour, and the market in which he so delightfully operates does not appear to him as an epiphany of reason, but as an imperfect cauldron in which the homo oeconomicus finds constant obstacles to rational calculation. Playfulness, 'great joys' and foolishness are all part and parcel of economic success.

Thomas Mann describes his novel as picaresque, perhaps alluding to the fact that the acquisitiveness of his hero is both legitimate and illegitimate, and that his adventures take place in a moral void, as picaresque crime occurs in situations marked by an institutional void (McIntosh, 1975). He also believes that his work is a 'story of formation' (a *Bildungsroman*) – though it is difficult to say whether the *Bildung* ever occurs. The hero seems to disintegrate rather than construct himself as subject (Moretti, 1996), or perhaps it is exactly 'the subject as a con man' that is the final stage of that formation process.

Action and change

Accomplishment may impoverish our capacity to charm, 'since only he who desires is amiable and not he who is satiated' (*Felix Krull*: 54). Hence Felix's insatiability for change, movement and disguise. The pursuit of one goal alone, in his view, hides a coarse notion of enjoyment, a crude and illusory quest for the satisfaction of one's appetite. His goals are broader and never precisely defined, and for this reason, he feels, he remains 'so long innocent and unconscious, a child and dreamer indeed, my whole life long' (55).

This childish posture, and the vagueness of the goals pursued, distance Felix from the rational *homo computans*, while his playfulness enhances experimentation and increases the rhythm of action. The maximization of benefits, however, is achieved less by means of rational choice than through perpetual caprice. He finds it tiresome to be known by the same name for an entire life, and to scribble documents and papers with the same signature. To be able to give oneself a new name and to hear oneself called by it is refreshing and stimulating, a restorative tonic enjoyed by women that Felix envies. In contrast, for men any such change is forbidden by law, a circumstance which, as we shall see, will not deter our hero from borrowing someone else's title and identity.

What should be noted here is the ability of Felix to supplement, as sociology of organizations would suggest, the technology of reason with a *technology of foolishness*, in that he does things for which he has no good reason, and because he appears to need to act before he thinks

(March, 1990). The notion of foolishness, as we saw in the last chapter in the case of Captain Ahab, conveys, again, that of playfulness, which entails a temporary relaxation or suspension of rules. This temporary absence of rules may favour the exploration of new possibilities, so that new, alternative rules may eventually be identified. Consistency is also suspended, and Felix adopts a sort of transitional hypocrisy, whereby he is forced to ignore the growing gulf between the value he officially endorses and his actual behaviour. He floats in a moral limbo and, making a sharp distinction between natural inheritance and the achievement of will, is convinced that it is not morally reprehensible if deceit takes over from honesty. When praised for the agreeable tone of his voice, he feels that, had he been less hypocritical (or, euphemistically, had his soul been less watchful), his voice might have turned out common, his eyes dull, and his legs crooked. 'He who really loves the world shapes himself to please it' (*Felix Krull*: 73). Constant change – of environment, goal, title, clothes, identity, name, and indeed of voice – is the irresistible propellant for Felix's action, which, while unfolding, moulds consistent forms of rationalization, a device that makes him live comfortably with his deeds.

Techniques of neutralization

While shaping himself to please the world, Felix undergoes a learning process in respect of both the techniques of defrauding and those which sociologists of deviance describe as techniques of neutralization. The latter are said to permit delinquents to come to terms with the problem of guilt and ease the commission of crime. The denial of victims, for example, may neutralize guilt through the argument that those victimized deserve their fate or that they suffered no real loss (Sykes and Matza, 1957). 'It might be argued that higher loyalties were at stake or

that those who condemn action are in no moral position to judge'
(Downes and Rock, 1988: 35). Here is a brief account of the learning
process undergone by Felix Krull.

Felix devotes considerable thought to the unpleasant issue of his
military obligations, and, after gathering information about the practices,
criteria and the nature of regulations adopted by the recruiting office,
discovers a 'publication of clinical character', which he reads with
enthusiasm and profit. He uses what he learns in that publication when
the health councillor is required to ascertain his fitness for military
service. After claiming that what kept him home from school was
described by his family doctor as migraine, he explains that this manifests itself with 'a kind of roaring in both ears and especially a great
feeling of distress and fear or rather a timorousness of the whole body,
which finally turns into a spasm of choking so violent that it almost
hurls me out of bed' (Felix Krull: 106). As the conversation goes on, and
the curiosity of the health councillor grows, Felix makes all further
questions redundant by simulating a fit which precisely qualifies the
type of migraine he is subject to. He stammers foolishly, changes colour,
his face becomes contorted in a terrifying fashion, as if under a satanic
influence. His features are thrust apart in all directions while his eyeballs
seem to be on the point of popping out.

> To recount in detail the distortions of my features, to describe completely
> the horrible positions in which mouth, nose, brows, and cheeks – in
> short, all the muscles of my face – were involved, changing constantly,
> moreover, so that not a single one of these facial deformities repeated
> itself – such a description would be far too great an undertaking. (Felix
> Krull: 110)

He explains that these physiognomic phenomena must belong to an
infernal region where our passions, magnified to monstrous propor-
tions, would find themselves horribly reproduced. Whether deriving

from an infernal inner region or from a long apprenticeship in deception, this astonishing *mise en scène* leads the military authority to pronounce the unappealable word 'rejected'. And Felix is left with a subtle
sense of loss, because he would perhaps have cut an admirable figure
in a uniform; but he soon comes to his senses and ponders that he was
not born under the sign of Mars. For although martial discipline and
danger are characteristics of his existence, these are shaped by one
central concern: freedom.

Felix avoids companionship and human contact and is compelled to
follow his own path, in pursuit of rigorous self-sufficiency. However,
after a short relationship with Rozsa, he secretly 'superintends' the
conquests she makes on the street, and at times even lies in hiding
while she receives her paying customers. Although he does not disdain
to 'accept a reasonable share of the proceeds', he warns readers to refrain
from calling his business pimping. It is too simple a procedure to label
two individuals acting identically with an identical word, and even
labels such as drunkard, gambler or wastrel 'not only do not embrace
and define the actual living case, but in some instances do not even
touch it' (*Felix Krull*: 127). Moreover, the relationship with Rozsa is of
the most crucial importance for his education: 'I could never have borne
myself with so much subtlety and elegance in the many vicissitudes of
my life if I had not passed through Rozsa's naughty school of love' (128).

On arrival in France he acts amiably with customs officials, and after
praising their country is given the warmest of welcomes. While repacking his luggage he notices a certain object in an adjacent suitcase
open for inspection. The suitcase belongs to a lady wearing a mink coat
and a velvet cloche adorned with heron feathers. The object is a case
containing jewellery, which slips into his luggage – an occurrence rather
than an action; the case just smuggles itself in. Eventually, he is to find
out more about that lady.

Felix is enveloped in a self-perception which excludes any possibility that his behaviour be termed criminal. Physical elegance and intellectual sophistication indicate that his status is well above material need, and his undertakings do not damage anyone: the army can do without him, and Rozsa is compensated with the beauty of his body and the pleasures of his intellect. As for that glamorous lady, her jewels must be part of an enormous collection, and she will hardly detect the negligible loss. He is chosen to achieve, and will do so without 'dull toil and labour', while enjoying freedom and apparent idleness. However, while applying these techniques of neutralization to his undertakings, he also, if un- wittingly, endorses a notion of crime as the result of consumerist ac- quisitiveness, of the urge to possess commodities generated by publicity, and, ultimately, as the result of relative deprivation. In the big city he observes 'this youth in ragged clothes', alone, lost in the crowd, with no money to take part in the enjoyment of goods, whose qualities are proclaimed on advertising placards. He sees 'the portals of the theatres festively open and dares not join the crowd that goes streaming in'. Temptation is accentuated by that 'happy institution', the shop window:

> How lucky that stores, bazaars, salons, that market places and emporia of luxury do not stingily hide their treasures indoors, but shower them forth in glittering profusion, in inexhaustible variety, spreading them out like a splendid offering behind shining plate glass. (Felix Krull: 84–5)

This 'splendid offering' causes an inner turmoil in young Felix, who turns it into 'good purpose for his education, his enthusiastic researches', and one wonders whether his 'researches' in fraud are illegitimate ways of pursuing legitimate goals (Merton, 1968). When the fence he contacts to sell the stolen jewellery shows appreciation for his talents, Felix senses yet again that, legitimately or otherwise, his purposes and the style with which he achieves them, protect his behaviour from moral judgement.

God of thieves

As a lift boy in a Paris hotel, Felix changes his name to Armand, thus experiencing the emotion he envies in women who are offered such fortune. In the hotel he recognizes the owner of the jewels, who finds him so young, so beautiful, so insolent; she entices him to her room, to admire his noble ribs, narrow hips and, as if in premonition, Hermes legs. When Felix confesses that he took and sold her missing jewels, the godly similarity extends from the body to the mind, and Felix–Armand is awarded the title of 'god of thieves'. The lady finds it sublime, a marvellous humiliation, an exciting circumstance, and remarks that the thief is more precious to her than what he took: 'Hermes, Hermes!', she shouts. She then has a wonderful idea: while she pretends to be asleep Felix, her thievish god, will steal from her; she will watch him, and her excitement will produce the most enchanting fulfilment of their love. As Felix obeys, her exhilaration triggers a climactic injunction:

> This is your booty of love and theft. Put it in your pockets, get dressed and vanish, as is proper! Hurry and flee! I heard it all, I heard you breathing as you stole ... *Adieu*, Armand! Farewell, farewell forever, my idol! Do not forget your Diane, for in her you will survive. (*Felix Krull*: 93)

This identification of social ascent with theft offers a desecrating complement to the Weberianism of Thomas Mann, whose parody strengthens the moral ambiguity with which he describes the business career of his hero. Hermes is a distinguished member of the Greek pantheon, and is regarded as the patron of the upwardly mobile Athenian merchant entrepreneurs (McClelland, 1961). He makes a lyre out of a tortoise that he finds in the doorway of his cave and invents wicker sandals in order not to leave footprints on the road. 'He not only wants to get ahead in the world; he gets real pleasure out of the schemes he devises for doing so' (McClelland, 1961: 302). Like Felix, Hermes exhibits the most vivid characteristics of entrepreneurship: the capacity to innovate. He too makes his innovations and pursues his career in a spirit of restless energy, and in his life there is much motion and little waste of time. He produces change and avoids repetition, but he is also a thief: as soon as he is laid in his cradle he jumps up and goes looking for Apollo's cattle, which he steals. He lies to the point of persuading Apollo to let him keep the cattle. He is dishonest: on closer examination, his sandals are in fact worn backwards in order to deceive those who follow him after being cheated. He is an innovator and at the same time the trickster hero. He belongs to an ostracized group, and while Felix is the son of a suicidal bankrupt businessman, Hermes is the product of a casual relationship between Zeus and Maia. He reacts to ostracism with his 'need for discovery and invention – which means invention also in the sense of deceit' (Kerenyi, 1958: 10). While Apollo is tragically dignified and his deeds are noble, Hermes is somewhat comical, and likes ambiguity and shady deals, colourful lies and serendipitous finds (Citati, 1996). His voice enchants and heals, gives pleasure and arouses heretic desire; he gives peace with his elusive art of deception. While Apollo is found on the front of temples, in epic poems and in Aeschylus' tragedies, Hermes is adjacent to the market place and in Pompeii he appears on the threshold of shops in via dell'Abbondanza, wearing a cloak and holding a bagful of coins.

Thomas Mann follows Socrates' demand that the same author should write tragedies and comedies, so that the combination of tragic and comic makes both relative. Humorous and roguish as he may be, Felix combines with Dr *Faustus* and displays an inner kinship with him; he is also a complement, an ironic counterpart, to others of Thomas Mann's heroes, and to the author's humanism (Cayrol, 1996).

In the *Joseph* novels Thomas Mann took up and treated one of the chief
problems of the classical period, namely the self-enjoyment of personality.... Self-enjoyment of personality appeared as the natural consequence,
the inevitable by-product of a successfully waged life; it acquired a slightly
more independent emphasis as a humanist, this worldly polemic against
a medieval or puritanical asceticism. (Lukács, 1964: 117)

To lose pleasure in oneself is also the concern of other of Mann's
characters, and ultimately the author appears to suggest that with entrepreneurs and their class observing moral and material decline, 'only
the confidence man can fulfil himself in pleasure' (Lukács, 1964: 127).
Felix Krull, like Hermes, pursues such fulfilment, though it is unknown
whether Mann sees in his hero the signs of entrepreneurial descent or
those of the necessary steps for ascent.

An a priori individual

Felix is not drawn by sheer material acquisition, and his purpose to
deceive is not pure enrichment. He becomes a con man in order to
make his life resemble his imagination, 'to impose on life his image of
himself' (Lukács, 1964: 129). Social rank and money are only the means
to provide him with the necessary circumstances for the free deploy-
ment of his talents.

Felix believes in predisposition and feels that his success is due to
the acknowledgement by others of the finer clay from which he is
made. For this reason, he despises those whose aspirations are not
prompted by adequate predispositions and consistent social origin. His
climbing to the status of man of the world, and even his elegant clothes,
are the natural outcome of his outstanding individual qualities. Without
such qualities one would appear out of place in his position, like those
factory workers 'awkwardly striving to be fashionable' (*Felix Krull*: 200).
The image he nurses of himself makes him reject the proposal of his

co-worker in the hotel to break into a villa in Neuilly. His colleague perhaps thinks that someone 'possessed of childish cunning and skilled fingers' like him would make a perfect partner in theft, and does not realize that Felix cannot be anyone's accomplice. That his is a different mission in life also becomes clear when he is invited to move in with a Scottish gentleman, who is 'childless and master of [his] own affairs'. A sort of adoption would make Felix wake up one day as Lord Strath-bogie and heir to his possessions. Although tempting ideas start swirling in his mind, he senses that to acquire lordship just because it is dangled before him implies the abandonment of his dreams, free play, inde-pendent imagination and self-created career.

His dreams and free play do in fact continue when, while still working in the hotel, he rents a room in town, where he spends some time after work and where, more importantly, he keeps his elegant clothes. Appearance, again, takes over from reality, and Felix cherishes his fine shirts, silk socks and bow ties, along with his dinner jacket with satin lapels, that he wears when he dines at some restaurants on the rue de Rivoli or the avenue des Champs-Élysées, 'by way of experi-ment and practice in living the higher life' (Felix Krull: 244). His dual existence therefore proceeds as ever, and he is charmed by the ambi-guity of his own making: which is the real Felix and which the masquerade? But this is only the prelude to the final events, when his theatrical gifts are played 'in a decisive and gratifying, indeed almost intoxicating, manner' (245).

The young Marquis de Venosta, a customer of the hotel who admires the gifted Felix, is desperately in love with Zaza, whose social back-ground does not match that of her lover. The parents of the Marquis believe that the only way to 'pry him lose' is to send him on a long journey across the world. Felix does not take much convincing: he will take the trip and cash the cheque which goes with it; he will be the

Marquis, who will relinquish his money, milieu and personality to him. Finally life gives substance to airy nothings and brings 'childhood dreams to pass'. 'Had not I in boyhood tasted in imagination those delights of incognito I fully savoured now?' (*Felix Krull*: 270). The mind games of Felix become reality, as he meets people of high social status, and with the patent of nobility in his pocket he mingles with a world that he feels belongs to him. Frivolity is not his style, 'especially in the matter of jokes', and because a 'good joke does not come off unless one approaches it with complete seriousness' Felix embarks on the new adventure with the conscientious attitude which characterizes him at work as well as in fraud.

Among his encounters one finds the bearers of illuminating philosophies who partly confirm and partly accentuate Felix's convictions. For example, Professor Kuckuck reminds him that, true, there is progress, from pithecanthropus to Shakespeare, but all stages of nature and evolution are always present at the same time, and all conditions of culture and morality exist side by side. Readers may find in the professor's words a description of the very activities conducted by Felix, who joins the elite through fraud (or is it business?) Again, the silliest and the wisest, the most barbaric and the most delicately evolved, forms of behaviour cohabit sometimes in the same individuals: 'often indeed the finest becomes tired of itself and infatuated with the primitive and sinks drunkenly into barbarism' (*Felix Krull*: 294). Self-discipline cannot be aimed at preventing such 'sinking', but should encourage it with a view to success. Only transitory, episodic acts and goals are worthy of sympathy, as only a transitory and episodic morality can aspire to dwell in the human soul. In a dialogue with mademoiselle Zouzou, beauty is described as being part and parcel of self-discipline, the outcome of the care for oneself. Ugliness, like failure, should be punished, as the result of carelessness, offensive to decorum and to the eye. Finally, in a remarkable confirmation of how individual and organizational careers are formally inspired by manifest goals and actually promoted by operative goals, Felix experiences the final 'great joy' with Maria, while apparently aiming for her daughter.

Perhaps Felix is a subject who lives in an alleged condition of nature and acts egoistically, though managing, after all, to develop a peaceful mental order through techniques of rationalization. These techniques allow him to come to terms with his conduct and to impute to others the origin of that conduct. He is an a priori individual, oriented towards clear personal aims, who competes with other individuals, but unlike the Hobbesian individual he does not relate to them by using either force or deception, or both intermittently. His fraud excludes force and manifests itself in a variety of actions which make it redundant. His range of possibilities includes the full Weberian typology: instrumentally rational, value-rational, affectual or emotional and traditional acts, in a constant competition between logical and non-logical objectives (Joas, 1996). While climbing the social hierarchy, Felix combines purposeful with non-purposeful actions, as if at times lying were not geared to achievement, but rather constituted a restful withdrawal from it. His life, however, does not enable him to avoid the relentless demands of business and to commit himself gracefully to nothing (Lukács, 1964). Rather, his commitment embraces both nothing and business, and, like business, he acts both 'in order to' and 'for the sake of'.

8

Mark Twain and
the Corruption of a Town

Hadleyburg is the most honest town in its region. This reputation has remained untainted for three generations, and the town is prouder of it than of any other of its qualities or possessions. Even babies in the cradle are taught the principles of honest dealing, and such principles accompany them throughout their education for years. Temptations are kept at bay during their formative period, so that honesty can grow strong and become part of their bones. In *The Man that Corrupted Hadleyburg* Mark Twain ([1901] 1993) tells the story of how the town is corrupted by a passing stranger because some of its citizens have the ill luck of offending him, possibly without knowing it, certainly without caring, 'for Hadleyburg was sufficiently unto itself, and cared not a rap for strangers or their opinions' (400).

The stranger is a bitter and revengeful man, and keeps the injury in his mind for a long time, before contriving a plan which would hit the town as a whole, leaving none of its inhabitants unhurt. It is with 'evil joy' that he commits himself to corrupting the town.

He calls at the house of the old cashier of the bank, with a sack, and asks if he can leave it in his care. He introduces himself as a stranger passing through to 'discharge a matter' which has been long in his mind: 'my errand is now completed, and I go pleased and a little proud, and you will never see me again'. A note attached to the sack will explain everything.

The note says that he is a foreigner going back to his own country to remain there permanently. He is grateful to America for what he has received during his long stay, and is especially grateful to one of her citizens, a citizen of Hadleyburg, 'for a great kindness done' to him one or two years back. He used to be a gambler, and had arrived in the town one night, hungry and penniless. He had asked for help, in the dark, as he was ashamed of begging in the light. A man gave him twenty dollars; he gave him life, and also made his fortune, because with that money he became rich 'at the gaming-table'. That man made a remark which was destined to remain with him for the rest of his days, a remark that saved him and led him to give up gambling for ever. He has no idea who that man might be, but he asks that he be found and given the money contained in the sack.

> It is merely my way of testifying my gratitude to him. If I could stay, I would find him myself; but no matter, he will be found. This is an honest town, an incorruptible town, and I know I can trust it without fear. This man can be identified by the remark which he made to me; I feel persuaded that he will remember it. (*Hadleyburg*: 402)

A sealed envelope in the sack contains a transcription of the remark; the candidate coming forward with a remark that perfectly tallies with it will be the right man. Reverend Burgess is named in the letter as the man chosen to hold and deliver the money.

Mr Richards, the bank cashier, is one of the nineteen 'important citizens' of Hadleyburg. However, he and his wife Mary are very poor, and looking at the mysterious sack the man complains that he is 'always at the grind, grind, grind, on a salary', and that he is another man's slave, the slave of a man sitting at home in his slippers, rich and comfortable. In brief, the two are tempted: all they have to do is to bury the money and burn the papers, and if the gambler returns, they will make him look foolish, telling him that he is talking nonsense. Hesitation, which will accompany their conduct throughout the story, soon comes to rescue them: that is gambler's money, the wages of sin, therefore they cannot touch it. They finally decide to contact the local paper and have the letter published.

Who might the anonymous benefactor ever be, in a town that the Richards believe to be honest, but also narrow, self-righteous and stingy? Readers slowly start to appreciate that behind its reputation Hadleyburg hides hatred, jealousy and crafty plots. The Reverend is the most hated man in town, and his unpopularity has its foundation in 'that one thing – the thing that made so much noise' (*Hadleyburg*: 404). The reader will never know what that thing is, but is informed that Mr Richards could have helped him, because he had proof of the Reverend's innocence, but failed to intervene, for fear of having everybody in town against him. The Reverend, in his turn, does not suspect that he might have been saved, and in fact is grateful to Mr Richards for his suggestion that he should leave the town for a while and return when things calmed down.

Silent assertions

Our first impression is that *The Man that Corrupted Hadleyburg* is the story of the 'stealthy despoliation of an idyllic town by a cunning stranger' (Ozick, 1996: xxxvi). But we soon realize that the stranger, a Mephistophelean emblem, resembles the citizens he corrupts, who are already degraded, to the point that the 'evil joy' of the schemer is not worse than 'the greedy dreams of the townsfolk who scheme to enrich themselves through lies' (Ozick, 1996: xxxvii).

Mark Twain is said to have made Americans unafraid to reject European models of civilization as tainted or corrupt, and at the same time 'helped them recognize their own insularity, boorishness, arrogance, or ignorance, and laugh at it' (Fisher Fishkin, 1996: xii). Regarded as remarkably prescient about political affairs, Twain is admired for uncompromisingly dealing with the struggle for integrity in the face of the seductions of power, status and material things. Some of his work reads like a precursor of sociological analysis of white-collar criminals, and readers learn that poor people do not exercise a monopoly on criminal activity. People who think of themselves as exemplarily moral, admirable citizens, often lie, steal, and even kill. They do so as a result of communicative processes and interactions whereby they learn the techniques of illegal behaviour along with the rationalizations that help them come to terms with that behaviour. As Sutherland (1939; 1983) would put it, they are exposed, during the course of their occupation, to an excess of definitions favourable to violation of law.

Within white-collar criminal activity, however, corruption occupies a specific position. It would appear, for example, that corrupt behaviour only exists, and causes intimate discomfort, when it becomes public knowledge. For generations Hadleyburg has learned through secrecy to deflect attention from the unorthodox dealings and shady exchanges in which its citizens engage, thus succeeding in establishing a reputation as an exemplarily honest town. The learning process through which its citizens have managed to establish such a reputation produces the acceptance of mutual hatred and gratitude, of wrongs and favours, and an equilibrium apparently benefiting all is reached. In this respect, it might be argued that corruption exists when something goes wrong, namely when those involved in it find reason to express some form of resentment for being denied the benefits they expect from their own corrupt behaviour (Ruggiero, 2000c). Hence their decision to expose it, as if by doing so they singled out those whose corrupt behaviour yields more revenue than their own.

Twain possesses a subtle ability to dissect social lies, not only through novels and short stories, but also through pamphlets and essays. He describes the 'lie of silent assertion', that we can tell without saying a word. 'In the magnitude of its territorial spread it is one of the most majestic lies that the civilizations make it their sacred and anxious care to guard and watch and propagate' (Twain, 1996a: 169). For example, 'it would not be possible for a humane and intelligent person to invent a rational excuse for slavery', but 'from pulpit and press all the way down to the bottom of society', thanks to the clammy stillness created and maintained by the lie of silent assertion, humane and intelligent people find nothing wrong in it. Similarly, 'from the beginning of the Dreyfus case to the end of it all France, except a couple of dozen moral paladins, lay under the smother of the silent-assertion lie that no wrong was being done to a persecuted and unoffending man' (169). The universal conspiracy of the silent-assertion lie, Twain continues, is hard at work always and everywhere, and always in the interest of a stupidity or a sham, 'never in the interest of a thing fine or respectable'. Lies mutely labour in the interest of 'despotisms and aristocracies and chattel slaveries, and military slaveries, and religious slaveries', all kept alive by them.

> When whole races and peoples conspire to propagate gigantic mute lies in the interest of tyrannies and shams, why should we care anything about the trifling lies told by individuals?... Why should we help the nation lie all day long and then object to telling one little individual private lie in our own interest to go to bed on? (Twain, 1996a: 170–71)

In sum, the honesty of Hadleyburg is based on a conspiracy to propagate a lie, from which every citizen thinks to reap some sort of benefit. Higher immoralities are tolerated, provided they generate some advantage for all, including those who limit their immorality to the 'little individual private lie'. The town, therefore, is not corrupted by a stranger: that stranger simply activates a situation in which silence is broken, and as a consequence the town starts to acknowledge the features of its own corruption.

The principal citizens

When given the letter by Mr Richards, the editor of the local paper wonders whether a secret deal can be struck whereby they share the content of the sack. In this way they would benefit, but all the other citizens, if indirectly, would benefit too, because the town's reputation as a paragon of honesty would remain intact. Unfortunately, he discovers that the paper is already in press, and he cannot stop the letter becoming public.

Mr Richards is torn, and starts recognizing that the type of honesty in which the children of Hadleyburg are trained, from the very cradle, is artificial honesty, 'as weak as water when temptation comes' (*Hadleyburg*: 409). He is convinced that the town's honesty is as rotten as his and that its 'mean, hard, and stingy' inhabitants, under great temptation, would bring it 'to ruin like a house of cards'.

After the publication of the letter, however, the name of Hadleyburg the Incorruptible 'was on every lip in America, from Montreal to the Gulf, from the glaciers of Alaska to the orange-groves of Florida'. The town wakes up astonished, happy and vain. Its 'nineteen principal citizens and their wives went about shaking hands with each other, 'beaming, and smiling, and congratulating, and saying this thing adds a new word to the dictionary – *Hadleyburg*, synonym for *incorruptible* – destined to live in dictionaries forever' (410). The lesser and unimportant citizens go around acting in much the same way, participating in the wild intoxication of pride and joy. This soon gives way to a sweet, silent delight, 'a sort of deep, nameless, unutterable content'.

After a few days, Jack Halliday, the 'loafing, good-natured, no-account irreverent fisherman, hunter, stray-dogs' friend, who always made fun of everything, no matter what', begins to notice that people are no longer looking so happy, and that slowly they are taking a 'sick look'. Everybody seems 'so moody, thoughtful, and absent-minded that he could rob the meanest man in town of a cent out of the bottom of his breeches pocket and not disturb his revery' (411). He goes about laughing, but his laugh is the only one left in the town, which falls 'upon a hollow and mournful vacancy and emptiness' (412). Everybody stops chatting, paying or receiving visits: the whole village sits at home, silent, trying to guess the fateful remark made to the stranger.

A second letter appears, giving a sudden twist to the story. It is sent to Mr Richards, but also to each of the principal citizens of Hadleyburg, nineteen letters in all. The letters all reveal the remark that changed the gambler's life and fortunes: 'You are far from being a bad man: go, and reform.' The wives of these important citizens mentally start to spend the money, and in their investment plans in one night only they spend 'an average of seven thousand dollars each out of the forty thousand in the sack – a hundred and thirty-three thousand altogether'. The faces of the nineteen chief citizens and their wives, as Jack Halliday notices, bear that expression of peaceful and holy happiness again. Some of them do not limit themselves to planning to spend, but really spend money, on credit. 'They bought land, mortgages, farms, speculative stocks, fine clothes, horses, and various other things, paid down the bonus, and made themselves liable for the rest – at ten days' (417–18).

At the town hall, where the public disclosure of the name of the benefactor and his remark finally takes place, Reverend Burgess finds that he has nineteen envelopes in his pocket, sent to him by as many candidates to the sack. In a pandemonium of delight, the ordinary citizens of Hadleyburg realize that all their top fellow citizens claim they have made exactly the same remark to the gambler and have helped him change his life. The only envelope that the reverend does not open is the one sent to him by Richards, thus sparing the poor bank employee the derisive jeers of the crowd. Richards maintains his reputation of honesty untarnished because, in the circumstances, an untold secret agreement with the Reverend saves him from the public stigma.

Imaginable mutual accusations between the powerful citizens are loudly exchanged, revealing how the purported cohesiveness of an elite seemingly exemplifying the honesty of the town is but a thin layer of conventionalism. Fierce competition among the principal citizens replaces the superficial harmony displayed by them for so long, as if that harmony were the mere result of lack of opportunities. For example, Mr Harkness and Mr Pinkerton are running as opposing candidates in the local elections, and it is a close race, but fair. Both have bought a piece of land and are determined to have the new railway located on their property. The two, aiming at the sack, plot against each other; it is unclear who becomes more discredited as a result.

Mark Twain focuses on temptation, which in sociological jargon would amount to opportunity. How do variables such as opportunity, moral choice and competition explain corruption? Let us briefly review some relevant analyses found in the specialistic literature.

Corruption and development

Before the arrival of the vindictive stranger, Hadleyburg's citizens operate within a political machine that satisfies basic latent functions. The needs of the diverse groups of inhabitants are adequately attended to through an exchange of favours which establish bonds of gratitude and mutuality.

Although the establishment of such bonds does not follow officially approved and legally orthodox modalities, it allows for conflict and competition to be defused of its potentially dysfunctional effect. Moreover, the ties cementing the community of the town make every individual embrace the conventional, general, view of that community as exemplarily honest. And this convention – or shared lie, as Twain would put it – provides alternative channels of social mobility and advancement, so that everyone feels the recipient of some beneficial outcome in accord with his or her expectations. In other words, the well-being of the town, prior to the arrival of the canny stranger, represents the triumph of amoral intelligence over morally prescribed failure (Merton, 1968).

The stability of Hadleyburg, therefore, is based on a 'silent-assertion lie' which humanizes and personalizes social relationships, encourages cooperation and keeps fragmentation at bay. Contrary to analyses associating corruption with poverty, however, the town, which is already corrupt, enjoys an acceptable standard of living; when the contours of its corruption are unveiled, the revelation is caused not by poverty but by unexpected, and highly contested, wealth. The sudden appearance of wealth, perhaps, could be interpreted as a signifier of social transition, which in academic studies of corruption occupies a central explanatory role. It is suggested, for example, that corruption flourishes in periods of rapid growth, when unorthodox practices constitute a price societies pay for social progress and economic development (Bailey, 1966; Huntington, 1968; Scott, 1969). Surely, Mark Twain would hardly agree that corruption is a vestigial survival of the past, and that it is destined to be swept away by progress and development (Wilson, 1990). On the contrary, corruption in Hadleyburg reaches maximum visibility when opportunities for development are offered and competing actors who are prospective leaders of such development unleash their economic initiative. Mr Harkness and Mr Pinkerton are poised to build a new railway, and presumably this will foster trade, mobility, material and cultural exchange; the town will perhaps lose that dormant self-righteousness, that static stinginess, while its dull inhabitants will create a more vibrant community.

Elitist access to resources

Mr and Mrs Richards, who temporarily maintain a reputation as honest people, become the beneficiaries of the sack, as the citizens of Hadleyburg are led to believe that their behaviour in the whole affair has been inspired by the proverbial town integrity. They could have kept the money for themselves, instead of giving it to the Reverend; and as for that improbable letter, they could have thrown it away. When someone proclaims that that money should go to the 'cleanest man in town, the one solitary important citizen who didn't try to steal' it, the proposal is passed by acclamation. Again, the Richardses are sorely tempted, and they fall, for 'we are very poor, we are old, and have no chick nor child to help us' (Hadleyburg: 430).

Reverend Burgess, after hiding Richards's letter claiming their entitlement to the money, himself writes a letter to the man, in which he explains that he has saved him because he was once saved by him.

> It was at the cost of a lie, but I made the sacrifice freely, and out of a grateful heart. None in this village knows so well as I know how brave and good and noble you are. At bottom you cannot respect me, knowing as you do of that matter of which I am accused, and by the general voice condemned; but I beg that you will at least believe that I am a grateful man; it will help me to bear my burden. (Hadleyburg: 438)

This tie of gratitude, which is based on a misunderstanding, hides the fact that it was Richards who had exposed the culpability of the Reverend before rescuing him with the advice to leave. Moreover, the very reason why Richards receives the note revealing the remark of the benefactor, thus enabling him to claim the money, is also the result of a misunderstanding. The stranger exploits this second misunderstanding to test the honesty of Richards and ultimately to trouble his conscience to his deathbed. The benefactor is a man named Goodson, now dead, but always deeply grateful to Richards, who is therefore repaid with the revelation of the remark.

But why is Goodson so grateful? We finally learn that Goodson, years before, came close to marrying a pretty girl named Nancy, and that that girl 'carried a spoonful of negro blood in her veins'. Richards remembers that it was he who found out, and that he told everyone in town, thus saving Goodson from pairing with a 'tainted girl'. Richards, in brief, has done a great service without knowing he was doing it. But 'Goodson knew the value of it, and what a narrow escape he had had, and so went to his grave grateful to his benefactor and wishing he had a fortune to leave him' (Hadleyburg: 416).

Mark Twain asserts that one should perhaps have no special regard for Satan, but at least one has to hold no prejudice against him. His ecumenism includes the Devil: how could he tolerate racism? About the different human races, he says: 'All that I care to know is that a man is a human being – that is enough for me; he can't be any worse' (Twain, 1996b: 254). Not only is Hadleyburg entangled in a mesh of lies, bonds of mistaken gratitude and false favours, but those very lies are embedded in petty provincialism and repugnant feelings harboured against parts of the human race. These feelings are shared by the elite as well as by poor, old, people like Edward and Mary Richards, and while the man recollects the good deed he has performed by denouncing the 'tainted girl', the woman is lost in her fantasy about how to invest the money: six thousand dollars on a new house for herself and a pair of slippers for her pastor.

At the end, however, the Richardses are prostrated by excitement, but also shattered by remorse. The old couple become seriously ill, and as the news goes around the town is sincerely distressed, because those two old people are 'all that is left to be proud of'. The doctor hears Edward Richards talk about Satan and the money he sent him to 'betray him to sin', and in his final hours the man falls 'to gabbling strange and dreadful things which were not clearly understandable' (*Hadleyburg*: 440). These 'gabblings' are soon spread across the town, and finally everyone learns that Richards is among those who had claimed the sack for himself. After a day or two 'Mrs Richards's delirious deliveries were getting to be duplicates of her husband's', and the town reaches the ultimate conviction that its pride in 'the purity of its one undiscredited citizen' is destined 'to dim down and flicker toward extinction' (441).

The Richardses are the only victims of the town saga, as if the effects of corruption were selective and discriminatory. They are poor, a circumstance which tempts them into dishonestly claiming the money, but simultaneously leads them to serious illness and ultimately to death. The other 'important citizens' who make the same claim are exposed and ridiculed by their fellow citizens, but at the end they carry on with their business, despite the fact that their reputation and that of the town as a whole is irretrievably tarnished. One could suggest that underprivileged people cannot compete in corruption with their powerful counterparts, as those who have easier access to resources find the way to neutralize the negative impact of their misconduct. The Richardses make a naive mistake, namely that of believing corruption to be an 'equal opportunity' illegal act. Let us elaborate on this final point.

The victims of corruption

Hadleyburg, as we have seen, was a corrupt town long before being tempted by a vindictive stranger. Its citizens engage in corrupt exchange, and in so doing they participate in the political life of their town and contribute to the establishment of peaceful cohesion within their community. When new resources are suddenly made available, corruption becomes too competitive a game for its cohesion to be safeguarded. Initially, self-interest is geared to the well-being of the citizens' families and close peer groups, in an apparent fair arrangement that benefits all. Although the reputation of the town as honest is undeserved, Hadleyburg manages to channel self-interest into consensual social organization. Whether we call it greed or utility maximization, corruption allows the town to temper its internal conflicts, until the silent agreement, or lie, among its citizens is nullified by unprecedented material opportunities. Endemic corruption thus turns into destructive corruption only when the town fails to translate self-interest into collective purposes and achievements.

Classical analysis posits that societies with highly personalized relations have difficulty developing economically and politically. These societies are also said to be unable to establish modern bureaucracies led by individuals, hired on the basis of their skills, who are capable of separating their official role from their personal interest. In Hadleyburg, instead, there is a sense that a substantive equilibrium is maintained precisely thanks to the existence of interpersonal links, of a web of mutual feelings of gratitude, and an exchange of genuine or false favours. The town offers an exemplary model of democratic systems as described by sociologists such as Vilfredo Pareto (1966: 67), who sees all societies, irrespective of the regime, as governed by a minority elite. The governing class is not a tight, close-knit and clearly circumscribed organization. It is a very unsystematic system – much like the feudal system. In such a system, democratic participation is achieved by courtesy of 'a vast number of mutually dependent hubs of influence and patronage, which keeps together by the fact that each hub is dependent to some extent on the good graces of another such hub'. The task of these systems, in order to maintain their stability, is to aggregate the various centres of patronage, the various clienteles, in such a way that they are all satisfied. Hadleyburg maintains its social stability as long as it manages to make the interests of its groups compatible: it thrives on personalized relations, and seems to satisfy all centres of patronage and clientele, until an external, artificial, force unsettles its equilibrium.

In a broad distinction, it has been argued that archetypical competitive markets transmute self-interest into productive activities that lead to efficient use of resources. Dysfunctional markets, on the other hand, are said to resemble war, where a destructive struggle over wealth 'ends up destroying the resource base that motivated the fight in the first place' (Rose-Ackerman, 1999: 2). In between, commentators see situations where people use resources both for productive purposes and to gain an advantage in dividing up the benefits of economic activity, benefits which are said to characterize rent-seeking systems. Hadleyburg proves unable to keep its collective system of rent-seeking in place, and disadvantaged participants in corrupt exchange pay severe costs for their participation. Their fragility in the market makes their corruption unproductive, while more powerful actors are able to turn their own corruption into a supplementary competitive tool. Mr Haskell, for example, links his corrupt behaviour to the future of his business, and in defeating his competitor proves that corruption is but an extra resource to be used in the market. The only cost he pays is the one that the town pays as a whole: namely the re-christening of Hadleyburg and the change of the motto that for many generations had graced the town's official seal. The 'not' from 'Lead us not into temptation' disappears.

Surely, when observed against the backdrop of sociological analysis, Hadleyburg possesses some anomalies. In the town, petty corruption is pervasive, though this does not affect the levels of trust in public institutions among citizens. In fact, pride is the prevailing feeling, and routine corruption does not seem to generate 'negative consequences for commitment to collective projects, civic behaviour, levels of crime and public order' (Doig and Theobald, 2000: 6). The fact that Hadleyburg hides its corruption from the outside world is the result of the lack of opportunities the town experiences in interacting with that world. This leads us to some of the contemporary dilemmas troubling students of corruption.

It is often argued that the actual incidence of corruption is even more problematic than its definition. 'Our thinking about the level of corruption is somewhat impressionistic, based upon our own perceptions (or prejudices), or those of journalists, diplomats, politicians, and businessmen' (Doig and Theobald, 2000: 6). Efforts to rank countries according to how their level of corruption is perceived meet with difficulties because of the varying number of transactions in which countries themselves are engaged. More transactions also means more opportunities for corrupt practices, or at least for practices so perceived by the individuals and groups involved. Hadleyburg is a relatively isolated town, a circumstance which allows the persistence of its reputation as honest. However, as soon as a stranger engages with its citizens in a transaction of sorts, corruption is revealed, and, retroactively, is proven to have always been there.

In witnessing a variety of corrupt exchanges, the citizens of Hadleyburg become unaccustomed to public welfare and collectively shared benefits. This process is favoured by the limited benefit that even its poorer inhabitants might enjoy from corrupt exchange. Opportunities granted to ordinary citizens from minor episodes of corruption lead to their partial condoning of large-scale corruption: the little lies of Richards lead to his acceptance of the 'big lie' about the town's reputation. The tolerance of petty immorality on the part of the elite paves the way for the acceptance of their own higher immorality by the non-elite (Mills, 1956). This mutual acceptance between different social groups affects the perception of corrupt exchange in the town, where corruption causes the loss of an agreed yardstick whereby its impact can be measured. The involvement in it of non-elite groups contributes to this process, which results in overlooking the quality and quantity of social damage caused by different episodes. Those involved in petty corrupt exchange hesitate to condemn those involved in large-scale corruption, for fear of losing the small benefits their own behaviour brings. The victims of corruption, in this way, miraculously disappear, while the degree of harm caused to each, which is incommensurable, becomes symbolically equal. Edward and Mary Richards die; this is the retribution inflicted on them for having overlooked how participation in corrupt exchange translates, for poor people like them, into victimization.

Mark Twain strips the town of 'the last rag of its ancient glory', and in doing so he also strips American suburban life of its hypocrisy. The mourning of Hadleyburg 'was not showy, but it was deep'.

9

Hugo, Mirbeau and Imprisonment

Prisons are scandalous, but they make people dream. This paradox encapsulates the ways in which imprisonment is dealt with in classic literature, where notions of punishment appear so frequently that their collection in a text would make a wonderful volume, putting dry socio-legal volumes to shame (Brombert, 1975). Prisons are not in nature, but 'man never ceases to pervert his own nature through the tragic pride of condemning his brother' (Hugo, 1969: 1718). The history of society, according to Chekhov (1966), is the history of how we incarcerate our fellow creatures. However, the prison cell is also the space of dream and poetry, of meditation and religious fervour. Calderón de la Barca (1967) has his hero secluded in a castle, where he learns that dreaming surpasses living, while Pirandello's (1922) eponymous Henri IV, after a brief excursion outside, rather than face the ruthlessness of those surrounding him, returns to the reassuring, maddening, tower where he has buried himself.

Students of prison and literature may argue that much of our cultural tradition took shape under conditions of incarceration or involuntary exile. Davies (1990: 3), for example, argues that it is perhaps impossible to understand Western thought 'without recognising the central significance of prison and banishment in its theoretical and literary composition'. Bender (1987: 3), who considers literature as an advanced form of knowledge, anticipating and contributing to institutional formation, suggests that in certain periods fiction enabled the conception and construction of actual penitentiaries. Classic literature, especially in prose form, subjected the old practices of confinement to corrosive critique and in doing so 'set the stage for their rejection and reformulation even when reform of the social function of prisons was not explicitly at issue'.

This chapter avoids formulating general claims. It confines itself, first, to a brief overview of how prisons are presented in some influential literary classics and how authors relate to the debates within the sociology of punishment and the prevailing philosophies of incarceration. Second, the chapter repeats a similar exercise while focusing on two authors, namely Victor Hugo and Octave Mirbeau.

Suffering and ascesis

Benvenuto Cellini, a pupil of Michelangelo, an admired goldsmith and sculptor, is incarcerated in Rome, and in his (fictional?) autobiography there is no concession to theories of rehabilitation or individual deterrence. The guards receive the instruction to just do their 'duty and see that he doesn't escape' (Cellini, [1728] 1956: 189). He is unable to see a connection between his conduct and the punishment imposed upon him; nor does he seem to endorse the consequentialist argument whereby the harm he is suffering is meant to prevent the greater harm he would otherwise produce through his crimes (Duff and Garland, 1994). As soon as he is arrested he begins to plan his escape. A soldier, who never enters his cell without insulting him, inspects the hinges of the door as if Cellini had made up his mind to flee from the outset. The prisoner is reluctant to accept that the guards should be the agents of his re-education, but rather sees in them an arbitrary, unwritten power inflicting a discretional supplement of pain to the pain of imprisonment itself. For example, he does not tolerate their touching his bed, and deems this a vexing, motiveless intrusion performed for the pure pleasure of humiliating him. In his view the guards are not worthy to touch the bed of a man of his sort, to dirty and spoil it. All prison does, in his circumstances, is to ignite his sense of rebellion: 'You filthy cowards! I'll grab one of your swords and give you a whack that you won't forget in a hurry ... I don't mind risking my life, since I'll have yours first' (Cellini, 1956: 201). He asks to be left alone with his suffering and misery, and intimates that no more burdens should be added to the ones he is already bearing, or else he will show them what a desperate man can be driven to.

Imprisonment is experienced as unjustified infliction of pain; the escaping of such pain recurs in Stendhal, as well as in Alexandre Dumas and Victor Hugo, who warns that there are numerous Cellinis in jail, all engaged in refining the incredible art of climbing. The physical destruction of prison buildings is a counterpoint to such incredible art, and is seen as legitimate when symbolizing the collapse of a decrepit social and institutional order. Dumas (1926: 236) describes the Bastille as a dark tomb, which detains not only bodies but also thoughts: 'the explosion of thoughts made the Bastille explode'. Destroying this archetypical prison establishment is an act of faith: Bastille and tyranny are synonyms all over the world. Michelet (1847–53) argues that in revolutionary France there were many other prisons, but that only the Bastille was the symbol of arbitrariness, despotism, 'bureaucratic and ecclesiastic inquisition', and that it was the prison of ideas, the residence of free spirits.

Dostoevsky, who himself served a sentence in a labour camp, lamented that all prisoners smell like pigs, and that they cannot avoid behaving like pigs, performing dirty tricks, in order to feel that they are alive. Experienced as sheer retribution, imprisonment does not generate the impulse, once freedom is regained, to lead a virtuous life, but merely to live a life. From the outset, as Dostoevsky notes, prisoners count the time they have left: this is their preferred occupation. Instinctively, they refuse to regard theirs as a definitive, concrete condition, and prison as part of their existence. They feel as if they are 'visiting' the establishment holding them, and are convinced that, once released, at the age of (say) fifty, they will be the same as when incarcerated at thirty: 'I'll still have time to enjoy myself.' Even those serving a life sentence believe that sooner or later an order from St Petersburg will allow them out; while 'elderly men with white hair keep thinking that, once their sentence is over, then...' (Dostoevsky, 1977: 36).

In distancing themselves from their condition, prisoners can hardly engage in a communicative process inducing their reconciliation with society: they just withdraw from that process in order to retreat into their own self, oblivious to the acts and social interactions which brought them there. In Dostoevsky's *House of the Dead* ([1860–61] 1985), however, prisoners work hard, as if punishment consisted of a form of retaliation for their having escaped, in the free world, from the duties of a productive life. According to a materialistic analysis of the 'house of the dead', it could be argued that prisoners are kept in the labour camp because they constitute a redundant population that is not employable outside (Rusche and Kirchheimer, 1968). On the other hand, as redundant population, convicts are not simply held with the prospect of being eventually received back in the labour market; they are also trained to work under humiliating rules, and simultaneously forced to perform, under those rules, their productive capacity.

Training prisoners to lower their social expectations requires physical and mental pain, but also the participation of prisoners themselves in the punishment inflicted on them. The inmates must be caught in a power relation in which they themselves are actively involved (Foucault, 1977). A two-way current is set up between dominators and dominated, an interaction between the two poles of the disciplinary universe, without which the mechanism of punishment could not function. This situation is well described by Camus (1947) in a crude metaphor: those about to be executed are highly concerned about the proper functioning of the guillotine; accidental faults may necessitate the operation being repeated over and over again. This metaphor also finds literary expression in Kafka's penal colony (1973), where the sentencee looks so beastly resigned that he can be left free to run about on the hills, a simple whistle being sufficient for him to return, on time for the execution.

Prisoners' participation in the infliction of suffering implicitly demonstrates that they are non-persons who bow to any form of humiliation, even to self-destruction (Levi, 1986). Humiliation may be inflicted through the incessant, sinister noise characteristic of some prisons (Cervantes, 1998), or the maddening silence that leads Casanova ([1825] 1973) to the 'illness of solitude'. An unforgettable character in Sue's Les Mystères de Paris brutalizes himself, seemingly for the unconscious necessity of exculpating his guilt. In fact he does it because his physical and mental state performs a message to his torturers: stop vexing me, I have given up my physicality, and thus my rebellion. His humiliation is complete, he is a wreck, a sign of accomplished reconciliation, via the degradation of the self, with law and order (Sue, 1949).

Literary classics, however, oscillate between condemnation of prisons, for their inability to achieve their presumed functions in society, and their appreciation, for their ability to generate positive, spiritual effects on individuals. Dostoevsky, in *Crime and Punishment* ([1866] 1979: 473), after his descriptions of the inhumanity of incarceration, and despite treating crime as tragedy and justice as parody, forces Raskolnikov to kneel down 'in the middle of the square', bow to the earth, and kiss 'that filthy earth with bliss and rapture', because he has sinned against it too. It is not 'the horrors of prison life, not the hard labour, the bad food, the shaven head, or the patched clothes' that torment the murderer, but the difficulties he finds in feeling repentance, that 'burning repentance that would have torn his heart and robbed him of sleep, the repentance, the awful agony of which brings visions of hanging and drowning' (487). Tears and agony would at least make him alive again. Initially unaware, he is soon to become conscious of the fundamental falsity in himself and his beliefs, and a crisis will prepare a new life and his future resurrection. At the beginning his fellow prisoners appear total strangers to him, but after the initial refusal to look around at the 'loathsome and unbearable' environment in which they all live, Raskolnikov starts talking to the other inmates, who even answer in a friendly way, while the New Testament under his pillow renders the cell less unbearable. It is the beginning of a new story, 'the story of the gradual renewal of a man, the story of his gradual regeneration, of his passing from one world into another, of his initiation into a new unknown life' (493).

This notion of incarceration includes a variety of differing notions. On the one hand, while publicly declaring that he is a murderer, Raskolnikov seems to claim his 'right' to be punished. As German idealistic philosophy would posit, with punishment he is honoured as a rational being (Kant, 1953). He is entitled to retribution and his individual responsibility provides the moral basis for legitimate punishment (Norrie, 2000). On the other hand, the idea of regeneration through custody that we find in Dostoevsky is indebted to the notion of Plato's cave, in which men are held in chains and where only a dim light filters, so that prisoners are only able to see shadows of reality, blinded as they are by their spiritual inadequacy. This is part of the mythological image of individuals being imprisoned by their own senses and of their struggle to see the light, an image constantly feeding the Christian imagination and its views on custodial punishment. In his *Pensées* Pascal (1983) offers a particular, sublime rendition of these views, and although – or perhaps because – he abhors prisons and chains, he warns that life itself resembles a ghastly dungeon in which humans err, ignoring the fact that only divine light can rescue them from loss and bewilderment. 'Prison is the metaphor of the world and also of the act of striving for salvation' (Davies, 1990: 27).

Stendhal (1932) remarks that the protagonist of *La Chartreuse de Parme* is reluctant to escape from prison, and when he does he misses his happy solitude. Clelia and Fabrice, in a convent and a cell respectively, discover how they can grow indifferent to the tribulations of life, and that there are intimate regions of the self where spirituality can develop through renunciation. Only the vulgar noise of the guards' laughter, ugly and eerie, distracts prisoners from their spiritual exercise, a noise perhaps inflicted with the deliberate intent of annulling the beneficial effect of incarceration. In Stendhal, all forms of extreme happiness are connatural to shady and quiet environments, including prisons (Brombert, 1975).

Foucault terms such environments 'complete and austere institutions', where the convict can reflect in solitude, and when 'he has profoundly repented and made amends without the least dissimulation, solitude will no longer weigh upon him' (Foucault, 1977: 237). In the cell prisoners are confronted with their own conscience: it is the Philadelphia system of custody established in 1836, where absolute isolation is deemed to enlighten convicts from within. Prisoners, like Pascalian men and women, are handed to themselves, and in the silence of their cells they experience the awakening of moral feelings 'that never entirely perish in anybody'. Prisons, therefore, perform not a vindictive, but rather an educational function; they are not the response of power to crime in the form of a predetermined quantum of suffering, but a mechanism fostering a response from prisoners themselves, who in custody start communicating with that power and end up internalizing it. Prison 'provides an intimate exchange between the convict and the power that is exercised over him' (Foucault, 1977: 237).

Suffering and ascesis are intertwined in classical literature, and supporters of the beneficial effects of imprisonment are as persuasive as radical critics of it. The novels of Victor Hugo and Octave Mirbeau that I will now examine, on the contrary, are unambiguously critical of prison institutions, and their analysis may uncover a rich repertoire of sociological notions of incarceration.

Fear and escape

Hugo's prisoners conjure up humanity in pain: livid faces, flaming eyes, fists stretched out through the bars, pointing to the sky in anguished challenge. The effects of punishment are visible on the bodies and in the frantic gestures of those who suffer it, while prison is a sonorous experience, with its rattling of chains, shrill laughter and screeching voices, a cacophony akin to a witches' Sabbath. Prisoners are not heroes; they are frightened beings, victimized by this cacophony, by invisible devils laughing. Hugo seems to hear the ghastly yell of the thief under the branding iron, a spectacle he says he has witnessed personally, and which determined his vocation to fight legal injustice.

Scenes of garrotting and near-crucifixion had etched themselves on the
brain of the boy of ten, and the frequent manifestations of exemplary
justice that he could not help but witness barely a mile from his home
near the Louvre gave Hugo a distinctly uneasy conscience. (Woollen,
1992: viii)

With Beccaria, whom he mentions in more than one novel, he exposes
judicial murder, the cold vendetta performed without irascibility.

Time is intolerable, because exclusively experienced as present, with
no relation with the past and the future. Prison does not impose itself
as place, but as 'idea', chaining the inmates like a prison. Imprisonment, through time as pure present, becomes internalized, a psychological condition, an obsessive thought exuding from the surrounding
walls. In *Le dernier jour d'un condamné*, Hugo (1992) shows how 'the obsession of prison turns into the prison of obsession', how the cell is a
thought, and how prisoners hold the prison inside rather than being
held by it.

As an exile in Britain, Hugo tried to meddle with British affairs, and
when a murderer was condemned to death in Guernsey he published
an open letter which sparked off a mass protest against the death penalty (Kahn, 2001). He describes the execution 'in a gory, forensic manner
worthy of Edgar Allan Poe', and denigrates the composed hypocrisy of
Lord Palmerston, and for that matter of English mores, for tightening
'his cravat with one hand and the hangman's noose with the other'
(Robb, 1997: 342).

A poetics of escape is elaborated, in which prisoners are equated to
inspired artists striving for freedom, dazzling over the walls. Escaping
is a physical effort, but also symbolizes a spiritual ascent; it is like the
healing of a wound, the recovery from degradation. Hugo's prisoners
turn fear into rage, and – as in Beethoven's *Fidelio* – for them breaking
the fetters is tantamount to emerging from darkness into light.

Rejecting the rejectors

In Les Misérables (Hugo [1862] 1982) we are told that freedom is not fully appreciated until we see a guillotine with our own eyes. The name of this 'ultimate expression of law' is vengeance, and like law it is not neutral, nor does it allow us to remain neutral. It is not merely a framework, a machine, a lifeless mechanism made of wood, iron and rope. It is a being with its own dark purpose; that arrangement of wood, iron and rope expresses a will, namely to solve all social questions by means of a blade.

Hugo's invective against legal suffering, however, is not confined to the death penalty, but embraces all forms of custodial punishment, behind which he sees the perpetuation, and aggravation, of social injustice. When Les Misérables was first published, critics branded it a 'dangerous' novel, perhaps because persistent criminals are described as 'a product of the criminal justice system, a human and therefore monstrous creation', and because in the novel 'the burden of guilt lies with society' (Les Misérables: 382). The story of Jean Valjean is, in this sense, emblematic.

A convict on parole, after nineteen years in prison, Jean is looking for a place to sleep: not even the prison would take him back. When he finally knocks on the bishop's door, he is addressed as 'monsieur', a courtesy which is 'like fresh water to a shipwrecked man'. Ignominy thirsts for respect, says Hugo, even after nineteen years of 'the red smock, the ball and chain, a plank to sleep on, heat, cold and hard labour, the galleys and the lash. The double chain for a trifle, solitary for a single word. Chained even when you are sick in bed' (Les Misérables: 96). Valjean was tried for housebreaking and robbery, and the prison sentence made him 'like a tree sawed down at the root'. Hunger, claims Hugo, is the direct cause of four robberies out of five.

In prison, Jean withdraws into his own conscience and reflects. He reaches the conclusion that he is not the only one at fault, and that the punishment is more ferocious than the offence. In prison he feels that he is the weak victim of a strong assailant:

> Was it not a serious matter that a man willing to work should have been without work and without food?... Had not the scales of justice been over-weighted on the side of expiation? And did not this weighting of the scales, far from effacing the crime, produce a quite different result, namely, a reversal of the situation, substituting for the original crime the crime of oppression, making the criminal a victim and the law his debtor, transferring justice to the side of him who had offended against it? (*Les Misérables*: 97)

In the study conducted by Sykes (1958: 67), now a classic of the sociology of imprisonment, the loss of civil rights is pinpointed as the crucial aspect of custody, along with the loss of that more diffuse status which defines individuals as trustworthy and morally acceptable. Prisoners suffer this loss, and while the walls seal them off as contaminated persons, their self-conception is constantly threatened, as if they were daily reminded that they must be kept apart from 'decent' men and women. This degradation or rejection, Sykes suggests, is somehow warded off, turned aside, rendered harmless by prisoners, who, in order to endure psychologically, must find a device for 'rejecting their rejectors'. Let us see how this device takes shape in *Les Misérables*.

In prison Jean lives as though in darkness, fumbling like a blind man. Only occasionally is he overtaken by a burst of furious rage, rising within him or provoked from without. Rage is the outcome of an overflow of suffering, a swift, searing flame illuminating all his soul and 'shedding its ugly light on everything that lay behind him and ahead' (*Les Misérables*: 99). After these sudden flashes, darkness closes in again, and the 'pitiless', brutalizing punishment to which he is subjected gradually erodes his mind. Prison 'turns a man into an animal, sometimes a ferocious one', and like a caged wolf Jean dashes madly for the door whenever he finds it open. Instinct prompts him to run where reason would have bidden him stay: in the face of that overwhelming impulse, reason vanishes.

> There are prisoners, obsessed with the thought of escape, eternally en-
> vious of the birds and the flies, who make a positive cult of the physical
> sciences, daily performing a mysterious ritual of exercises. The climbing
> of a sheer surface, where scarcely any hand or foothold was to be dis-
> cerned, was to Valjean a pastime. (*Les Misérables*: 100)

Jean speaks seldom and never smiles. When shattered by extreme emotion, perhaps once or twice a year, he emits the 'sour convict-chuckle that is like the laughter of demons'. The sight of him suggests that he is continually absorbed in the contemplation of something terrible. When he looks upward, beyond the pallid light in which he is crouched, he sees, with mingled terror and rage, an endless structure rising above him, 'a dreadful piling-up of things, laws, prejudices, men and facts, whose shape he could not discern and whose mass appalled him, and which was nothing else than the huge pyramid that we call civilisation' (*Les Misérables*: 100).

Jean is an 'outcast of the law', and feels upon his neck the whole weight of society. He finds his condition inconceivable, the world around him grotesque. He says to himself, this is a dream, and stares at the warder standing a few feet away as though he were seeing a ghost – until suddenly the ghost deals him a blow. As prison shapes him, he becomes capable of two kinds of ill deeds: 'first the heedless, un-premeditated act executed in a blind fury, as some sort of a reprisal for the wrongs he had suffered; and second, the deliberate and considered crime, justified in his mind by the thoughts inspired by those wrongs'. Thus, Jean starts 'rejecting his rejectors'; his impulses are governed by resentment, bitterness and a profound sense of injury. These translate into hatred for society as a whole, rage against all humans, all created things, into 'a savage and obsessive desire to inflict harm on no matter what or whom' (*Les Misérables*: 101).

Prisons as incubators of crime

Victor Hugo denounced the way the system grinds the poor between the millstones of need and excess – need of work and excess of punishment – finding it monstrous that society should treat in this fashion precisely those least favoured in the distribution of wealth. Similarly, Jean passes judgement on society, and condemns it to his hatred. Hatred is his only weapon, and he resolves to sharpen it in prison and carry it with him when he leaves.

The description of the chain gang conjures up an implicit justification of this hatred. There is a sound like the rattle of chains, and as the procession draws nearer, with sounds and outlines growing more distinct, something approaches as if in a dream. As the details become clearer, darkly silhouetted heads appear, bathed in the pallid glow of the rising sun, resembling the heads of corpses. Each convict has his own collar, but the chain is shared by all of them, so that they have to move in concert 'like a body with a single backbone, a sort of centipede'. The procession is escorted on both side by a line of troops of infamous aspect, with 'dirty and bedraggled pensioners' tunics, tattered trousers, something between grey and blue', armed with axes, muskets and clubs. 'Mercenary soldiers bearing themselves with the abjectness of beggars and the truculence of prison-guards.' A crowd of spectators springs up in an instant, and gathers on either side of the road to stand and stare. Men call their mates to come and look, and the clatter of clogs is heard, all rushing to see that 'variegated picture of misery, a harlequinade in tatters', those men with tattoos, sores and blotches of disease, their eyes expressionless, apathetic or gleaming with an evil light, some darting venomous looks to the jeering children.

The chain gang displays every aspect of misery, 'every animal face'. All convicts bear the stamp of ignominy, that dreadful leveller. 'Dante might have seen in them the seven circles of Hell on the move' (Les Misérables: 785). Urchins swarm around the procession like flies around an open wound.

Hugo does not limit his condemnation to the officially stated functions of imprisonment, such as rehabilitation and re-education; he argues that prisons are dysfunctional modes of dealing with social problems, truculent ways of encouraging criminal careers. Like penal reductionists or abolitionists, he expresses this view in a section of Les Misérables tellingly titled 'The hatching of crimes in the incubator of prison' (Les Misérables: 743). Here he remarks that 'criminals do not cease their activities because they have fallen into the hands of the law; they are not to be deterred by trifles.' In prison many learn new skills, sharpen their ability to avoid apprehension, and plan their future exploits. Prisoners are like artists who hang their latest painting on the wall while keeping busy in the studio, working at new paintings. In the last page of the novel, Hugo appears to endorse a conflictual notion of prison, and for that matter of crime, when he suggests that delinquency and custodial punishment are the reflection of social differences and interests, of the 'sombre confrontation of egoists and outcasts' (1232). On the one hand we have the egoists, with their prejudices, their rich education, their appetite that grows with intoxication, their complacency and prosperity which blunt their feelings, their fear of suffering which translates into hatred for all sufferers. On the other hand we have the outcasts, with their resentment, fatalism, their hearts filled with misery and needs, 'the turmoil of the human animal in search of personal fulfilment'.

Hugo describes the two prison systems and philosophies prevalent in his years as strikingly antithetical: cellular incarceration and communal detention. In the first system, prisoners are thrown together at random: children of seventeen with old men of seventy, the youngster who stole apples with the highway killer. 'And here, in filthy, dirty workshops, they work side by side in semi-darkness at stale and sordid tasks, deprived of air and daylight, wordless, sightless, mindless, like hideous, dull spectres of whom the ones are terrifyingly old, and the others terrifyingly young'. In the second system, he sees a 'hive of monastic activity': each worker in a cell and each 'soul in its own compartment'. In this 'town of multiple retreats' prisoners 'have work, study, tools, books, eight hours' sleep, one hour's rest, and one hour's recreation in a small, walled courtyard, prayers morning and evening, and their thoughts at all times' (Hugo, 1992: 163). Although he terms this system praiseworthy when compared with the system of communal detention, Hugo exposes all systems of incarceration and punishment as fundamentally unjust.

Pages of murder and blood

Octave Mirbeau is guided by a similar desire to expose prison systems as barbaric and dysfunctional. He wrote at a time when the transportation of offenders to Algeria, Guyana and New Caledonia proceeded simultaneously with the establishment of a new republican prison system in the urban areas of France (Petit, 1984; Petit et al., 1991; Perrot, 1980; 2001). He dedicates his *Torture Garden* ([1898] 1995), those pages of murder and blood, to 'the priests, the soldiers, the judges, to those people who educate, instruct and govern men'. Like Anatole France, the author abandons his conservative heritage to embrace a fierce radicalism: he becomes a devout anarchist (Stableford, 1995). His purpose is to expose the hypocrisies of the establishment and society at large by showing how many of the institutions and practices which are commonly taken for granted, and even regarded as pillars of civilization, are in fact cruel and repelling. In other novels Mirbeau draws on his own experience of the Franco-Prussian war to describe the ferocious stupidity of soldiers and national states supporting them. *Torture Garden* is homiletic in tone, though the division of the novel into two sections allows for a differentiation of styles, whereby satire is followed by disturbing, allegorical denouncement. Similarities with the work of the Marquis de Sade are reduced to detailed descriptions of sophisticated methods of inflicting pain, and to the use of 'butchery of human flesh' as a way of approaching issues around human morality. If there is no God, as Sade implies, it does not necessarily follow that moral boundaries are drawn by individual choice and arbitrary aesthetic preference, but rather that the morality determining the death of God should be exposed and a new, alternative one tentatively prefigured. Mirbeau strips away all the lies hiding the real nature of punishment, and the perversity of 'civilized' institutions: 'Where Sade had set out slyly to create moral unease, Mirbeau set out forthrightly to call forth moral outrage' (Stableford, 1995: 13).

Indigestible though the novel may be, the incipit contains sarcastic conversations and ironic allusions that are as crude in their content as unbearably light in their formulation. At a gathering of 'famous authors', after bountiful feasting, what can be discussed if not murder? A pompous Darwinian classifies murder among the very foundations of social institutions, the most imperious necessity of civilized life, something to cultivate with intelligence and perseverance: 'And I don't know a better means of cultivation than laws' (*Torture Garden*: 19). Our innate need for murder may be curbed, and violence may be attenuated by giving it a legal outlet, for example through colonial trade, hunting, racism, war, because it would be dangerous to abandon oneself to violence immoderately, outside the law. So goes the conversation of cultivated minds and refined natures, who list among their favourite pleasures 'fencing, duelling, violent sports, abominable pigeon shooting, bullfights, varied manifestations of patriotism, hunting' (24). One of them, after calling for fresh cigars and drinks, tells the story of a period of his life that for a long time he has been reluctant to make public.

Politicians and traders

The journey of the narrator to the torture garden in China could not have originated from a more apposite source. His friend and mentor, a corrupt politician who is temporarily unable to offer him a position, suggests going abroad, which would take him away from the political scene for a while and prepare the grounds for his return in a changed political situation. The journey, therefore, is a pretext, officially aimed at studying foreign penal systems and assessing if they might be applied at home. The politician is the epitome of 'our current age', where 'ostentatious dishonesty assumes the place of finer qualities', and 'the more infamous a man is, the more disposed we are to credit him with intellectual force and moral value' (Torture Garden: 39). 'I've stolen, I've stolen', he proclaims in the streets and on public squares, and similar proud claims he publishes in his political manifestoes, election posters and confidential circulars.

The narrator describes his father as a rough, vulgar dealer of grain, a man with a sharp business sense and a reputation for deviousness which consists of 'getting people where you want them'. His principles are to mislead people about the quality and weight of his merchandise, charge two francs for what cost him two sous and, whenever possible (if it does not entail too much of a row), make them pay twice over for the same thing. The moral atmosphere in which the protagonist is brought up is exemplified by arguments of the following nature: 'If you take something from someone and keep it for yourself, that's theft. But if you take something from someone and pass it on to someone else for as much as you can get, that's business.' After such an upbringing, our hero mixes with politicians, that 'pack of starving carnivores', who take a sensual delight 'in the stench of human decay' (*Torture Garden*: 49).

The companion he meets on his journey, Clara, is the daughter of an opium trader who lives in China, where she convinces the protagonist to join her. While on board ship, murder recurs as a central point of conversation. The use of infallible arms is advocated, so that, in war, incalculable savings could be made by abolishing surgeons, nurses, ambulances and military hospitals.

Meat for the prisoners

Clara loves going to feed the convicts, an odd, amusing pastime, and the only original, elegant distraction for the inhabitants of that lost corner of China.

> When I see the convicts, I go all dizzy and my whole body quivers in the same way as it does in love. It seems to me, you see ... it seems to me that I am descending into the depths of my flesh, right to the dark depths of my flesh. (*Torture Garden*: 106)

All that is needed for this elegant distraction is a meat basket woven by the best Chinese artisan, and a pitchfork with teeth of platinum encrusted with gold and a handle of green jade. Every Wednesday, amid a considerable crowd of elegant people, the Convict-Meat-Market is held. Vendors shout: 'Here! Here! Come on by! Look and choose! You'll not find anything better anywhere.... No one has anything more rotten!' (112). Clara inhales decay with delight, as though it was perfume. 'But it's not a bad smell, my love. It smells of death, that's all' (114).

The crowd at the prison entrance is restless, and no sooner has the door opened than tumult starts: Clara throws herself in the 'melee of chattering, cries, sounds of suffocation, rustling of fabrics and clatter of parasols and fans' (122). And behind those doors, the clamour of the crowd is covered by the cries, the 'muffled wailing, the clanking of chains, the panting of breaths, like bellows, the strange and prolonged groaning of beasts' (124). The prisoners have their necks gripped in iron collars, and are squatting in their own filth; hands and feet in chains, they can neither lie down nor rest. 'The slightest movement displaced the iron collar, causing shooting-pains in their throats and their bleeding necks, and causing them to shriek in such suffering and to utter violent insults against us mingled with supplications to the Gods' (125).

Delicately, accompanying her shivers with exquisite gestures, Clara rummages in the basket with her fork, then lifts out some scraps of meat that she graciously flings through the bars into the cage. Ten heads begin swinging simultaneously, and twenty bulging eyeballs cast flushed looks on the meat – looks of terror and hunger. The prisoners cannot eat, explains Clara, because they cannot reach the meat, theirs is the torture of Tantalus. People passing by the cages laugh and 'abandon themselves to impassioned mimicry'. A blonde woman with a blank, cold look, holds a revolting greenish fragment of meat with the end of her parasol, which she alternatively offers and withdraws. The convicts draw back their lips, baring their teeth like mad dogs, with famished expressions, no longer human, and try to snatch the food which always evades their mouths, 'sticky as they were with dribble'.

Prisons are not for prisoners

But what crimes have these prisoners committed to deserve such torment? No idea, is the reply. Perhaps none at all, or probably something trivial. 'Petty theft, I expect. They are vagrants from the harbour, vagabonds, paupers' (*Torture Garden*: 126). At first sight, crime and punishment seem to have lost any relationship here: the latter not only finds no justification in terms of its 'beneficial' effects, but also shows no commensurability in respect of the type of crime it addresses. Punishment is both non-consequentialist and a way of disposing of the social residue, the unemployable vagrants and paupers. There is, however, something more in the torture garden, namely a Durkheimian sense that prisoners are tormented for the sake of spectators, who are assumed to be law-abiding individuals, and that through the spectacle of suffering they reinforce their feelings of solidarity and set of values. Prisons, therefore, are not addressed to offenders, but are a means for boosting the common moral order, the *conscience collective* (Garland, 1990).

It could be argued that prison appears to be the legal form of sadistic pleasure in inflicting pain. However, even pain as torture, paradoxically, can hide a principle of 'proportionality'. As Nietzsche (1956) suggests, sadism can be translated into the notion of 'legalized equivalence', whereby offenders, as creditors, give away a deposit or a pawn, something which belongs to them – for instance, their freedom, their body, their very life. In ancient societies, creditors could cut limbs and bits of flesh as appropriate and equivalent with the entity of the debt. 'And soon precise evaluations were provided, legitimately established, as to the exchange value of limbs and parts of the body.'

In the final pages of *Torture Garden* sadism mingles with Durkheimian principles of punishment as reinforcement of the *conscience collective*. It is interesting to examine what values Mirbeau ascribes to such conscience.

Torture is mingled with horticulture and blood with flowers. In the torture garden the extraordinary vigour of the vegetation is activated by the prisoners' excrement, by the blood of the tortured and by all the organic debris left each week by the crowd: the beauty of wealth is built on this powerful compost, of which plants are voracious. Nature is made complicit with the refinements of cruelty. All this cruelty, however, is part of civilization, and is akin to the devastation caused by civilizing 'cultures'. Mirbeau, while describing torture, recalls the streets of Calcutta, the fresh Himalayan villas of Darjeeling, and the magnificent mansions of Bombay, which give the impression of mourning and death left 'by the atrocity of clumsy massacre, vandalism and senseless destruction'. Wherever it appears, he concludes, 'civilisation shows this face of sterile blood and forever dead ruins':

> Wherever there is spilt blood to justify, acts of piracy to be consecrated, violations to bless, hideous trade to protect, you're sure to see him, that British Tartuffe, pursuing the work of abominable conquest on the pretext of religious proselytism or scientific study. His cunning and ferocious shadow hangs over the desolation of conquered peoples, tied up with that of the cut-throat soldier and vindictive Shylock. In virgin forests, where the European rightly inspires more dread than the tiger, on the threshold of humble straw-huts that have been devastated, between the burnt-out shacks, he appears after the massacre, like a scavenger, to plunder the dead the evening after the battle. (*Torture Garden*: 141–3)

Catholic missionaries, in their turn, are said to bring civilization 'on the end of torches and at the point of sabres and bayonets'. In brief, the torture garden contains the passions, appetites, personal interests, hatred and lies, along with the laws and social institutions which shape justice, glory, heroism and religion. A final vision hits the protagonist at the climax of his considerations: he sees the face of his friend, the corrupt politician, grimacing over the shoulder of the fat executioner.

Fiction offers invaluable materials for sociological analyses of imprisonment. Classic novels alternate exposure of prison systems as destructive and unjust with some appreciation of the introspection and regeneration that the prison cell may induce. This chapter has focused on two authors who put 'prison on trial' and find it indefensible (Mathiesen, 1990). For Victor Hugo, poverty, social disadvantage and scandalous inequity are the main sources of crime, and prisons reproduce injustice while causing the reproduction of crime. His arguments echo conflict-theory texts on crime and punishment, as well as reformist, reductionist and abolitionist analyses. Mirbeau's arguments, instead, present us with a repertoire of notions that we are used to associating with Durkheim and Nietzsche, namely that punishment reassures and regenerates the righteousness of the law-abiding community, whilst also meting out in legally sanitized fashion our desire to inflict pain.

In my final chapter, pain is located more generally in criminal justice processes, and in broader mechanisms generating legal suffering.

Manzoni and Legal Suffering

If institutional punishment, as Nietzsche (1956) proclaimed, is a vulgar substitute for irascibility, vulgarity is also required for the perception or shaping of events and acts as deserving such punishment. Among such events, plague epidemics have long provided the scene for irascibility and vulgarity to deploy their devastating power.

The belief that cholera and plague have been deliberately spread among the population is ancient. The Roman historian Livius records this belief, noting that in the year 428, under the reign of Claudius Marcellus and Caius Velerius, in times that he terms 'coarse', the propagation of plague was attributed to an unlikely conspiracy of malicious matrons. Later, however, plague became the manifestation of God's ire or the result of the movement of celestial bodies. When a fierce plague epidemic hit Milan in 1630, a fall back into 'vulgarity and obscurity' is not enough to explain the violent return of conspiracy theories. In this respect, Sciascia formulates a captivating hypothesis: this credence in plague propagators re-emerged as ideological retaliation against the new concept of *raison d'état*, when the separation between the political and the moral spheres was tentatively being established and 'codified', and when residues of the old social and institutional order bounced back in revenge (Sciascia, 1985: iv).

Large epidemics were also to be interpreted as Malthusian provisions, and even the ravaging Spanish flu that killed thousands after the First World War was regarded as a necessary extension of the war, which presumably had not been completely effective in eliminating the excessive population (Sciascia, 1985: v). The plague that decimated the population of Milan in 1630, however, was not merely attributed to Malthusian governmental calculations. Bad governments, when faced with situations they cannot tackle or are unable to resolve, may always identify external enemies to blame; therefore the public opinion of Milan might well have been directed against France, which was then inimical to Spain, of whose dominions Milan was a part. But in the event, blame for the outbreak was laid not on some political conspiracy (either internal or external), but on a conventional delinquent conspiracy: it was said to be orchestrated by a group of 'plague-spreaders' aiming at provoking social disorder, robbery and looting.

Alessandro Manzoni's *Storia della colonna infame* ([1842] 1964) is a historical novel based on judicial documentation of the Milan outbreak, interspersed with fictional elements and meditations on the criminal justice system – condemned by the author, who staunchly advocated reform. The central focus of this condemnation is the practice of torture, a practice without which the delinquent conspiracy carried out by plague-spreaders could never be realistically 'proven'. Manzoni's meditation focuses on the iniquities of procedures, the heartlessness of investigators and judges, and finally on the hasty vindictiveness of the public. He seeks individual responsibilities, and appears to be surprised that similar 'miscarriages of justice' might have been provoked by 'honest and intelligent' prosecutors. As Sciascia (1985: vi) comments, he is unaware that torturers are very often good family men, sentimental human beings, music lovers, and respectful of animals: they are mere bureaucrats of evil.

Much of the documentary material used by Manzoni derives from the classic *Osservazioni sulla tortura* written by Pietro Verri in 1777, which concluded the intense reformist cycle in the arena of penal justice set off by Cesare Beccaria in 1764. But while Pietro Verri is a man of the Enlightenment, and condemns the obscurity of the times and the judicial apparatus as a whole, Manzoni, a Catholic, investigates personal inadequacies and failures, neglecting the institutional make-up generating them. After presenting the story of the *colonna infame* I will examine some aspects of the controversy between the two authors, who, speaking in two different centuries, perhaps did not anticipate that their arguments would also bring an echo in centuries to come.

The column of infamy

At 4:30 in the morning of 21 July 1630, a woman called Caterina Rosa, while looking out of the window, saw a man in a black cloak, a hat hiding his eyes, with a piece of paper in his hand that he touched as if he were writing. She noticed that the man grazed the wall and touched it while walking. Another spectator to the scene, Ottavia Bono, saw the man halting at a nearby garden; she also noticed a piece of paper on which the man rubbed his hand as if he wanted to write, then she saw him raise his hand and stroke the wall. He was probably only trying to clean his hands, because it seems that he was actually writing. As for grazing the wall, one could suggest that that morning it was raining. But the two women thought their sleepless night had been compensated by an unexpected find, and their civic awareness made them disclose that find to as many neighbours as they could approach. The rumour spread fast, and it was found that the man was Guglielmo Piazza, a health officer. Soon the belief took shape that deadly smearing had been applied to walls and doors of houses that morning, and, after rumours turned into 'deplorable certainty', this belief was transmitted from the people straight to the magistrates.

This is the incipit of Manzoni's historical novel, which centres on how unscrupulous judges failed to ascertain truth rationally, and condemned the defendants to atrocious suffering, deeming them guilty of propagating plague with 'silly as well as horrible substances'. These judges felt that they also had to give their sentence a memorable appendix, and after decreeing a supplement of torture for one of them, instructed that his house be demolished, 'and in its place a column be erected, to be called the column of infamy, and on this pillar an inscription written where all posterity might read of the crime which they had prevented and the punishment they had imposed' (Storia: 103).

It was customary, almost universal, that 'lies' told by suspects when interrogated − or, rather, that the feeling on the part of judges that lies were being told − would trigger torture. In other words, legitimate evidence of the necessity of such practice arose from the personal conviction of those interrogating suspects. Torture, for example, could start its course when suspects appeared to tell implausible stories, and the use of violent means against them was deemed instrumental in conferring some plausibility to their stories. It was implausible, for example, that Guglielmo Piazza ignored the circumstances in which the walls of that town area had been spread with poisonous ointment, and his ignorance of those circumstances could only be won with some energetic reminder that false testimony was a sin.

Alessandro Manzoni argues that Piazza's lies had to be proven through a proper legal procedure, not inferred through personal conjecture. His criticism of the legal modus operandi appears to target individual prosecutors who are unable to apply procedural norms fairly. His argument takes inspiration from the Roman Law, according to which, in effect, torture was not to be the investigative tool with which the judicial process was to start. Torture was to be inflicted only when evidence had reached the 'clarity of midday', because such violent practice determined the fate of human lives: *agitur de hominis salute*. Manzoni also draws on Beccaria, who regarded torture as the legal remains of an old conquering people, and warns that such barbaric practice reconciles certainty with doubt, making innocent people guilty and inducing them to confess predetermined things.

Like judges of the Holy Inquisition, prosecutors did not search for truth; they only wanted a confession. Think of Verdi's *Don Carlo*, where the people celebrate their king, while the monks lead the culprits to the Holy Office, glad that 'the day has come, the day of terror, the tremendous day, the feral day, They'll die, they'll die, the rigour of the Immortal is just. But the supreme voice of pardon will succeed over anathema if the sinners will repent' (Méry and Du Locle, 1978: 44). The plague-spreaders were more unlucky than the heretics condemned by Don Carlo, for although repenting they were not pardoned.

The judges wanted Piazza to admit to being a liar once, so that they would gain the right not to believe him when he claimed he was innocent. Unlikely and implausible things were added one to another, in order to depict a man inured to lying. Each session of torture led to the same result, with Piazza saying he had told the truth. Therefore, judges felt obliged to decree that 'the suspect be submitted to *tortura grave*, this time tied by the rope – a very cruel addition, since it meant that now his hands, as well as arms, would be dislocated' (*Storia*: 130).

The Milan judges acted under the pressure of public anger, or so Manzoni implies, and the two women accusing Piazza became the guides of their action. Blame is, here, laid upon popular superstition and its impact on institutional representatives. The judges became the victims of rudderless passion, and 'where passion calls the tune, it is only natural that the blind should be leaders' (Storia: 140).

Piazza's head was shaved, and he was dressed in penitent's attire and purged. As Verri (1988) explains, it was believed that in the hair, in clothing or even in the intestines of suspects there might be an amulet or some marks of a pact they had established with the Devil; therefore they were shaved, undressed and purged with the purpose of setting them free. The use of penitential garments, however, ominously reminded Piazza of his sacrificial status.

The second type of torture then started. Piazza was promised impunity in exchange for the complete truth, a promise intended to make him say that which the judges − and, for that matter, part of public − wanted. Manzoni's indignation here is addressed to the prosecutors, who used the legislation too discretionally, as promises of impunity could only be pronounced by the general governor of Milan. Deliberately failing to inform the general governor, judges promised impunity verbally, so that no official document was ever issued. Piazza, in brief, was required to accuse some of his accomplices in a deed he did not commit. His hopes of escaping a horrific death lay in the prospect of causing the death of another innocent. He did not believe that those judges would abandon one prey without getting hold of another. They could not conclude their performance without a conviction. He thought that he had to find a type of circumstance as weak as the one which made him a suspect. The only person he could think of was Giangiacomo Mora, a barber who prepared and sold an unguent against plague. He claimed that the poison had been given to him by Mora, who had told him to spread it on the walls and then come back for 'his payment'.

In the barber's shop some human excrement was found, which, it was assumed, was mixed with the unguent manufactured by Mora to make it more lethal. It was believed that, to be effective, the excrement had to be from people who had contracted plague.

After collaborating, Piazza soon became aware that his position would worsen. Having confessed to his guilt he had implicitly provided evidence of his unreliability; therefore his confession regarding accomplices had to find solemn confirmation in a new session of torture. And while the veracity of Mora's claims were 'ascertained', he was also told that what he was saying was 'implausible', a terrible adjective signifying forthcoming torture. He ended up confessing that he intended to spread the plague in order to provide his terrified customers with an antidote, the unguent he was actually preparing.

> By the terms of the hellish sentence passed on them, Piazza and Mora were to be taken in a cart to the place of execution, being torn with red-hot pincers on the way; their right hand cut off in front of Mora's shop; their bones broken on the wheel; and, while they were still alive their bodies twisted into the wheel and lifted from the ground; and after six hours, their throats to be cut, their corpses burned and the ashes thrown into the river. Mora's house was to be demolished and in the place where it had stood a column erected ... with the prohibition of ever building in that place again. (Storia: 188)

The two men thought that they were dying because of the cruelty, ignorance and pettiness of judges, who found the prospect of not finding a culprit a calamity. However, they accepted death as a penalty for other sins they had committed. Before dying, they had accused a third man as the mastermind of the whole enterprise, Signor Padilla, the son of a castle owner and a soldier, whose lifestyle and status obviously disqualified him as a conspirator.

Fury against innocence

Manzoni's legal argument takes shape through an excursus on torture in which historians and philosophers are called upon as testimonies to the ambiguity of such investigative practice and its statutory regulation. The statutes of Milan, for example, did not indicate norms or conditions governing the use of torture, though the faculty of using violence during interrogation was implicitly admitted, and regarded as connatural to the right to judge. The use of torture was recommended for particularly deadly offences and in the presence of some 'moderate evidence' of culpability. Roman Law, on the other hand, warned that under no circumstance could torture be inflicted at the beginning of the investigative process, but only after a verisimilar accusatory argument had been built and sufficient evidence gathered. Torture had to be the final procedural device leading to truth, when truth was already, if partially, revealing its contours. Manzoni questions the type of truth the Milan judges were pursuing, rather than their legitimacy in pursuing it through torture. His is an invective against ignorance and superstition, in which he reminds readers that, before plague and cholera, other allegedly inexplicable events were also attributed to the deliberate acts of evil conspirators. Bushfires in Normandy, for example, were believed to be the product of ruthless arsonists taking pleasure in flames and destruction. Men found at the scene of a fire would be immediately taken and, frightened by a crowd eager to find culprits, would perhaps plead their guilt while accusing someone else of hiring them for the deed. These unfortunate men, Manzoni says, would be executed on the spot by a multitude as ignorant as they were thirsty of summary judgement. Incidentally, there must be some atavistic need to ascribe fires to deliberate destructive desires, if a few centuries on, the 'incendiary other' is still deemed responsible for firestorms and arsons, blazes of mysterious origin whose purpose is the creation of social disorder (Davis, 1998).

Manzoni had no lack of intellectual sources for an uncompromising condemnation of torture and the system allowing it. As a Catholic, he could have drawn on Montaigne, who 'cruelly hated cruelty', both by nature and judgement, as the worst of all vices. 'I hardly pity the dead, I rather envy them; but I feel great pity for the dying.' In an argument coalescing rationality and faith, Montaigne argued that 'We ought to take care that souls be sent to heaven in a state of grace; which cannot be, if they have been shaken and driven to despair by insufferable tortures' (Montaigne, 1958: 184). He also praised the Egyptians, who thought that their divine justice would be sufficiently satisfied if effigies rather than human beings were sacrificed.

> I live in an epoch when, owing to the licence of our civil wars, we abound in incredible examples of this vice: there is nothing to be found in ancient histories more extreme than what we witness every day. But this has by no means reconciled me to it. I could hardly persuade myself, before I had actual evidence, that there exist any souls so unnatural as to commit murder for the mere pleasure of doing so; as to hack and chop off men's limbs, as to sharpen their wits for the invention of unusual tortures and new forms of death; and all this without enmity or gain, but merely for the enjoyment of the pleasing spectacle afforded by the pitiful gestures and motions, the lamentable groans and cries, of a man dying in anguish. This is the extreme limit to which cruelty can attain, 'that one man should kill another, not in anger or in fear, but solely to enjoy the sight' (Seneca). (Montaigne, 1958: 186)

These aspects of torture are not considered by Manzoni, whose indictment of the judges is limited to their using casual discretion in considering the quality and validity of evidence. Manzoni's indictment centres on this casual attitude, which is coupled with the arbitrary departure from traditional ways of inflicting pain and the invention of new techniques of legal suffering. While innovative practices are seen by Manzoni as illegitimate, they are described by Verri (1988) as the result of professional pleasure (*propter delectationem*), the outcome of institutional perversion hidden behind the light of virtue. Institutional perversion finds its suitable agents in individuals who take pleasure in gashing human flesh, apparently for extracting a confession, but actually for the intimate desire to butcher members of their species.

Manzoni, however, seems to agree with those critical historians who regarded judges responsible for the death of defendants as murderers, because such judges kill not in order to set an example or to seek judicial compensation, but merely to gain glory (*propter gloriam erorum*). These judges he sees as executioners who vaingloriously pursue their career while imposing torments on others. Voluptuous pleasure and the quest for glory, subjugating imprisoned men while tormenting them: these all belong to the realm of 'passion', which Manzoni believed should play no role in the criminal justice process. But passion is, unfortunately, able and brave in finding new routes, in order to avoid that of law, which is long and uncertain. The judges started with the torture of affliction; they then moved on to a different type of torture, around a promised impunity, and this convinced Piazza to accuse falsely, and associate others as innocent as he in his atrocious fate.

Although judges proved to be both representatives and accomplices of the multitude, namely of people who were blinded by ignorance, malignity and fury, they could still claim a degree of neutrality by adhering to the precepts of divine law, of which they officially described themselves as faithful adepts. But in Milan judges were going against their own rules, and they knew what they were doing: they resorted to that ignorance that men assume and discard at will. They became responsible for personal and voluntary injustice, rationally determined agents of a gigantic miscarriage of justice. It was a cruel fight, and a horrific victory of error against truth, of powerful fury against disarmed innocence.

Blank norms

The contemporary debate on miscarriages of justice hinges around some recurrent problems. Attention is drawn to how evidence is concocted or falsified by investigators, how facts are concealed and events are not disclosed to the defence. 'These faults have implications for the rules on confessions and the controls on police investigations, and for the ethical orientation of the police, prosecution lawyers, and the Forensic Science Service' (Ashworth, 1994: 13). However, the derogation from ethical rules rests on professional rationalizations attributing to rule-makers an inability to understand practical problems, while claiming freedom of operation as the only prerequisite for effectiveness. Finally, 'when cases are dropped or a court gives a lenient sentence, this is bad for morale' (Ashworth, 1994: 82) – a statement that sounds like a commitment to future, more radical, derogation from rules.

Manzoni claims that the Milan judges who condemned the alleged plague-spreaders to unspeakable fury were honest and intelligent, though they were blinded by their passion. Sciascia retorts that the two qualities could not coexist, because it is possible that they were honest but imbecile, or that they were dishonest while being intelligent. The problem is that those judges thought they were acting under a public mandate and a general, abstract, injunction to allocate responsibility for a serious situation of public disorder. Their 'miscarriage of justice' took embryonic shape in the general social climate surrounding them as well as in the vagueness of the legislation they were required to apply. They were faced with ambiguous rules and jurisprudence, with contradictory precedents and controversial legal exegesis, and finally with contrasting ethical expectations by their own professional enclave and society at large. Moreover, their arbitrariness was akin to that one finds in many contemporary organizations, where unwritten forms of power and incentives are granted in order for members of that organization to strengthen their loyalty. Their incentive to continue in their job included the possibility of taking pleasure while inflicting pain.

Like agents of criminal justice systems today, they were faced with law as an 'artificial horizon', its symbolic value, and its capacity to shape and allocate labelling resources (Ferrajoli, 1989; Ceretti, 1992). The Milan judges experienced a situation that judges may well experience in most contemporary societies, in the sense that the law, whether addressed to plague-spreaders or to other conspirators, possesses a specific *disregard*, which is apparent in its inability to recognize its own violence when responding to others' alleged violence (Girard, 1980; 1987). This self-deception manifests itself in the exclusion, separation and social exile of some members of society: all expressions of the sacrificial practices prevailing in modern societies. The ambivalence of the Roman Law in respect of torture is akin to that of contemporary legal procedure causing damage while attempting to respond to damage. This ambivalence can be associated with the ambivalence of violence itself (Resta, 1992), in the sense that violence destroys and renovates, condemns and saves, kills and cures at the same time. This combination is conveyed by the Greek term *pharmakon*, which designates a poison and an antidote simultaneously, a *drug* which causes illness and cures at the same time. Poor Mora, the barber who became a sacrificial victim of this ambivalence, was himself an ambivalent figure, because whereas he was trying to market an antidote against plague, which arguably was going to be ineffective, he was accused of producing, at the same time, the lethal unguent that propagated plague.

This ambivalence, however, is compounded by something else accompanying particularly harsh laws responding to particularly problematic emergencies. When such emergencies arise, the law becomes replete with blank disposals, with measures *à la carte*, namely with harsher

additions to the high severity statutorily established. These are part of
the unwritten measures that shape the uncodified dimension of the law,
that is to say disposals which cannot be translated into statutory law
but constitute an unspoken section of it. Between law and practice, in
other words, something is lost in translation (Dimock, 1996). This is
particularly the case when severe legislative provisions are available,
because they are interpreted as a mandate to augment at will the harsh-
ness they already incorporate.

Manzoni, unlike Verri, seems unaware of this dynamic; he fights
miscarriages of justice, while the latter fights 'justice'. Verri is involved
in a battle that shows no sign of abating, because torture is still with
us, irrespective of passion or controversial jurisprudence.

Theological hatred

A neglected classic of Italian literature, *Storia della colonna infame* contains
a problematic nucleus which re-emerges in contemporary legal debate
each time social or political emergencies provide justification for harsher
legislation. Issues such as the reversal of the burden of proof, the promise
of impunity, the use of supergrasses, the ideological nature of offences,
culpability by personal contiguity or by cultural affinity: all of these
issues are still the object of heated debate when criminal justice systems
attempt to respond to forms of organized political violence or of organized crime deemed particularly alarming.

In most contemporary systems, despite the formal prohibition from
being a witness against oneself, confession is still a factor mitigating
punishment, and 'the refusal to confess will on the contrary aggravate
the sanction, and – perhaps even worse – prevent reintegration into the
community' (Brooks, 2000: 2). Confession is charged with moral
overtones signifying contrition, recognition of wrongdoing, and

acceptance of amendment. While relieving prosecutors from establishing the dynamics, motives and personal responsibility for acts, confession constitutes a verbal act of reintegration, and when accompanied by denunciation of accomplices it signals participation in, rather than refusal of, the investigative process. This participation marks the defendant's desire to prepare a basis for rehabilitation, to end ostracism, and ultimately to regain a place in the human community. Those who refuse confession display obduracy and callousness, revealing resistance to atonement and defiance of judges, 'whereas confession allows those judges to pass their sentences in security, knowing that the guilty party not only deserves and accepts but perhaps in some sense wants punishment, as the penance that follows confession' (Brooks, 2000).

As Manzoni says, prosecutors may invent the crime and then find the culprit; therefore interrogations must be conducted with a high degree of certainty of guilt. Confession releases defendants from interrogation and judges from moral uncertainty. The Fourth Lateran Council of 1215 developed the doctrine that confession to heresy was necessary to save the heretic's soul and preserve the purity of the Church:

> one had to stand condemned by one's own word – even if that word had to be extracted by the rack and the pinion and other ghastly techniques of torture.... If partial proofs – indicia – were abundant enough, this justified proceeding to seek full proof by way of torture, in order to produce a confession. (Brooks, 2000: 15)

The 'ignominy and horror' felt by Verri, however, are not restricted to that infamous Lateran Council, but extend to those human agents and institutional apparatuses granting philosophical continuity to its doctrine and precepts. He observes with horror those refined historians exposing their views on the acceptability of torture, or presenting those repugnant lists of torments, and describes as beastly those judges inventing new techniques, supplementing with their own ferocity that ferocious list. 'Obscure and private', those men constructed a system and developed a science aimed at tormenting other men, 'with the same tranquility that is used to remedy the ills of the human body'; and they were obeyed and highly regarded as legislators. Their theoretical treatises were welcomed in legal libraries, proud of hosting writers who taught how to disconnect with industrious spasms the limbs of live humans.

Ignorant and ferocious, judges are accused by Verri of failing to examine the source of their right to punish and the aims of that right. If Manzoni focuses on a precise historical period when the criminal justice system had rather rest in error than agitate itself in doubt, Verri pessimistically ponders on the capacity of that system to reproduce itself and to overshadow future reform throughout the intervening centuries.

Against facile juxtapositions between past and present, between the age of darkness and the age of light, Verri is sceptical about the inevitability of human progress, and 'the gloomy, tragic, events of the previous century appear to project a shadow on the current epoch, which has not completely ridden itself of fanaticism and error' (Carnazzi, 1988: 18). Criminal justice systems, in his view, find it extremely difficult to abandon superstition, obscurantism and violence – in brief, the *theological hatred* on which they are based.

State crime and the Church

Law, justice and violence have been linked together by authors as varied as Walter Benjamin ('Critique of Violence' in Benjamin, 1979), Jacques Derrida (1994) and Giorgio Agamben (1995), who have unravelled the sacred mission of judicial systems as well as their innate need to destroy and immolate sacrificial victims. Plague epidemics are ideal events in this respect, and they have also been studied as crucial determinants of social and political change in law enforcement and in the judicial process. In a study conducted by Cordero (1984), plagued cities, in the seventeenth century, witnessed the role of sanitary police becoming paramount, and because sanitary policing was a dirty job, it ended up in undignified hands. At the lowest level of the police apparatus, the 'monatti' were found, the removers of corpses, 'and from dawn to dusk in the streets of Milan the charts clanged, while the little bells attached to their feet warned passers-by of their arrival'. They became omnipotent, as they could grab 'suspects' as well as corpses, and could lay their hands on everything, 'humans and things, alive or dead; cheat, extort, rape' (Cordero, 1984: 9). A bounty was put on those who reported about suspect plague-spreaders. In Cordero's study the plague-spreaders are described as 'politically necessary' for the restructuring of law enforcement agencies and the judicial system. Daniel Defoe's ([1722] 1983) description of the plague in London offers similar examples of how municipal powers regroup and authorities find revitalization, while even xenophobia receives a boost, in the face of such a mysterious calamity. Responsibility for the propagation of the plague in London was attributed to goods arriving from the Netherlands, while among those exploiting the emergency situation people from southern Europe were singled out, cheats who sold improbable antidotes or phoney magic items to naive Londoners.

The plague is a powerful metaphor of crime as dirt, of crime-miasma, of delinquents as infected bodies, and of punishment as disinfection. Some criminologists look to this disinfecting power of punishment, and to the theological hatred described above, to support their arguments around the future of penal systems. Who would have thought, some argue, that the Roman Empire, which lasted for more than a millennium, would collapse? And that slavery was to be abolished?

(Scheerer, 1986; Mathiesen, 1990). Similarly, who would have predicted the vanishing of the Holy Inquisition in Spain or the end of the witch-hunt? Penal abolitionists take inspiration from the collapse of former judicial systems and the decline of their philosophies to prefigure the withering of custodial punishment as a form of responding to problematic situations. Advocating a provisional 'freeze', a 'standstill' or a moratorium on the use of imprisonment, Mathiesen looks to examples that could lead to full penal abolition: 'Are there, finally, examples of full abolition, in which total penal or sanctioning systems have been abolished? There are, and we see them if we distance ourselves a little more from our own present' (Mathiesen, 1990: 156).

Manzoni's classic historical novel, however, may inspire not only penal abolitionists but also theorists devoting their analytical efforts to state crime. The zones of obscurity and ambiguity in which judges prosecuting plague-spreaders operated are said to remain in present law systems, allowing for the proliferation of elite illegality or state-sponsored crimes. 'The rise of the powerful modern state does not eliminate illegality, and often stimulates it' (Heyman and Smart, 1999: 8). While presenting itself in the guise of a rational set of norms, the law is said simultaneously to provide opportunities for illegal practices.

> Critical legal theorists, and the legal realists before them, hold that the law is not a definite system of rules (as legal positivists had held) but an indeterminate system of meanings manipulated in actual social practice. The critical legal theorists go on to contend that the law in its particular social context is reified, appearing as if it were definitive, unimpeachable and logical.... [T]he state appears to be the very embodiment of reified legality, while varied actors inside and around states manoeuvre actual legality and illegality in complex ways. (Heyman and Smart, 1999: 11)

In this perspective, states are studied as ideal entities on the one hand – namely as the embodiment of the perfection of the law – and as empirical entities on the other – that is to say, as apparatuses struggling for their own survival through the relentless search for practices and alliances, be they legitimate or otherwise (Abrams: 1988). States, in other words, are conceptualized as not only victims or mediators but also as perpetrators of crimes. One feels an echo of the Manzoni–Verri controversy when contemporary analysts concentrate their efforts on describing and in some cases outlining the causes of state crime (Barak, 1991; Friedrichs, 1998; Ross, 1995). Whether the causes of this type of crime are to be associated with individual deviation or with systemic violation remains a central focus of debate, the aetiology of state crime being 'varied and its study fraught with difficulties and challenges':

> In the main, the greatest impediments to the study and control of state crime are definitional, conceptual, theoretical and methodological in nature, as well as the design of practical methods to combat this type of behaviour, provision of adequate resources to accomplish this task, and the proper implementation and monitoring of mechanisms of control. (Ross, 2000: 1)

From a different perspective, it could be suggested that difficulties in explaining state crime derive from the ability of the elite to escape criminal labelling and increasingly strengthen their power to impose it on others. This power is embedded in inquisitorial philosophies which – optimistically regarded by penal abolitionists as superseded – have in reality never been abandoned. The stronger the capacity of powerful groups to manifest theological hatred against the vulnerable, the stronger their efficacy in diverting that hatred from themselves. The fact that such hatred still permeates current criminal justice systems is, in itself, a form of state crime.

Interrogation and torment may still activate guilt, because contemporary justice systems continue to hinge on the notion of *suspicio*, a pivotal idea behind state intervention. Suspicion combines with *indizia* (or limited, mild, evidence), and with *dubitatio incerta* (doubtful uncertainty): *suspicio non est cognitio certa sed dubitatio incerta.* 'Studying suspicion one encounters a sort of festival of adjectives: suspicio can be *modica, levis, probabilis, magna, urgens, temeraria, violenta, vehemens.* Discussions revolve around the adjective, never around the noun' (Mereu, 1979: 131). This combination of suspicion, limited evidence and uncertainty is a constant of penal legislations since the Middle Ages, mostly underlain by the presumption of guilt. According to Mereu, suspicion is a pathological state of mind that can turn into obsessive neurosis. State neurosis resembles the state of individuals suspecting their partner of betrayal, who act and react irrationally, link incongruent episodes with one another, associate inconsistent facts and unite them into a sole 'criminal project'.

Contemporary sensibility still finds difficulties in avoiding the assimilation of deviance to declared heresy, and it is hard, when hearing terms such as 'persistence' coupled with the word 'offending', not to hear the echo of the inquisitorial similar term *pertinacia*, addressed to resilient heretics. Nor, when discussing issues around offenders' rehabilitation, can one avoid thinking of how heretics were expected to gain some form of resocialization through a public *declaratio fidei*. In the same way, looking in particular at contemporary anti-terrorism legislation, the thought comes spontaneously that the treatment of 'accomplices' – namely, of passive individuals who fail to inform on the possible commission of a terrorist act – is as harsh as the inquisitorial law destined for so-called *fautores*. And do not the mass gatherings presided over by the authorities, where the commitment to combat international evil is proclaimed, resemble those collective meetings called *auto-da-fé*, in which heretics were exposed to public disgrace, divinity was placated and the offended institution glorified? Finally, observing contemporary legislations one may find a varied range of *specialia*, that is special provisions to tackle alleged emergencies, and numerous examples of *normativa rinnegante*, whereby 'legislators situate in the same normative context two principles which are contrasting or opposed to each other, while leaving to those who wield power the possibility of availing themselves of one or the other' (Mereu, 1979: 54). Manzoni and Verri were faced, as we are today, with self-denying norms, designed for social emergencies, but subjected to the discretionary power of individuals who might well view emergencies as permanent features of social systems. Perhaps this is the price we are still paying for the shift from the 'Church of hope' to the 'Church of law' – a shift which provides the foundational basis for penal systems (Cordero, 1985). Perhaps in the Church as *societas iuridica* there are many traces of the Church as *societas spiritualis*, and of its theological hatred that we still find in the law.

Post scriptum

After going through the exploits of political conspirators and conventional organized criminals, drug-takers and prostitutes, violent racists, crooks, elitist corruptors and ship captains, I hope readers will not detect in this book a suggestion that such a colourful array of offenders deserves to be dealt with by a similar new Church as *societas iuridica*.

References

Abrams, P. (1988), 'Notes on the Difficulty of Studying the State', *Journal of Historical Sociology*, 1: 58–89.

Adler, F. (1975), *Sisters in Crime*, New York: McGraw-Hill.

Adorno, T. and Benjamin, W. (1999), *The Complete Correspondence*, Cambridge, MA: Harvard University Press.

Agamben, G. (1995), *Homo sacer. Il potere sovrano e la nuda vita*, Turin: Einaudi.

Albanese, J. (1985), *Organized Crime in America*, Cincinnati: Anderson.

Anonymous (1851), 'The Whale', *Athenaeum*, 1252: 1112–13.

Archer-Straw, P. (2000), *Negrophilia: Avant-Garde Paris and Black Culture in the 1920s*, London: Thames & Hudson.

Aristotle (1925), *Nicomachean Ethics*, Oxford: Oxford University Press.

Arlacchi, P. (1998), 'Some Observations on Illegal Markets', in V. Ruggiero, N. South and I. Taylor (eds), *The New European Criminology*, London: Routledge.

Artaud, A. ([1956] 1976), *Oeuvres complètes*, Paris: Gallimard.

Ashworth, A. (1994), *The Criminal Process*, Oxford: Oxford University Press.

Atwood, M. (1998), 'Introduction', in C. Wolf, *Medea*, London: Virago.

Bailey, D. (1966), 'The Effects of Corruption in a Developing Country', *Western Political Quarterly*, 19: 719–32.

Baldwin, J. (1965), *Blues for Mister Charlie*, London: Corgi.

Baldwin, J. (1993), *The Fire Next Time*, New York: Vintage International.

Balzac, H. de ([1831–47] 1958), *La Comédie humaine*, Paris: Gallimard.

Barak, G. (ed.) (1991), *Crimes of the Capitalist State: An Introduction to State Criminality*, Albany: State University of New York Press.

Barak, G. (1998), *Integrating Criminologies*, Boston: Allyn & Bacon.

Barnes, A. and Ephross, P. (1994), 'The Impact of Hate Violence on Victims: Emotional and Behavioural Responses to Attack', *Social Work*, 39: 247–52.

Baudelaire, C. (1975), *Oeuvres complètes*, Paris: Gallimard.

Baudelaire, C. (1999), *Artificial Paradise*, Harrogate: Broadwater House.

Beattie, J.M. (2001), *Policing and Punishment in London, 1660–1750. Urban Crime and the Limits of Terror*, Oxford: Oxford University Press.

de Beauvoir, S. ([1954] 1999), *America Day By Day*, Berkeley: University of California Press.

Becker, H. (1963), *Outsiders: Studies in the Sociology of Deviance*, New York: Free Press.

Becker, H. (1995), 'Introduction', in A. Candido, *On Literature and Society*, Princeton: Princeton University Press.

Bender, J. (1987), *Imagining the Penitentiary: Fiction and the Architecture of Mind in Eighteenth-Century England*, Chicago: University of Chicago Press.

Benjamin, W. (1972), *Über Haschisch*, Frankfurt: Suhrkamp Verlag.

Benjamin, W. (1979), *One-Way Street and Other Writings*, London: New Left Books.

Bird, D. and Walker, B. (1993), *Killing Women: Rewriting Detective Fiction*, Pymble: Argus & Robertson.

Blau, P.M. (1994), *Structural Contexts of Opportunities*, Chicago: University of Chicago Press.

Blee, K.M. (2001), *Inside Organized Racism*, Berkeley: University of California Press.

Bonger, W.A. (1936), *An Introduction to Criminology*, London: Methuen.

Borges, J.L. (1980), *Labyrinths: Selected Stories and Other Writings*, Harmondsworth: Penguin.

Borges, J.L. (1999), *The Total Library: Non-Fiction 1922–1986*, Harmondsworth: Penguin.

Bourgois, P. (1996), *In Search of Respect: Selling Crack in El Barrio*, Cambridge: Cambridge University Press.

Bowling, B. (1998), *Violent Racism: Victimisation, Policing and Social Context*, Oxford: Oxford University Press.

Box, S. (1983), *Power, Crime and Mystification*, London: Tavistock.

Brecht, B. ([1928] 1979), *The Threepenny Opera*, London: Methuen.

Breton, A. (1988), *Nadja*, in *Oeuvres complètes*, Paris: Gallimard.

Brombert, V. (1975), *La Prison romantique. Essai sur l'immaginaire*, Paris: Librairie José Corti.

Brombert, V. (1999), 'The Voice of Camus', in *In Praise of Antiheroes*, Chicago: University of Chicago Press.

Brooks, P. (2000), *Troubling Confessions: Speaking Guilt in Law and Literature*, Chicago: University of Chicago Press.

Buchanan, I. and Marks, J. (eds) (2000), *Deleuze and Literature*, Edinburgh: Edinburgh University Press.

Buchanan, J. (1980), 'A Defence of Organized Crime', in R. Andreano and J. Siegfried (eds), *The Economics of Crime*, New York: John Wiley.

Buell, L. (1986), 'Moby Dick as Sacred Text', in R. Brodhead (ed.), *New Essays on Moby Dick*, Cambridge: Cambridge University Press.

Butler, J. (1990), *Gender Trouble: Feminism and the Subversion of Identity*, London: Routledge.

Calasso, R. (2001), *La letteratura e gli dèi*, Milan: Adelphi.

Calderón de la Barca, P. (1925), *Life's a Dream*, Cambridge: Heffer.

Campbell, J. (1991), *Talking at the Gates: A Life of James Baldwin*, Berkeley: University of California Press.

Camus, A. (1947), *L'Étranger*, Paris: Gallimard.

Camus, A. (1965), 'L'Homme révolté', in *Essais*, Paris: Gallimard.

Camus, A. (1984), 'The Just', in *Caligula and Other Plays*, Harmondsworth: Penguin.

Candido, A. (1995), *On Literature and Society*, Princeton: Princeton University Press.

Carlen, P. (1988), *Women, Crime and Poverty*, Milton Keynes: Open University Press.

Carnazzi, G. (1988), 'Introduzione', in P. Verri, *Osservazioni sulla tortura*, Milan: Rizzoli.

Casanova, G.G. ([1825] 1973), *Memorie*, Milan: Rizzoli.

Castoriadis, C. (1999), *Figures du pensable*, Paris: Seuil.

Cayrol, M. (1996), 'Thomas Mann. La conquête de l'humain', *Magazine Littéraire*, 346: 38–40.

Cellini, B. ([1728] 1956), *Autobiography*, Harmondsworth: Penguin.

Ceretti, A. (1992), *L'orizzonte artificiale*, Padua: Cedam.

Cervantes, M. ([1605, 1615] 1998), *Don Quixote*, New York: W.W. Norton.

Cervantes, M. (1952), *Three Exemplary Novels*, London: Cassell.

Chambliss, W. (1978), *On the Take: From Petty Crooks to Presidents*, Bloomington: Indiana University Press.

Chase, R. (1949), *Herman Melville: A Critical Study*, New York: Macmillan.

Chekhov, A. (1987), 'Ward n. 6', in *Collected Works*, Moscow: Raduga.

Citati, P. (1996), *La luce della notte. I grandi miti nella storia del mondo*, Milan: Mondadori.

Citati, P. (2000), *Il male assoluto. Nel cuore del romanzo dell'Ottocento*, Milan: Mondadori.

Clinard, M. (1979), *Illegal Corporate Behaviour*, Washington, DC: US Department of Justice.

Cloward, R. and Ohlin, L. (1960), *Delinquency and Opportunity*, New York: The Free Press.

Coleridge, S.T. (1956) *Collected Letters*, Oxford: Clarendon Press.

Colesanti, M. (ed.) (1998), *Baudelaire. Tutte le poesie e i capolavori in prosa*, Rome: Newton.

Cordero, F. (1984), *La fabbrica della peste*, Bari: Laterza.

Cordero, F. (1985), *Criminalia. Nascita dei sistemi penali*, Bari: Laterza.

Cornell, D. (1993), *Transformations: Recollective Imagination and Sexual Difference*, New York: Routledge.

Cressey, D. (1969), *Theft of the Nation: The Structure and Operations of Organized Crime*, New York: Harper & Row.

Cruickshank, J. (1984), 'Introduction', in A. Camus, *Caligula and Other Plays*, Harmondsworth: Penguin.

Davies, I. (1990), *Writers in Prison*, Oxford: Basil Blackwell.

Davis, D.B. (1957), *Homicide in American Fiction, 1798–1860: A Study in Social Values*, Ithaca: Cornell University Press.

Davis, M. (1998), *Ecology of Fear: Los Angeles and the Imagination of Disaster*, New York: Metropolitan Books/Henry Holt.

Defoe, D. ([1722] 1983), *A Journal of the Plague Year*, Harmondsworth: Penguin.

Defoe, D. ([1725] 1986), *The True and Genuine Account of the Life and Action of Jonathan Wild*, Harmondsworth: Penguin.

Delahaye, E. (1925), *Souvenirs familiers à propos de Rimbaud*, Paris: Messein.

Deleuze, G. (1998), *Essays Critical and Clinical*, London: Verso.

De Quincey, T. ([1822] 1985), *Confessions of an English Opium Eater*, Harmondsworth: Penguin.

Derrida, J. (1994), *Force de loi. Le fondement mystique de l'autorité*, Paris: Galilée.

Dickens, C. (1850), *Sketches by 'Boz'. Illustrative of Every-day Life and Every-day People*, London: Ward, Lock.

Dickens, C. (1870), *The Mystery of Edwin Drood*, London: Ward, Lock.

Dimock, W.C. (1996), *Residues of Justice: Literature, Law, Philosophy*, Berkeley: University of California Press.

Doig, A. and Theobald, R. (2000), *Corruption and Democratisation*, London: Frank Cass.

Dolin, K. (2000), *Fiction and the Law: Legal Discourse in Victorian and Modernist*

Literature, Cambridge: Cambridge University Press.

Dostoevsky, F. ([1872] 1971), The Devils, Harmondsworth: Penguin.

Dostoevsky, F. (1977), Lettres à son frère, Paris: Gallimard.

Dostoevsky, F. (1979), Crime and Punishment, London: Book Club Associates.

Dostoevsky, F. (1985), The House of the Dead, Harmondsworth: Penguin.

Douglas, M. and Ney, S. (1998), Missing Persons: A Critique of Personhood in the Social Sciences, Berkeley: University of California Press.

Dow, P.E. (1980), Criminology in Literature, New York/London: Longman.

Downes, D. and P. Rock (1988), Understanding Deviance: A Guide to the Sociology of Crime and Rule Breaking, Oxford: Oxford University Press.

Doyle, A.C. ([1890] 1986), The Sign of Four, Harmondsworth: Penguin.

Drake, St. C. and Cayton, H.R. (1945), Black Metropolis: A Study of Negro Life in a Northern City, Chicago: University of Chicago Press.

Driscoll, L. (1999), 'Something Strange but Not Unpleasant: Freud on Cocaine', in J. Lilienfeld and J. Oxford (eds), The Languages of Addiction, London: Macmillan.

Du Bois, W.E.B. ([1903] 1996), The Souls of Black Folk, Harmondsworth: Penguin.

Duff, A. and Garland, D. (1994), A Reader on Punishment, Oxford: Oxford University Press.

Dumas, A. (1926), Ange Pitou, Paris: Nelson.

Dumas, A. ([1844] 1997), Le Comte de Monte-Cristo, Paris: Gallimard.

Durkheim, E. (1960), The Division of Labour in Society, Glencoe, IL: The Free Press.

Duyckinck, E. (1851), 'Moby Dick', Literary World, 251: 403–4.

Eaton, M. (1986), Justice for Women?, Milton Keynes: Open University Press.

Eaton, M. (1993), Women after Prison, Buckingham: Open University Press.

Eco, U. (2000), 'Sur quelques functions de la littérature, Magazine Littéraire, 392, November: 58–62.

Eco, U. (2002), Sulla letteratura, Milan: Bompiani.

Edwards, S. (1981), Female Sexuality and the Law, Oxford: Robertson.

Elias, N. and Scotson, J.L. (1994), The Established and the Outsider, London: Sage.

Escobar, R. (1997), Metamorfosi della paura, Bologna: Il Mulino.

Feldman, H. (1968), 'Ideological Supports to Becoming and Remaining a Heroin Addict', Journal of Health and Social Behaviour, 9: 131–9.

Ferrajoli, L. (1989), Diritto e ragione, Rome and Bari: Laterza.

Fielding, H. (1751), An Inquiry into the Causes of the Late Increase of Robbers, quoted in B. Loughrey and T.O. Treadwell, 'Introduction' to J. Gay, The Beggar's Opera, Harmondsworth: Penguin, 1986.

Fielding, H. ([1743] 1978), 'The History of the Life of the Late Mr Jonathan Wild the Great', in *Jonathan Wild and a Voyage to Lisbon*, London: Dent.

Finestone, H. (1957), 'Cats, Kicks and Color', *Social Problems*, 5: 15–24.

Fisher Fishkin, S. (1996), 'Foreword', in M. Twain, *The Man that Corrupted Hadleyburg and Other Stories and Essays*, New York: Oxford University Press.

Flint, K. (1993), *The Woman Reader: 1837–1914*, Oxford: Oxford University Press.

Forster, E.M. (1927), *Aspects of the Novel*, New York: Harcourt, Brace.

Foucault, M. (1977), *Discipline and Punish*, Harmondsworth: Penguin.

Franzwa, G. (1999), 'Aristotle and the Language of Addiction', in J. Lilienfeld and J. Oxford (eds), *The Languages of Addiction*, London: Macmillan.

Freud, S. ([1884] 1974), *Cocaine Papers*, New York: Stonehill.

Friedrichs, D.O. (ed.) (1998), *State Crime*, Aldershot: Ashgate.

Gambetta, D. (1992), *La mafia siciliana. Un'industria della protezione privata*, Turin: Einaudi.

Garland, D. (1990), *Punishment and Modern Society*, Oxford: Oxford University Press.

Garofalo, R. (1914), *Criminology*, Boston: Little, Brown.

Gay, J. ([1728] 1986), *The Beggar's Opera*, Harmondsworth: Penguin.

Gelsthorpe, L. and McWilliam, W. (eds) (1993), *Minority Ethnic Groups and the Criminal Justice System*, Cambridge: Cambridge University Institute of Criminology.

Gibson, D.B. (1996), 'Introduction', in W.E.B. Du Bois, *The Souls of Black Folk*, Harmondsworth: Penguin.

Giddens, A. (1976), *The New Rules of Sociological Method*, London: Hutchinson.

Gilmore, M. (1985), *American Romanticism and the Marketplace*, Chicago: University of Chicago Press.

Gilroy, P. (1993), *The Black Atlantic: Modernity and Double Consciousness*, London: Verso.

Girard, R. (1972), *La Violence et le sacré*, Paris: Bernard Grasset.

Girard, R. (1982), *Le Bouc émissaire*, Paris: Bernard Grasset.

Girard, R. (2001), *Celui par qui le scandale arrive*, Paris: Desclée de Brouwer.

Goldman, H. (1988), *Max Weber and Thomas Mann: Calling and the Shaping of the Self*, Berkeley: University of California Press.

Goldman, H. (1992), *Politics, Death, and the Devil: Self and Power in Max Weber and Thomas Mann*, Berkeley: University of California Press.

Goldstein, P.J. (1985), 'The Drugs–Violence Nexus: A Tripartite Conceptual Framework', *Journal of Drug Issues*, 15: 493–506.

Goldstein, P.J. (1986), 'Homicide Related to Drug Traffic', *Bulletin of the New York Academy of Medicine*, 62: 509–16.

Gordon, D.R. (1994), *The Return of the Dangerous Classes*, New York: W.W. Norton.

Gottfredson, M. and Hirschi, T. (1990), *A General Theory of Crime*, Stanford, CA: Stanford University Press.

Green, G. (1993), *Occupational Crime*, Chicago, IL: Nelson-Hall.

Hagen, E. (1980), *The Economics of Development*, Homewood, IL: Irwin-Dorsey.

Hall, S., Critcher, C., Clarke, C., Jefferson, T., and Roberts, B. (1978), *Policing the Crisis*, London: Macmillan.

Hamburger, M. (1996), 'Thomas Mann. Un sens de comique', *Magazine Littéraire*, 346: 44–5.

Hamm, M. (ed.) (1994), *Hate Crimes: International Perspective on Causes and Control*, Cincinnati: Anderson.

Harnishmacher, R. and Kelly, R. (1998), 'The Neo-Nazi and Skinheads of Germany: Purveyors of Hate', in R. Kelly and J. Maghan (eds), *Hate Crime: The Global Politics of Polarization*, Carbondale: Southern Illinois University Press.

Hay, D. (1975), 'Property, Authority and the Criminal Law', in D. Hay, P. Linebaugh, J.G. Rule, E.P. Thompson and C. Winslow, *Albion's Fatal Tree*, Harmondsworth: Penguin.

Heidensohn, F. (1985), *Women and Crime*, London: Macmillan.

Heidensohn, F. (1994), 'Gender and Crime', in M. Maguire, R. Morgan and R. Reiner (eds), *The Oxford Handbook of Criminology*, Oxford: Oxford University Press.

Heilbrun, C.G. (1994), *La madre di Amleto e le altre*, Milan: La Tartaruga.

Heilbut, A. (1995), *Thomas Mann: Eros and Literature*, London: Papermac.

Heyman, J. and Smart, A. (1999), 'States and Illegal Practices: An Overview', in J. Heyman (ed.), *States and Illegal Practices*, Oxford: Berg.

Highsmith, P. (1980), *Little Tales of Misogyny*, Harmondsworth: Penguin.

Holden, G. (1972), 'Introduction', in É. Zola, *Nana*, Harmondsworth: Penguin.

Hood, R. (1992), *Race and Sentencing*, Oxford: Clarendon Press.

Hudson, B. (1993), 'Penal Policy and Racial Justice', in L. Gelsthorpe and W. McWilliam (eds), *Minority Ethnic Groups and the Criminal Justice System*, Cambridge: Cambridge University Institute of Criminology.

Hughes, P. (1977), *Behind the Wall of Respect. Community Experiments in Heroin Addiction Control*, Chicago: University of Chicago Press.

Hughes, P., Crawford, N., Barker, N., Shumann, S. and Jaffe, J. (1971), 'The Social Structure of a Heroin Copping Community', *American Journal of Psychiatry*, 128: 43–50.

Hugo, V. (1969), *Oeuvres complètes*, Paris: Le Club Français du Livre.

Hugo, V. ([1862] 1982), *Les Misérables*, Harmondsworth: Penguin.

Hugo, V. ([1847] 1992), 'The Condemned Cells at La Roquette', in *The Last Day of a Condemned Man and Other Prison Writings*, Oxford: Oxford University Press.

Huntington, S. (1968), *Modernization and Corruption*, New Haven: Yale University Press.

Hutchings, P.J. (2001), *The Criminal Spectre in Law, Literature and Aesthetics: Incriminating Subjects*, New York: Routledge.

Jefferson, T. (1993), 'The Racism of Criminalisation: Policing and the Reproduction of the Criminal Other', in L. Gelsthorpe and W. McWilliam (eds), *Minority Ethnic Groups and the Criminal Justice System*, Cambridge: Cambridge University Institute of Criminology.

Jenness, V. and K. Broad (1997), *Hate Crime: New Social Movements and the Politics of Violence*, New York: Aldine De Gruyter.

Joas, H. (1996), *The Creativity of Action*, Cambridge: Polity.

Kafka, F. (1973), *In the Penal Settlement*, London: Abacus.

Kahn, J.F. (2001), *Victor Hugo un révolutionnaire*, Paris: Fayard.

Kant, I. (1948), *Groundwork of the Metaphysic of Morals*, London: Hutchinson.

Kefauver Committee (1951), *Report on Organized Crime*, New York: Didier.

Kelly, R. and Maghan, J. (eds) (1998), *Hate Crime: The Global Politics of Polarization*, Carbondale: Southern Illinois University Press.

Kerenyi, C. (1958), *The Gods of the Greeks*, Harmondsworth: Penguin.

Kerr, C., Dunlop, J.T., Harbison, F.H. and Myers, C.A. (1964), *Industrialization and Industrial Man*, New York: Oxford University Press.

Knox, S.L. (1998), *Murder: A Tale of Modern American Life*, Durham, NC and London: Duke University Press.

Kundnani, A. (2001), 'From Oldham to Bradford: The Violence of the Violated, *Race & Class*, 43: 105–110.

Lara, M.P. (2000), 'Narrating Evil', *Soundings*, 16: 122–30.

Lawrence, D.H. (1923), *Studies in Classic American Literature*, New York: Thomas Seltzer.

Legambiente (2000), *Rapporto sulle ecomafie*, Rome: Legambiente.

Leverenz, D. (1989), *Manhood and the American Renaissance*, Ithaca: Cornell University Press.

Levi, P. (1980), *The Drowned and the Saved*, London: Abacus.

Levin, J. and McDevitt, J. (1993), *Hate Crimes: The Rising Tide of Bigotry and Bloodshed*, New York: Plenum Press.

Lewis, R.W.B. (1955), *The American Adam: Innocence, Tragedy and Tradition in the Nineteenth Century*, Chicago: University of Chicago Press.

Lilienfeld, J. and Oxford, J. (eds) (1999), *The Languages of Addiction*, London: Macmillan.

Lombroso, C. (1876), *L'uomo delinquente*, Turin: Bocca.

Lombroso, C. (1894), *Gli anarchici*, Turin: Bocca.

Lombroso, C. and Ferrero, G. (1893), *La donna delinquente: la prostituta e la donna normale*, Turin: Roux.

London, J. ([1913] 1998), *John Barleycorn: 'Alcoholic Memoirs'*, Oxford: Oxford University Press.

Loughrey, B. and Treadwell, T.O. (1986), 'Introduction', in J. Gay, *The Beggar's Opera*, Harmondsworth: Penguin.

Lukács, G. (1964), *Essays on Thomas Mann*, London: Merlin Press.

Lukács, G. (1989), *Studies in European Realism*, London: Merlin Press.

McClelland, D.C. (1961), *The Achieving Society*, Princeton, NJ: Van Nostrand.

McCrudden, C., Smith, D.J. and Brown, C. (1991), *Racial Justice at Work*, London: Policy Studies Institute.

McIntosh, M. (1975), *The Organisation of Crime*, London: Macmillan.

Magarshack, D. (1971), 'Introduction', in F. Dostoevsky, *The Devils*, Harmondsworth: Penguin.

Mann, T. ([1954] 1997), *Confessions of Felix Krull, Confidence Man*, London: Minerva.

Manzoni, A. ([1842] 1964), *The Column of Infamy*, Oxford: Oxford University Press.

March, J.G. (1990), 'The Technology of Foolishness', in D.S. Pugh (ed.), *Organization Theory: Selected Readings*, Harmondsworth: Penguin.

Marx, L. (1964), *The Machine in the Garden: Technology and the Pastoral Ideal in America*, Oxford: Oxford University Press.

Mathiesen, T. (1990), *Prison on Trial*, London: Sage.

Matthiessen, F.O. (1941), *American Renaissance: Art and Expression in the Age of Emerson and Whitman*, New York: Oxford University Press.

Mayhew, H. and Binney, J. (1862), *The Criminal Prisons of London*: London: Charles Griffin.

Melville, H. ([1851] 1998), *Moby Dick*, Oxford: Oxford University Press.

Mereu, I. (1979), *Storia dell'intolleranza in Europa. Sospettare e punire*, Milan: Mondadori.

Merton, R. (1968), *Social Theory and Social Structure*, New York: The Free Press.

Méry, J. and Du Locle, C. (1978), *Don Carlos* (music by Giuseppe Verdi), Milan: Ricordi.

Meyer, H. (1973), 'Introduzione', in B. Brecht, Teatro, Turin: Einaudi.

Michelet, J. (1981), Histoire de la révolution française, Paris: Nouvelle Librarie de France.

Miller, G. (1996), Search and Destroy: African-American Males in the Criminal Justice System, Cambridge: Cambridge University Press.

Millet, K. (1971), Prostitution: A Quartet for Female Voices, New York: Basic Books.

Mills, C.W. (1956), The Power Elite, Oxford: Oxford University Press.

Milner, M. (2000), L'imaginaire des drogues. De Thomas De Quincey à Henri Michaux, Paris: Gallimard.

Mirbeau, O. ([1898]1995), Torture Garden, Sawtry: Dedalus.

Montaigne, M. de (1958), 'On Cruelty', in Essays, Harmondsworth: Penguin.

Moore, L. (1997), The Thieves' Opera: The Remarkable Lives and Deaths of Jonathan Wild, Thief-Taker, and Jack Sheppard, House-Breaker, Harmondsworth: Penguin.

Moore, L. (2000), Con Men and Cutpurses: Scenes from the Hogarthian Underworld, London: Allen Lane.

Moretti, F. (1996), Modern Epic: The World System from Goethe to García Márquez, London: Verso.

Mulhern, F. (2000), Culture/Metaculture, London: Routledge.

Mumford, L. (1929), Herman Melville, London: Jonathan Cape.

Munt, S.R. (1994), Murder by the Book? Feminism and the Crime Novel, London: Routledge.

Muraro, L' (1984), 'Le ragioni che una donna può avere di odiare la sua simile', in P. Highsmith, Piccoli racconti di misoginia, Milan: La Tartaruga.

Murray, H. (1951), 'In Nomine Diaboli', New England Quarterly, 24: 435–52.

Naffine, N. (1997), Feminism and Criminology, Cambridge: Polity Press.

Nietzsche, F. (1956), The Genealogy of Morals, New York: Random House.

Norrie, A. (2000), Punishment, Responsibility, and Justice, Oxford: Oxford University Press.

Olson, C. (1947), Call Me Ishmael: A Study of Melville, London: Jonathan Cape.

Oz, A. (2000), The Story Begins: Essays on Literature, London: Vintage.

Ozick, C. (1996), 'Introduction', in M. Twain, The Man that Corrupted Hadleyburg and Other Stories, New York: Oxford University Press.

Pareto, V. (1966), Sociological Writings, London: Pall Mall Press.

Parsons, T. (1982), On Institutions and Social Evolution, Chicago: University of Chicago Press.

Pascal, B. (1983), Pensées, London: Grant & Cutler.

Passas, N. (1990), 'Anomie and Corporate Deviance', Contemporary Crises, 14: 157–78.

Paz, O. (1990), *Alternating Current*, New York: Arcade.

Pearce, F. (1976), *Crimes of the Powerful: Marxism, Crime and Deviance*, London: Pluto.

Pearce, F. and Tombs, S. (1998), *Toxic Capitalism: Corporate Crime and the Chemical Industry*, Aldershot: Dartmouth.

Pearson, G. (1987), 'Social Deprivation, Unemployment and Patterns of Heroin Use', in N. Dorn and N. South (eds), *A Land Fit for Heroin?*, London: Macmillan.

Perrot, M. (ed.) (1980), *L'impossible prison*, Paris: Seuil.

Perrot, M. (2001), *Les ombres de l'histoire. Crime et châtiment au XIX siècle*, Paris: Flammarion.

Perrow, C. (1961), 'The Analysis of Goals in Complex Organizations', *American Sociological Review*, 26: 854–65.

Perry, B. (2001), *In the Name of Hate: Understanding Hate Crimes*, New York: Routledge.

Petit, J. (ed.) (1984), *La prison, le bagne et l'histoire*, Geneva: Librairie des Méridiens.

Petit, J., Castan, N., Faugeron, C., Pierre, M. and Zysberg, A. (1991), *Histoire des galères, bagnes et prisons: XIII–XX siècles*, Toulouse: Privat.

Phoenix, J. (1999), *Making Sense of Prostitution*, London: Macmillan.

Pirandello, L. (1922), *Enrico IV*, Florence: Bemporad.

Plant, S. (1999), *Writing on Drugs*, London: Faber & Faber.

Poe, E.A. (1980a), *The Unknown Poe*, San Francisco: City Lights.

Poe, E.A. (1980b), *Selected Tales*, Oxford: Oxford University Press.

Preble, E. and Casey, J. (1969), 'Taking Care of Business: The Heroin User's Life in the Street', *The International Journal of the Addictions*, 4: 1–24.

Putnam, S. (1952), 'Translator's Introduction', in M. Cervantes, *Three Exemplary Novels*, London: Cassell.

Rawson, C. (2001), *God, Gulliver, and Genocide: Barbarism and the European Imagination, 1492–1945*, Oxford: Oxford University Press.

Reiner, R. (1993), 'Race, Crime and Justice: Models of Interpretation', in L. Gelsthorpe and W. McWilliam (eds), *Minority Ethnic Groups and the Criminal Justice System*, Cambridge: Cambridge University Institute of Criminology.

Resta, E. (1992), *La certezza e la speranza. Saggio su diritto e violenza*, Rome and Bari: Laterza.

Reynolds, D. (1992), 'Its Wood Could Only Be American: Moby Dick and Antebellum Popular Culture', in B. Higgins and H. Parker (eds), *Critical Essays on Herman Melville's Moby Dick*, New York: G.K. Hall.

Rimbaud, A. ([1873]1965), 'Une saison en enfer', in *Oeuvres*, Paris: Baudouin.

Robb, G. (1997), *Victor Hugo*, London: Picador.

Roebuck, J. and S.C. Weeber (1978), *Political Crime in the United States: Analysing Crime by and against Government*, New York: Praeger.

Rose-Ackerman, S. (1999), *Corruption and Government: Causes, Consequences, and Reform*, Cambridge: Cambridge University Press.

Ross, J.I. (ed.) (1995), *Controlling State Crime*, New York: Garland.

Ross, J.I. (ed.) (2000), *Varieties of State Crime and Its Control*, New York: Criminal Justice Press.

Ruggiero, V. (1991), 'The Disrespect of Prison', paper delivered at Respect in Prison, Lincoln, 11–14 July.

Ruggiero, V. (1992), 'Realist Criminology: A Critique', in J. Young and R. Matthews (eds), *Rethinking Criminology: The Realist Debate*, London: Sage.

Ruggiero, V. (1993), 'The Camorra: "Clean" Capital and Organised Crime', in F. Pearce and M. Woodiwiss (eds), *Global Crime Connections*, London: Macmillan.

Ruggiero, V. (1996), *Organised and Corporate Crime in Europe: Offers that Can't Be Refused*, Aldershot: Dartmouth.

Ruggiero, V. (2000a), *Crime and Markets: Essays in Anti-Criminology*, Oxford: Oxford University Press.

Ruggiero, V. (2000b), 'Daniel Defoe and Business Crime', in *Crime and Markets: Essays in Anti-Criminology*, Oxford: Oxford University Press.

Ruggiero, V. (2000c), 'Corruption as Resentment', in *Crime and Markets: Essays in Anti-Criminology*, Oxford: Oxford University Press.

Ruggiero, V. (2001), *Movements in the City: Conflict in the European Metropolis*, New York: Prentice Hall.

Ruggiero, V. (2002), 'Fuzzy Criminal Actors', in V. Ruggiero (ed.), *Is White Collar Crime Organised Crime?*, special issue of *Crime, Law and Social Change*, 37: 177–90.

Ruggiero, V. and N. South (1995), *Eurodrugs: Drug Use, Markets and Trafficking in Europe*, London: UCL Press.

Rusche, G. and Kirchheimer, O. (1968), *Punishment and Social Structure*, New York: Russel & Russel.

Salt, H. (1892), 'Marquesan Melville', *Gentleman's Magazine*, 272: 252–4.

Scarman, Lord (1981), *The Brixton Disorders 10–12 April*, London: HMSO.

Scheerer, S. (1986), 'Towards Abolitionism', *Contemporary Crises*, 10: 5–20.

Schelling, T.C. (1967), 'Economic Analysis of Organized Crime', in The President's Commission on Law Enforcement and the Administration of

Justice, *Task Force Report: Organized Crime*, Washington, DC: Government Printing Office.

Sciascia, L. (1985), 'Introduzione', in A. Manzoni, *Storia della colonna infame*, Milan: Bompiani.

Scott, J. (1969), 'Corruption, Machine Politics and Social Change', *American Political Science Review*, 63: 1142–59.

Search, P. (ed.) (1957), *Great True Crime Stories*, London: Arco.

Selby, N. (ed.) (1998), *Herman Melville: Moby Dick*, Cambridge: Icon Books.

Sellin, T. (1938), *Culture Conflict and Crime*, New York: Social Science Research Council.

Shaw, C. (1930), *The Jack-Roller: A Delinquent Boy's Own Story*, Chicago: University of Chicago Press.

Sivanandan, A. (2001), 'Poverty is the New Black', *Race & Class*, 43(2): 1–6.

Slapper, G. and Tombs, S. (1999), *Corporate Crime*, Harlow: Longman.

Smart, C. (1977), *Women, Crime and Criminology*, London: Routledge & Kegan Paul.

Smart, C. (1989), *Feminism and the Power of Law*, London: Routledge.

Smith, D.J. (1994), 'Race, Crime, and Criminal Justice', in M. Maguire, R. Morgan and R. Reiner (eds), *The Oxford Handbook of Criminology*, Oxford: Oxford University Press.

South, N. (ed.) (1995), *Drugs, Crime and Criminal Justice*, Vol. II, Aldershot: Dartmouth.

South, N. and P. Beirne (eds) (1998), 'For a Green Criminology', special issue of *Theoretical Criminology*, 2: 147–285.

Stableford, R. (1995), 'Introduction', in O. Mirbeau, *Torture Garden*, Sawtry: Dedalus.

Stanko, E. (1993), *Men and Crime*, Buckingham: Open University Press.

Stark, R. (1987), 'Deviant Places: A Theory of the Ecology of Crime', *Criminology*, 25: 893–909.

Stendhal (1932), *La Chartreuse de Parme*, Paris: Seuil.

Stigler, G. (1970), 'The Optimum Enforcement of Law', *Journal of Political Economy*, 78(3): 526–36.

Sue, E. (1989), *Les mystères de Paris*, Paris: Laffont.

Sutherland, E. (1939), *Principles of Criminology*, Chicago: Lippincott.

Sutherland, E. (1983), *White Collar Crime: The Uncut Version*, New Haven: Yale University Press

Sutherland, J. (1998), 'Introduction', in J. London ([1913] 1998), *John Barleycorn: 'Alcoholic Memoirs'*, Oxford: Oxford University Press.

Sutherland, J. (2001), 'The Narrator as Witness', *Times Literary Supplement*, 23 February.

Sutter, A. (1966), 'The World of the Righteous Dope-Fiend', *Issues in Criminology*, 2: 177–222.

Sykes, G.M. (1958), *The Society of Captives: A Study of a Maximum Security Prison*, Princeton: Princeton University Press.

Sykes, A. and Matza, D. (1957), 'Techniques of Neutralization: A Theory of Delinquency', *American Sociological Review*, 22: 664–73.

Tanner, T. (1988), 'Introduction', in H. Melville, *Moby Dick*, Oxford: Oxford University Press.

Tatum, B. (1996), 'The Colonial Model as a Theoretical Explanation of Crime and Delinquency', in A.T. Sutton (ed.), *African-American Perspectives on Crime Causation, Criminal Justice Administration, and Crime Prevention*, Boston: Butterworth–Heinemann.

Thrasher, F. (1927), *The Gang*, Chicago: University of Chicago Press.

Tonry, M. (1995), *Malign Neglect: Race, Crime, and Punishment in America*, New York: Oxford University Press.

Turk, A.T. (1982), *Political Criminality: The Defiance and Defence of Authority*, London: Sage.

Twain, M. ([1901]1993), *The Man that Corrupted Hadleyburg*, in *Short Stories*, Harmondsworth: Penguin.

Twain, M. (1996a), 'My First Lie, and How I Got Out of It', in *The Man that Corrupted Hadleyburg and Other Stories*, New York: Oxford University Press.

Twain, M. (1996b), 'Concerning the Jews', in *The Man that Corrupted Hadleyburg and Other Stories*, New York: Oxford University Press.

Vergès, J. (1988), *Beauté du crime*, Paris: Plon.

Verri, P. ([1777] 1988), *Osservazioni sulla tortura*, Milan: Rizzoli.

Vold, G.B., Bernard, T.J. and Snipes, J.B. (1998), *Theoretical Criminology*, 4th edn, New York: Oxford University Press.

Wassenaar, I. (2001), 'Can the Ideals of 1905 be Made to Live in 2001?', *Times Literary Supplement*, 23 February: 19.

Weber, M. (1947), *The Theory of Social and Economic Organization*, New York: Free Press.

Weber, M. (1948), 'The Protestant Sects and the Spirit of Capitalism', in H.H. Gerth and C.W. Mills (eds), *From Max Weber: Essays in Sociology*, London: Routledge.

Whyte, F.W. (1943), *Street Corner Society*, Chicago: University of Chicago Press.

Wilde, O. (1974), *Salomé*, in *Plays*, Harmondsworth: Penguin.

Williams, R. (1976). *Keywords: A Vocabulary of Culture and Society*, London: Fontana.

Wilson, J.Q. (1990), 'Corruption: The Shame of the State', in A. Heidenheimer, M. Johnson and V. LeVine (eds), *Political Corruption: A Handbook*, New Brunswick: Transactions.

Witte, R. (1996), *Racist Violence and the State*, London: Longman.

Wolf, C. (2001), 'Je n'écris que sur ce qui m'inquiète', *Magazine Littéraire*, 395, February: 98–103.

Woollen, G. (1992), 'Introduction', in V. Hugo, *The Last Day of a Condemned Man and Other Prison Writings*, Oxford: Oxford University Press.

Wright, R. (1945), 'Introduction', in St. C. Drake and H.R. Cayton, *Black Metropolis: A Study of Negro Life in a Northern City*, Chicago: University of Chicago Press.

Wright, R. (1981), *Native Son*, Harmondsworth: Penguin.

Yehoshua, A.B. (2000), *Il potere terribile di una piccola colpa. Etica e letteratura*, Turin: Einaudi.

Young, A. (1996), *Imagining Crime: Textual Outlaws and Criminal Conversations*, London: Sage.

Yourcenar, M. (1978), *Sous benefice d' inventaire*, Paris: Seuil.

Zedner, L. (1991), *Women, Crime and Custody in Victorian England*, Oxford: Oxford University Press.

Zola, É. ([1880] 1972), *Nana*, Harmondsworth: Penguin.

Index

abstraction, evil of, 26
adversarial narratives, 3
Aeschylus, 173
Afro-Americans, 'invisibility', 104
Agamben, Giorgio, 230
alcohol, 55, 59, 64, 68, 70, 73–4, 89
    alcoholism, 67, 72
anarchists, 16, 208
Andalusia, underworld, 30
anomie theories, 10, 19
anti-Semitism, 112
anti-terrorism legislation, 234
antiracist marches, 115
Apollo, 173
Artaud, Antonin, 57
authority, struggle for, 26
autocracies, 165
'automatic writing', 57

Bakunin, Mikhail, 11
Baldwin, James, 116, 133
    Blues for Mr Charlie, 105–15
Balzac, Honoré de, 55, 60, 80, 84
Bastille, the, 196
Baudelaire, Charles, 64, 72, 76
    Confessions, 65
    Écrits intimes, 67

Le Spleen de Paris, 73
Les Paradis artificiels, 6, 59–63, 66
Beauvoir, Simone de, 116–17, 121
Beccaria, Cesare, 218, 220
Becker, Howard, 3
Beethoven, Ludwig van
    Fidelio, 202
begging, 47
Bender, J., 195
Benjamin, Walter, 4, 58–9, 132, 230
Bentham, Jeremy, prison design, 2
bisexuality, 84
Borges, Jorge Luis, 8
Brecht, Bertolt, 28, 52
    The Threepenny Opera, 6, 46–50
Breton, André, 57
'British insincerity', 66
'Brotherhood of thieves', Seville, 29
bushfires, Normandy, 223
'business ethics', 2

Caius Valerius, 216
Calderón de la Barca, Pedro 194
Camus, Albert, 26–7, 198
    The Just, 20–25
Candido, Antonio, 3
capitalism, 144, 163

careers, criminal, 207
Casanova, G.G., 198
Caserio, Sante 14
Cassandra, 5
Cellini, Benvenuto, 195–6
Cervantes, Miguel de, 52
　　Novelas ejemplares, 28
　　Riconete and Cortadillo, 6, 29–38,
　　　45–6
chain gang, 206–7
Chekhov, Anton, 194
Chicago, sociologists, 130
chivalry, 92–3
Christianity, 6, 109–10
　　Greek Orthodox, 10
　　imagination, 200
Claudius Marcellus, 216
cocaine, 57–8
　　crack, 129
codes of conduct, vague, 151
Communists, 123
competitive markets, 191
confession, 228–9
conflict theory, 24–6
consequentialist argument, 195
cooperation, 147
Cordero, F., 231
corruption, 43, 181–6, 189–93
crime(s)
　　business, 2–3
　　careers, 36
　　corporate, 153
　　drug caused, 75
　　'families', 36
　　of the economy, 141–5, 152
　　organizational, 150
　　organized, see organized crime
　　picaresque, 166
　　professional, 28, 38
　　race bias, 128
　　racial bias, 130
　　racialized forms, 129

state-sponsored, 232–3
writers, 102–3
'criminal atavism', 17
criminal behaviour, redefinition, 25
criminal justice system, 7, 227, 230
　　legislation, 40
criminality
　　'self-inflicted', 132
　　elitist, 51
　　genetic attribution, 95
criminals, professional, 37, 43, 45–6,
　　52
criminology, 92
　　environmental, 153
　　positivist school, 9, 12, 16, 82,
　　　89
　　women practitioners, 95,
　　　100–101, 103
　　Zola's theories, 97
cruelty, 214
cultural materialistic analysis, 139

Dante Alighieri, 207
Darwinians, 209
Davies, I., 194
De Quincey, Thomas, 55, 64–6, 73
　　Confessions of an English Opium Eater,
　　　54
death penalty, 203
　　protest against, 202
deconstructive analysis, 139
Defoe, Daniel, 2, 44, 231
Deleuze, Gilles, 5
democracy, myth of, 139
Derrida, Jacques, 230
detectives: fictional female, 103
　　women invented, 102
deviance
　　ecological tradition, 130–31
　　sociology of, 10, 36, 58, 75, 92,
　　　152–3, 168
'deviant insiders', 165

Dickens, Charles, 55–6, 59
differential association, 149
Dolin, K., 3
Dostoevsky, Fyodor
    Crime and Punishment, 199
    House of the Dead, 197
    The Devils, 6, 11–20
Dreyfus case, France, 182
drug use, 53–4, 58–9, 72, 76
    literary productivity, 55

'sickness' model, 53
traditional analysis, 6
    varied, 74
drugs
    illicit markets, 75
    prohibition, 73, 129
Du Bois, W.E.B., 104
Dumas, Alexandre, 55, 81, 196
Durkheim, Émile, 19, 213, 215

economic practices, acceptable/
    unacceptable, 140–41, 154
elites, 188, 190, 192, 232–3
embezzlement, 149
emergency legislation, 228
entrepreneurs, 157–8, 162–3,
    172–3
    irrational, 165
epilepsy, 6, 17–18
eroticism, 83–4
ethnic minorities, 'problem', 105
'evil', 12, 85, 105, 135
    'unknown', 142
exclusion, perpetuation, 114

fear, 120, 122–4, 127, 133
    xenophobic, 129
femmes fatales, 101
Ferrero, Guglielmo, 82
fiction, orthodox crime, 102
Fielding, Henry, 39, 44–5

formalistic impersonality, 148–9
Forster, E.M., 138
Foucault, Michel, 200
Fourier, Joseph, utopianism, 85
Fourth Lateran Council, 229
France, Anatole, 208
France
    Napoleon III, 81
    Second Empire, 80
Franco-Prussian war, 209
Freud, Sigmund, 57
frivolity, 176
frontier, American myths, 139

Garibaldi, Giuseppe, 38
Garofalo, R., 13
Gay, John, 28, 52
    The Beggar's Opera, 6, 38–43, 46
gender, 92–3
Goldstein, P.J., 75
Grand Duke Sergei, Russia, 20
Green, G., 149

Harlem, 108, 116
hashish, 54–60, 62
    dreams, 63
hate crime, 111–15, 133
Hawthorne, Nathaniel, 136
Heidensohn, F., 93
Hermes, 172–4
Highsmith, Patricia, 94
hierarchy, oppressive, 147
historical inevitability, doctrines of,
    26–7
Holmes, Sherlock, 57
Holy Inquisition, 220, 232
homophobia, 112
'honour', 42
'hornets', 34
Hugo, Victor, 195–6, 201, 208, 215
    Le dernier jour d'un condamné, 202
    Les Misérables, 7, 203–7

illegality, elite, 232
illicit markets, racial hierarchy, 131
image, manipulation of, 161
imagination, 160, 174–5
imprisonment, sociology of, 204,
    214
individualism, 21, 138, 140, 147,
    154, 163
    Hobbesian, 177
    rugged myth, 139
inequality, 127
informers, 31, 40–41, 49
innocence, 'rhetoric of', 145
innovation, 152–3, 166, 173
irritability, 4

jealousy, sexual, 117
John the Baptist, 83
jury trial, right to, 130
justice, 21, 199, 230
    contemporary systems, 233
    injustice, 4
    miscarriages of, 226, 228
    social, 27

Kafka, Franz, 198
Kefauver Committee 1951, 36
King Herod, 83

labour, 145, 148
laudanum, 54, 60
law, violations of, 145
Lawrence, D.H., 137–8
lawyers, 41–2
'lie of silent assertion', 182, 186
Livius, 216
Lombroso, Cesare, 6, 13, 16–18,
    82–4, 89, 97
London, gin shops, 55–6, 59
    urban spacescape, 39
London, Jack, 73–4, 76
    John Barleycorn, 6, 59, 67–72

Lord Palmerston, 202
Lukács, Georg, 161
lynching, 118

malt liquor, 67
Malthus, Thomas, 217
Mann, Thomas
    Buddenbrooks, 161
    Dr Faustus 173
    Felix Krull, 156–77
Manolescu, Georges, 156
Manzoni, Alessandro
    Storia della colonna infame, 7, 217,
        219–33, 235
marginalists, 154
marginalization, 95
markets, 157
    dysfunctional, 191
    'the invisible hand', 144
Marxism, 20, 144
Mathiesen, T., 232
Medea, 5
    story of, 83
Melville, Herman
    Moby Dick, 7, 135–54
Mereu, I., 234
Merton, Robert, 58
    'innovation' concept, 6
Michelangelo, 195
Michelet, Jules, 196
Milan, plague of 1630, 7, 216–17
Millet, Kate, 94
minorities, crime rates, 130–31
Mirbeau, Octave, 195, 201, 215
    The Torture Garden, 7, 208–14
misogyny, societal, 94
missionaries, Catholic, 214
Mississipi, 116
Montaigne, Michel de, 223–4
Mora, Giangiacomo, 221, 227
moral entrepreneur, 73
moral insanity, 13, 17

Muraro, L., 94
murder, 209
  judicial, 202

Naffine, N., 101
National Association for the
  Advancement of Colored People
  (NAACP), 123
natural crimes, 12
naturalism, 80–81, 85, 97, 100
nature, dominion over, 138
Neapolitan Camorra, 38
Nechayev, Sergey, 11
'negrophilia', Parisian, 117
neo-colonial analysis, 131
neo-Nazis, 113
neutralization, techniques of, 168,
  171
Newgate prison, 42, 44
Nietzsche, Friedrich, 213, 215–16
nomos, 3
nymphomania, 89

Offenbach, Jacques, 81
opium, 55–6, 59–60, 64–6
organizations, sociology of, 152, 167
organized crime, 28, 37–40, 45, 47,
  50, 52
  bureaucracy, 36
  continuity, 35
  division of labour, 46
  stagnant forms, 51

Pareto, Vilfredo, 190
Pascal, Blaise, 200
penal philosophies, 7
'people, the', 71–2
perversion, institutional, 224,
Philadelphia, system of custody 1836,
  200
Piazza, Guglielmo, 219–22, 225
Pirandello, Luigi, 194

Piranesi, Giambattista, 2
pity, 12
plague epidemics, 216–17, 223,
  230–31
Plato, 53
  cave metaphor, 200
playfulness, 153, 165–8
Poe, Edgar Allan, 4, 55, 103, 202
police, the, 91
  'crimes', 12
  England, 40
political offenders, 6
politics
  criminal acts, 25
  legislative, 24
  violent, 9, 16, 18, 20, 228
positivist school, criminology, 9, 12,
  16, 82, 89
positivism, 19
prison, 2, 7, 194–7, 199–208,
  212–13, 215
  humiliation, 198

penal systems, 210
  use of, 232
probity, 12
'progressives', 19
prohibition(ism), 67, 71–2, 74
  drugs, 73
'propaganda of the deed', 25
'propensity event theory', 149
'proportionality', principle of, 213
prostitution, 81–2, 92, 95, 103
punishment, 27, 199, 201, 203–4,
  206, 209, 213, 216, 231

racial bias, 128–9
  sociology of, 195
Puritan ethic, bourgeois, 163

'rabble, the', 19
racial identity, anti-essentialist, 133

racism, 106, 108, 111, 114, 118, 188, 210
  exclusion, 112
  fear, 129
  southern USA, 119
  violent, 7, 113–15
rape, 118, 125
rationalization, 168, 181
  techniques of, 177
realism, 100
'reasonable culpability', principle of, 27
receivers/'fences', 40, 171
reciprocal dependence, 146
refugees, violence against, 113
relative deprivation, 6
religious hate, 112
rent-seeking, 191
retreatism, 6, 58–9, 73–4
revolt, 27
Revolution Surréaliste, La 57
Rimbaud, Arthur, 56–7
Roman Empire, 231
Roman Law, 220, 223, 227
rookeries, 39, 56
Russia, liberals, 10

sadism, 213
Saint Mark, 83
saloons, 68, 70
Schopenhauer, Arthur, 164
  The World as Will and Representation, 161
Sciascia, Leonardo, 216–17, 226
self-discipline, 176
Seville, 29, 35
  underworld, 33
sexism, 95
sexuality, women, 102
shamelesness, 84
Sheppard, Jack, 43–4
'sin' model, drug use, 53
slavery, 231

Society of National Retribution, Moscow, 11
Social Darwinism, 72
social equality, 110
social-problem theorists, 115
socialism, 72
Socrates, 173
South Side Boy's Club, 119
Spanish Flu, 217
St Giles, London slum, 39
state, organized, 24
Stendhal (Henri Beyle), 84, 196, 200
  The Red and the Black, 5
Stigler, G., 37
structural oppression, 131
subcultural theorists, 59
'substantive irrationality', 148
Sue, Eugène, 198
suffering, 201
suicide, 21, 70
superstition, 220, 223
surrealists, 57
surveillance, 39
suspicion, 233–4
Sutherland, E., 145, 149, 181
Sykes, G.M., 204

technology of foolishness, 167
temptation, 185, 191
The Russian Messenger, periodical, 10
thieves, jargon, 29
Toledo, 31
torture, 214, 219–24, 227–9
  torturers, 218
trade, principles of, 40
transition, periods of, 19
transportation, France, 208
Turgenev, Ivan, 11
Turk, A.T., 25
Twain, Mark, 179, 181–2
  The Man that Corrupted Hadleyburg, 7, 178, 180, 183–9, 191–3

vengeance, 141, 143, 147, 203
Verdi, Giuseppe
    Don Carlo, 220
Verri, Pietro
    Osservazioni sulla tortura, 218, 221,
        224, 228–30, 233, 235
victim blame, 109–10
victimization, rhetoric of, 115
violence, 45–6, 145, 210
    alcohol-fuelled, 70
    criminal, 132
    diseconomies, 132
    domestic, 93
    judicial, 223, 227, 230
    neo-Nazi, 113
    political, 9, 16, 18, 20, 228
    psycho-pharmacological, 75
    racist, 7, 111, 114–15
    revolutionary, 26
    terrorist, 112

war on drugs, 129
waste, illicit dumping, 153
Weber, Max, 148–9, 165–6, 172, 177
    The Protestant Ethic and the Spirit of
        Capitalism, 162

whaling industry, 139
white-collar crime/criminals, 51,
    153, 181
Wild, Jonathan, 38, 40–41, 43–5
Wilde, Oscar
    Salomé, 83
'will', 158–9, 161, 164, 166, 168
wine, 60–62, 65
Wolf, Christa, 5
women
    criminality, 95
    deviant, 93
    emancipated, 94
    fear of, 82–4, 92, 100, 102
    rights movement, 71
World Revolutionary Movement, 11
Wright, Richard, 105, 116–17
    Black Metropolis, 120
    Native Son, 7, 118–19, 121–8,
        132–3

xenophobia, 231

Zola, Émile, 84–5 100
    fiction theory, 81
    Nana, 77–80, 86–99, 101–3